The Early Modern World, 1450–1750

T0353219

The Early Modern World, 1450–1750

Seeds of Modernity

John C. Corbally and
J. Casey Sullivan

BLOOMSBURY ACADEMIC
LONDON • NEW YORK • OXFORD • NEW DELHI • SYDNEY

BLOOMSBURY ACADEMIC
Bloomsbury Publishing Plc
50 Bedford Square, London, WC1B 3DP, UK
1385 Broadway, New York, NY 10018, USA
29 Earlsfort Terrace, Dublin 2, Ireland

BLOOMSBURY, BLOOMSBURY ACADEMIC and the Diana logo are trademarks
of Bloomsbury Publishing Plc

First published in Great Britain 2022

Cover design: Terry Woodley

Cover image: Period map of Byzantium and Constantinople from an atlas.
(Photo by VCG Wilson/Corbis via Getty Images)

A catalogue record for this book is available from the British Library.

Library of Congress Cataloging-in-Publication Data.
Names: Corbally, John C. (John Christopher), author. | Sullivan, J. Casey, author.
Title: The early modern world, 1450-1750: seeds of modernity / John C. Corbally
and J. Casey Sullivan.
Description: London; New York: Bloomsbury Academic, 2022. |
Series: Making of the modern world | Includes bibliographical references and index.
Identifiers: LCCN 2021029025 (print) | LCCN 2021029026 (ebook) |
ISBN 9781474277730 (paperback) | ISBN 9781474277747 (hardback) |
ISBN 9781474277761 (pdf) | ISBN 9781474277754 (ebook)
Subjects: LCSH: World history. | History, Modern–16th century. |
History, Modern–17th century. | History, Modern–18th century.
Classification: LCC D209 .C67 2022 (print) | LCC D209 (ebook) |
DDC 909–dc23
LC record available at https://lccn.loc.gov/2021029025
LC ebook record available at https://lccn.loc.gov/2021029026

ISBN: HB: 978-1-4742-7774-7
PB: 978-1-4742-7773-0
ePDF: 978-1-47427-776-1
eBook: 978-1-4742-7775-4

Series: The Making of the Modern World

Typeset by Deanta Global Publishing Services, Chennai, India

To find out more about our authors and books visit www.bloomsbury.com and
sign up for our newsletters.

Contents

Figures

Acknowledgments

Special thanks to Troy Patton for his eagle eye and help in reviewing every page from a student's perspective.

Series introduction

This world history series comprises a unique, three-volume, set of books for use in the classroom or for those wishing to understand world history since 1500. It consists of three separate volumes:

The Early Modern World, 1450–1750: Seeds of Modernity

John C. Corbally and Trevor R. Getz

The Long Nineteenth Century, 1750– 1914: Crucible of Modernity (2018) *Trevor R. Getz*

The Twentieth-Century World, 1914 to the Present: State of Modernity (2018) *John C. Corbally*

The series is unconventional in its approach to understanding the world since 1500 through popular perspectives and experiences: those of common, ordinary people; of peasants, women, workers, slaves, serfs, and outsiders rather than of kings, generals, or politicians. In doing so, it aims to understand humanity's past by transcending the traditional emphasis on nations, empires, masculinity, war, or acquisition.

The authors intend for a diverse array of learners to appreciate just how connected our globalized world has been since 1500, instead of assuming separate peoples lived in separate nations with separate histories. They reveal rather than hide the complex and unappealing sides of history, outlining the history as it is understood, whether pleasing or not.

The series is purposely written in a nonacademic style, to invite students and general readers to enjoy the story while learning the broad outlines of world history. It is clearly organized, with short segments providing the opportunity for the reader to absorb one section at a time. Each chapter in each volume has a clear thesis, making a historical point supported by the sources, exploring a distinct period of the modern past through five different lenses: environmental, political, economic, intellectual, and technological history. Framed around social experience and cultural perspective, each chapter in each volume explores the development and contested construction of modernity. Together, the series forms an interpretation of the modern past that will help readers both understand and question the development of the world in which we live.

What is this book?

This book is the third of three volumes in the *Making of the Modern World* series. Each volume in the series is a tool for use in a world history classroom, covering one of three periods between c.1450 and the modern day. This volume covers the first period, 1450-1750 CE. Like later periods however, it does not claim to be the final word on this era. Instead, it is *one* potential model for understanding the global past in this period. More than anything, this book is based on the way we, the authors, teach world history courses, and it can be usefully used by instructors who have different approaches to this era and who want to contrast our work with theirs in a fruitful conversation. Such varying historical interpretations are good for students!

The key features of this book are:

> The approach is thematic, for this was a period when the planet first truly became tied together. Therefore, this is an era in which a number of themes can usefully be used to tell important stories about changes and continuities in this era.
>
> The main narrative of this book is its emphasis on the origins and growth of modernity. The thesis is that during the 250 years covered in its pages the world entered a new phase – the early modern era – that possessed a defining set of perspectives and experiences we can fruitfully explore and understand, at least more so than the more disparate medieval era.
>
> The chapters of this book group the major elements of modernity into five categories – environmental, political, economic, intellectual/philosophical and technological history. However, the approach we take is to focus on the social and natural environment within these categories. As a result, we seek to especially say something about how individuals and groups of people lived their lives and sought to manage and understand the changes going on around them.
>
> Finally, we see history as something that is living. Not only does it have an impact on how we live today, but it is also something that people try to understand in their everyday lives through nostalgia, traditions, memories, heritage projects, and popular culture.

The Early Modern World, 1450-1750 (Seeds of Modernity) is structured around five separate themes in eight chapters that group historical events into categories – environmental, political, economic, intellectual/philosophical and technological history. In our lives, these five overlapping aspects of our social environment seep into each other; combined, they shape our sense of reality, nature and life itself. Our approach is to explore continuity and change through individual and collective human experiences. The aim is to say something important about how individuals and groups lived their lives, how they sought to manage and understand the changes around them - to depict history in ways we can relate to as we live today.

Though the purpose is to relate to readers the essential stories of this era, all societies cannot be covered equally, both for practical purposes and due to disparities in available sources. What we can do is try to examine well-known events and historical processes from the perspective of the average person rather than the politician, general or priest. We can empathize with those who suffered rather than celebrate with the victors. We can question progress while acknowledging its virtues, and we can concede that our knowledge of the past is inherently limited.

Most of the events covered in this era still shape the mindsets and beliefs of people across the world today: Which societies despoiled the environment most in these centuries? Which nations made most use of it? Were Hernan Cortes and Christopher Columbus particularly evil compared to other men in this era? Were European rulers more benevolent to their subjects than Ming Emperors or Ottoman Sultans? Which kingdoms were most powerful or authoritarian? Which regions primed the newly global economy most? Who had the most ideas about making money? Which religions were most accepting of others they came across? What types of technology were adopted anew? Where did these ideas originate from: one place or many? So many historical questions. So many contested answers. Many bold interpretations of such questions are acceptable to the history student; any old interpretation is not acceptable though. Evidence must guide conclusions, not wishful thinking or beliefs.

One final note – it is often supposed that the purpose of history classes is to simplify the past and make it easier to comprehend. We feel it is important to write and teach histories that are understandable, but students must grasp how extraordinarily complex the real human past was. Often, we are left not with answers, but with more questions, questions that will hopefully stimulate an intellectual curiosity far beyond this book.

John Corbally and J. Casey Sullivan
Diablo Valley College

Introduction

The 'discovery' of rubber

In 1493 Christopher Columbus and his men walked around modern-day Haiti following their second voyage across the Atlantic. They noticed local Indians playing with a ball noticeably different to the hard, wooden balls familiar to Spaniards and Europeans. The bouncy, almost magical, rubber spheres the islanders possessed enchanted the Spaniards. Derived from a liquid material teased out of trees, this natural rubber stretched, bounced and responded to touch, unlike anything Eurasian hands had ever felt before. Indeed, the Spanish marvelled at much of what they saw in this New World before them, populated by unfamiliar peoples and blessed with a mindboggling diversity of natural resources unknown to those in the Old World. Europeans would soon turn from marvelling at this New World to exploiting it, and the peoples who lived there. In coming centuries, they would exploit the properties of rubber too, for tyres, industrial manufacturing, warfare and household goods.

Just one of many new substances that European explorers brought back from the Americas between 1500 and 1750, natural rubber was particularly unusual. Two centuries after Columbus, a French astronomer seeking to calculate cartographical meridians brought rubber from the Amazon to Europe. Its arrival in France in 1736 invited baffled headshaking at such unique properties. Now, of course, it is a major part of modern life.

This pliable rubber, with its unusual chemical composition, symbolizes well the New Worlds of thought and action that emerged across Eurasia in the early modern era after the 'discovery' of the Americas. Between 1500 and 1750, owing considerably to the strange New Worlds of people and plants, an unbounded inquisitiveness

Figure 0.1 Rubber tapping in Sri Lanka (Wikimedia Commons).

reframed human understandings of everything from massive starry heavens to minute microbes in air and water. Growing curiosity would later lead to systematic scientific thinking, which emerged as a new intellectual approach to observing the world in a coherent and organized way (Figure 0.1).

Between medieval and modern

Compared to previous centuries, the years between 1500 and 1750 brought vastly higher levels of human activity in the *environmental, political, economic, intellectual* and *technological* spheres – the five areas covered in this book. Aside from rubber, early modern humans would extract thousands of new products from the natural environment in this era, changing landscapes, bodies and reshaping whole regions.

As we shall see in the environmental chapters (1 and 2), natural destruction and modification increased in this era, bringing major population booms and greater use of earth's resources.

We shall see in the political chapter (3) how more flexible political systems emerged in some parts of the world, even introducing the radical notion that common people might partake in political decision-making. As the idea of political equality emerged in embryo, competition between states also increased in scale and ferocity.

Even greater changes emerged in the economic sphere. The economic chapters (4 and 5) will explore how theorists began developing a new logic for understanding commerce, money and profits. Moving past traditional economic understandings – in which gold, silver and solid land constituted wealth – new notions of liquid capital emerged, borne of innovative financial instruments such as national debts, interest fees and investments. This would create enormous affluence for some. In time economic systems devised by early modern thinkers allowed Europeans to dominate markets worldwide. Economic activity boomed as Atlantic crossings provided a consumerist bonanza for some, along with an astounding increase in economic violence oppressing countless more.

Perhaps even greater innovation, however, came in the spheres of religious, scientific and intellectual life (explored in Chapters 6 and 7). An earlier, more rigid worldview in which elites explained the world was challenged by new ways of open, critical and free thinking. This would both prompt ceaseless religious strife and encourage scientific innovation. Though most scientists and philosophers were religious and did not intend to critique revelation, the unintended consequences of freer thinking were colossal, eventually unleashing, for some, liberation from routine mental servitude required of traditional knowledge systems.

The final chapter (8) will focus on technological advances, highlighting the increasing use of earth's raw materials, minerals and ores, and exploring ways in which humans transformed them into entirely new products for popular consumption. Technological changes appeared in these centuries that seem almost contemporary to us, with industrial exploitation of steam, coal and combustion engines appearing and altering life on earth. This was the beginning of modernity.

The significance of all these transformations remain with us: exploitation of the environment and unremitting population growth continue, as do ongoing political rivalries with roots in this era; the enslavement of millions and the suppression of indigenous people worldwide continue to affect the lives of people around the globe; modern economic life consists of routinization and task-oriented labour regimes worldwide; and cultural wars over the value of science, free thinking and religion persist. Whether we should characterize this period as one of progress towards a modern world, or dismal decline and increased immiseration, is for the reader to decide.

Us and them

It is worth noting there is no straight historical line from medieval to modern, no clear demarcation between the two periods. No one at the turn of the sixteenth century had any idea they might be creating what future scholars would label the 'early modern world'. In addition, though commoners were seldom represented in historical records, the period after 1500 offers historians abundant source material about their lives compared to the medieval or ancient eras. We see more varied perspectives on human life, though they come mostly from literate cultures in Europe, East Asia, India and the Arab world, and usually from those in power. How much evidentiary accuracy these sources provide is a matter of debate, and such debate is central to the historical process. They rarely present the view of anybody but the victors or the powerful. Native Indians, African people, peasants, women and others considered subordinate rarely speak to us in the early modern historical record. Nonetheless, travellers' accounts, church records, diaries and letters, ordinances and narratives, among other sources, show interactions among classes, among societies, and, given rising literacy rates, gradually more insights into everyday life. As early modern states became more centralized and consolidated, they made increasing use of law court records, legal codes and decrees that tell us something about daily life. The rising numbers of books, protests, petitions and pamphlets produced also help, even if they tend to tell us more about the most literate societies and classes than anyone else.

This was a world very different from our own, one we have named in order to understand. In 1651 Thomas Hobbes famously lamented that life was 'nasty, brutish and short'. It was for most people, all over the world, throughout our period. For most human beings, little changed from the medieval centuries in this era. In 1750, when our volume concludes, most peasants still lived in villages or away from centralized cities. Most had nothing to spend and did not participate in the economy as consumers. Most simply produced for their own needs or for a local chief or grandee. European, Muslim, African or Asian peasants ate basic foods, wore very rough clothing and had no or few possessions. Some might own a bench, tools, a chair if lucky. Kitchens in more complex societies might consist of ceramic cups, spoons or bowls. Few people would have a bed, sleeping on straw floor mattresses or the ground. Animal skins provided warmth for people worldwide, serving as blankets into the nineteenth century. Very few people wore shoes, and, though wealthier people might possess towels, cushions and linens, discomfort was common for most. Anyone, rich or poor, might succumb to disease or illness at any time. A tiny minority lived in relative splendour in most societies, but food, clothing and shelter for the vast majority were scant, rough and basic.

This then remained a pre-industrial world where all societies continued habits, behaviours and practices that prevailed a thousand years prior. A new type of market economy approached though towards 1750, which greater utilized woods, water, land, crops and other environmental goods. Superstition and custom still informed land usage, preventing overuse in most places and limiting productivity. Even with new commercial links, trade in our era amounted to only a tiny amount of business compared to today. These two and a half centuries of commerce amounts to less than a year's international shipping volume in the twenty-first century.

In a period of unremittent cruelty and inhumanity by any standards, the Atlantic slave trade stands out. Many societies around the world have practised slavery (and many still do). Europeans began enslaving Africans and Indians in a late-fifteenth-century world where various forms of coerced servitude had been commonplace in all cultures for centuries, including by African and other indigenous rulers. It was, paradoxically, Europeans who towards 1750 began to abolish slavery – against the wishes of certain African, Muslim or Asian elites who considered it their own business who was freed or enslaved in their cultures. But the slave trade, run mostly by Europeans for the profit of European and Euro-American societies, was uniquely terrible. Where previously slaves had been low-status servants, the new type of 'chattel' slavery made humans objects of trade, to be profited from and worked to death. It was more modern, more lucrative, more calculated and more iniquitous in design and intent; it ruined millions of lives and impacted the ancestors of slaves for centuries.

Likewise, the imposition of new European attitudes towards land, labour and life in areas inhabited by Native Americans decimated Indian populations. Natives remain the poorest sector of American society today. Though Europeans did not intend to transmit bodily diseases or wipe out over 10 million indigenous people, they did intend to force Christianity on them, and to extract as much gold, silver and wealth as possible, at great cost to native societies they considered subhuman.

Europeans found new, morally dubious, ways of possessing and exploiting lands and peoples in the Americas, Africa and Asia, enabling them to harness more resources than any previous societies had done. Especially in North-western Europe, robust centralized governments began to purposefully promote economic growth. Political elites more often mobilized the labour inputs of wider swaths of the population. This created a feedback cycle of wealth and power that after 1750 empowered the strongest European countries to dominate global trade, and over time gain control of land and states in the Americas, Africa, Asia and Oceania.

By 1750 North-western Europeans took the lead in developing more efficient combinations of land, labour and natural resource inputs, to create great wealth and economic growth. The practice of saleable valuation of land and property became routine. More and more, European colonizers carefully measured the labour productivity of slaves and native peoples, pressuring them to perform under harsh supervision with minimal provisions. Ingenious new financial instruments allowed Europeans to create capital more effectively and invest it around the world.

Where in the medieval era, some elites enjoyed the produce of faraway markets, now elites and labourers yearned for and imbibed resources produced far away. All across the world, peasants and workers began to produce for distant markets, to be measured by profit sheets, when before they produced for their own local subsistence, working for and with people with whom they had long-standing social relations. These economic changes, once they spread from Europe to other regions of the globe, transformed human life and the natural environment virtually everywhere.

Early modern outcomes

How then might we arrive at a measured understanding of the early modern period and its legacy? This is a time which is in many ways familiar to us, but in other ways remarkably distant. Certainly, we can consider the long-term benefits that developments in this period brought to many peoples, especially those in Europe and leaders in other powerful societies. We can marvel at centuries of population growth and praise leaps in medical knowledge, rising life expectancies and standards of living. We can celebrate the emergence of more tolerant attitudes towards social lessors and foreigners; we can credit both elites and commoners who questioned political and religious abuses, and we might be grateful for innovations in scientific thinking and resulting technological developments that set us on the path to our comfortable techno-world today. We can even rejoice that all across Eurasia, a great many people benefitted from a huge energy subsidy derived from the Americas, from where resources were transformed into foods and products elsewhere.

But we can also dismay at the incessant war, famine, religious fury, inequality, hatred and suspicion that enveloped the centuries between 1500 and 1750. We can wince at a world of incredible violence, torture and pomposity, and the development of an Atlantic slave trade that forced over 10 million unfortunate souls into a life of misery or early death. We can blanch when considering the tragic ecological genocide that resulted from Eurasian diseases, which preyed on the defenceless immune systems of indigenous Americans. We can ponder the arduous lives of peasants all over the world, who continued to suffer under the domination of a small number of elites (Figure 0.2).

Clearly, cartographic understanding of the earth and cosmological comprehension of the skies improved vastly in the early modern period. By 1750, knowledge of the earth, thanks to the mathematical sciences of mapmaking and astronomy, brought power to those societies that developed it, and burdened those who did not with serious disadvantages. Indeed, such knowledge helped determine who would dominate whom into our time. Such domination did not occur overnight. Mongols, Muslims and Asian warriors were just as ferocious as Europeans, both before and after this era. But after 1750, the West would slowly prevail.

Figure 0.2 Medieval witch torture (© Bridgeman Images).

People clearly suffered everywhere. While American natives and African slaves endured European encroachments, nomadic populations that had roamed Central Asia for millennia were subjugated, too. As the growing Chinese and Russian empires enclosed the steppes, lesser-known indigenous populations were forced into humiliating subject status by these two powerful agricultural powers in the seventeenth and eighteenth centuries. The period's transformations pushed nomadic peoples onto marginal lands across Eurasia. The expansive Chinese state overcame numerous peoples, including Muslim Uighurs, Buddhist Tibetans and many tribes who still today consider themselves distinct from the dominant Chinese Han. After 1550, the small Russian state expanded from a region around Moscow, across Siberia, building forts and settlements to eventually control a vast portion of the continent. At the same time, African and Arabian nomads found themselves dominated or impoverished at the hands of Ottoman soldiers and settlers. Power abuses pervaded human history, as they always had.

There was far more interaction among distinct populations in this era. Better understanding of the earth, skies and seas moved populations more than ever after

1500, both in absolute numbers and in spatial distance. Of the roughly 500 million people on earth in 1500, most people lived in Eurasia, with two major empires, the Aztec and Inca, accounting for much of the population of the Americas. South Asia constituted about 20 per cent of the world, while in the Middle East, Africa and other parts of the world, smaller populations existed in mostly minor settlements. China represented about 40 per cent of humanity in 1500, and Europeans populated about 20 per cent of the world. By 1750, however, European numbers increased to represent about 30 per cent of the world, while those of China and India remained roughly the same. Europeans increased gradually in numbers but rapidly in power, settling new places and displacing natives as they did so.

Europeans, however, were not one orchestrated group, acting in conformity to plan and conquer areas of the world. They did not know they were crossing the Atlantic Ocean any more than Indians expected their arrival. The names of these bodies of water were constructed and labelled by Europeans – there were no actual Africa's, Europe's, Asia's, America's or Atlantic and Pacific Oceans. These were names later applied to the earth by Europeans, who would partially claim control over these lands and sea routes because of their newfound power. Across these expanses would flow millions of people, countless items and goods, immeasurable disease microorganisms, all of which prompted new intellectual approaches to life that would have seemed inconceivable before 1500. But nobody planned history to turn out this way (Figure 0.3).

Figure 0.3 Vulcanizing rubber in a factory in Paris, Ile-de-France, France (© Bridgeman Images).

In 1500 China remained the most complex economy and state on earth, the Ottoman Muslim dynasty ruled most of central Eurasia and innumerable other states traded with each other, unaware of even the existence of Europeans. Though they played a marginal role in world history before 1500, Europeans after 1750 began to have a far wider impact, encroaching upon ancient societies who had controlled trade and dominated vast regions for centuries. Yet by 1750, Britain, a tiny island situated on the edge of Europe, with a marginal impact in history thus far, would start to intimidate ancient empires with ease. How Britain, with a population of only 3 million in 1500, replaced China as the most flourishing economy on earth, with all the privileges of power that accompany affluence, is one of the central questions of the following chapters.

From 1750 well into the twentieth century, British traders controlled the production and sale of commodities such as rubber, using vast parcels of lands in India and south-eastern Asia to cultivate it, keeping the profits. This malleable product of the Americas, unknown to Eurasia in 1500, proved crucial in serving the industrial machines of European nations after 1750. Extracted from South America by European explorers in the early eighteenth century, it was, by the nineteenth century, becoming key to Western industrial production. By the twentieth century it represented a material integral to most households on earth, to transportation, infrastructure and to move machines of war and transit. One of the more significant and yet odder materials that arrived in the Old World from the New World, rubber is perhaps a fitting metaphor for the early modern era.

1

Exploiting nature – The early modern environment

Situating the chapter

Humans have always exploited and altered the environment. Our cognitive faculties enabled us to imagine changed surroundings, and then act to make them happen. Though they were weak powers in 1492, Western European states in this era began to chart, comprehend and measure geographical distances in new ways by 1750. Mariners and innovators made use of earlier innovations – derived from Islam, Africa, China and India – to sail the seas, and then to exploit and reshape traditional societies around the world in ensuing centuries.

Britons in this period had not yet developed their particularly calculated, profitable – utilitarian – attitude to land use and global land grabs. They remained committed to the preservation of nature locally, as did most people on earth across Afro-Eurasia and the Americas. The famed Japanese Haiku poet Basho (d. 1694) exalted a similar awe of the environment (and the importance of rest from life's travails).

From 1750, however, the small island of Great Britain, with relatively few people, would reshape the global environment more than any other by industrializing in the 1700s. This geographically tiny, unimportant nation, riven by internal conflict, would after 1750 become an imperial power and unleash the Industrial Revolution, the greatest assault on the environment in human history, prompting a world of rushed days, rushing power and, ultimately, the rush to modernity. In the nineteenth century, Japan too would industrialize at a great pace, with immense consequences for twentieth-century world history, as we shall see.

But first, between 1500 and 1750, the stage would have to be set for this dramatic transformation of human existence, mostly in societies far from England.

By the end of this chapter, readers should be able to:

- Understand how humans altered their environment in the early modern era.
- Suggest ways diverse populations made use of land and labour.
- Explain the consequences of greater global interaction for various societies.
- Appraise the effects of new connections on populations worldwide.
- Analyse whether connections were positive or negative for humanity.

Narrative

European avarice prompted the exploitation of new lands, particularly in the Americas. This spurred the development of a new harsher form of enslavement for African people, and the eradication of millions of indigenous Americans. By the twentieth century, Europeans had turned this zeal for exploration and profit towards Asia and the wider world. Once Western Europeans set foot in the Americas, new conceptions of life on earth emerged. European expansion in the early modern world set off a biological and geographical revolution, the environmental consequences of which we are still dealing with today.

Nature's mysteries

In 1968, the biologist Paul Ehrlich published *The Population Bomb*. He warned that humans might be on the verge of destroying life on earth through ceaseless population growth. Ehrlich predicted that the sheer number of humans, combined with overconsumption of nature's bounties, would condemn humanity to the way of the dinosaurs. Since then, global population has climbed from under 4 billion to 8 billion people, and the earth has been scarred and abused ever more. However, there have also been impressive attempts to reduce the damage of human actions. Persistent environmentalists have reshaped attitudes towards nature's limitations, and exposed the costs of the human capacity to exploit nature. Still, human births continue apace, putting increasing pressure on the earth's resources.

In the early modern era, the idea of overpopulating the planet seemed incomprehensible. The ecological bounty of the Americas nurtured millions of new lives, bringing forth a great population boom between 1500 and 1750, even accounting for vast deaths of African and American natives. Increasingly productive, effective use of the land in these centuries brought increases in food supplies, in lifespans and material expectations. Also, in this era, some began to grasp for the first time the great diversity of human societies inhabiting an increasingly connected earth. Few, if any, understood that nature was an active, dynamic linked system of species and processes that humans could defile.

By 1750, Europeans developed ever more efficient – if ultimately harmful – ways to exploit nature. A new moneymaking ethos, premised on a profit-seeking world view, propelled westerners to draw on the resources of *all* continents, primarily, if not wholly, for their benefit. Only around 1750 did some begin to slowly recognize the ethical and practical necessity of preserving lands and ecosystems for future use.

But well before Britain's late-eighteenth-century Industrial Revolution began polluting the planet at unprecedented levels, some English land lovers warned of overexploiting the earth, lettering the first known environmental tracts. In 1661, John Evelyn, in his 'Inconveniencie of the Aer and Smoak of London Dissipated', wrote of the negative health effects of smoke, arguing that planting trees would correct over-logging of native forests and improve London's dirty air:

> I am able to enumerate a Catalogue of native plants, and such as are familiar to our country and clime, whose redolent and agreeable emissions would even ravish our senses, as well as perfectly improve and ameliorate the Aer about London.[1]

By the 1760s British ecologists inaugurated the first focused attempts to protect forested islands in the Caribbean. In the late eighteenth century, Romantics and early environmentalists warned human actions were despoiling nature, and began to spread ecological awareness through poetry and print. These early environmentalists could not prevent vast levels of pollution between 1750 and the present, of course. At best they could slow the juggernaut of modernity that has now brought the world to possible environmental catastrophe.

Mapping and claiming – Understanding land

If there is one historical fact that most westerners know, it is that Christopher Columbus 'discovered' the Americas in 1492. The word 'discovered' implies that indigenous people did not know of their own existence. Native Americans had, of course, discovered the land millennia before Columbus stumbled upon the New World, unintentionally exposing Europeans to previously unknown peoples and unfamiliar lifeways, while exposing indigenous people by the millions to deadly diseases (Figure 1.1).

Columbus, like many early modern sailors, had little grasp of where he was going upon setting out. Sailors lived in a world of local geographical awareness, lacking accurate maps to guide them much further afar. The bounty of foodstuffs that would fill the bellies of much of the world for centuries to come was the result of wandering adventurers without a strong sense of their destination. What sailors such as Columbus did know about global navigation was mostly borrowed from knowledge developed by Muslim, Indian, African and Asian societies in previous centuries.

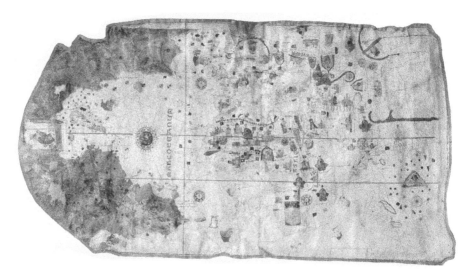

Figure 1.1 De la Cosa's map (Wikimedia Commons).

Indeed, the map Portuguese sailors relied on for the first all-important European voyages was made in Spain in 1375, by Jewish cartographers drawing on accounts of Muslim travellers interested in African gold and slaves. This was not simply a European endeavour, though they improved upon earlier efforts. The famous map of De la Cosa, from 1500, is thought to be the only map made by an individual who witnessed Columbus's voyages. Such visuals were more than the first attempt at mentally mapping the Americas; they were the first step towards recurrent European visits, colonization, settlement, centuries of exploitation of American people and resources, and at times genocide.

In the early modern world, though, geography consisted of a great deal of fantastical guessing. The English hero-pirate Francis Drake mistakenly assured himself in the 1570s that he had found a waterway to sail through the Americas, inspiring others over centuries to seek a passage through the Americas that did not exist (only with the opening of the Panama Canal in August 1914 could ships actually pass through the centre of the Americas). The art of mapping, and cartography as a science, remained essentially unchanged from ancient Greek, Islamic or Chinese efforts. Most were highly inaccurate.

This was a mental environment in which apparitions populated forests, demons haunted the outskirts of villages and monsters churned in the uncharted seas of unknown depths. Unbridled imagination and impossibly long distances shaped a world view that seems innocent to us today. It nonetheless brought the most important coming together of peoples in history, the **Columbian Exchange**. After European sailors stumbled into the Americas in the late fifteenth century, an incredible transatlantic exchange of ideas, goods and diseases began. This exchange benefitted Europeans above all, helping fuel a slow rise to Western global dominance that is only now shifting.

More accurate attempts at mapping and demarcating brought Western states new lands in this era. In the 1494 Treaty of Tordesillas, the Catholic Church and its staunch allies, the monarchs of Spain and Portugal, stamped claims on *all* lands west of an imaginary line down the Atlantic Ocean. As a result of this claim, in the long run, all of South and Central America would speak Spanish or Portuguese, and practice Catholicism. Other European landings in the Americas also had great impact over time. In 1497 John Cabot, an Italian adventurer living in England, raised investment capital from businessmen to fund exploration of what is today Newfoundland and Nova Scotia. Most Canadians and Americans now speak English as a result.

Native peoples in the Americas possessed remarkably different approaches to the natural world than did Europeans. The Aztec, for example, believed – like pre-Christian Europeans and countless societies worldwide throughout history – in respecting the fragility of the natural world, rather than exploiting it for profit. For the Aztec, the sun, wind and most importantly water (in the form of lakes, rivers and seas and rain) represented forces that must be respected to ensure long-term survival.

Dual devotion to sky and soil symbolized a holy life-giving force. Many cultures saw caves as the uterus of the earth. The earth's resources were not to be exploited in any way but a sustainable one. This was an environmental perspective that long predated modern, Western environmentalism.

After 1521, Hernan Cortes's defeat of the Aztec Empire challenged this Native American world view forever. Spain's growing dominance in the Americas and subsequent European mapping of continental lands initiated both a de-sacralization of lands and the ascendancy of an exploitative, utilitarian approach to land use. For early modern Christians, land was a gift from God, meant for them to control and exploit. Mapmaking, by using empirical methods and observation, helped Europeans understand geography and advance knowledge through science, with grave consequences for millions of indigenous people. Scientifically inclined Catholic Jesuit priests in the seventeenth century even mapped the Sonora desert in North America. They then worked to visualize and record parts of India, China, Japan and the Amazon. More accurate mapping fuelled Western domination.

Europeans wandering afar in the seventeenth and eighteenth centuries were remarkable only because elites in complex societies throughout Eurasia typically disdained exploration in this era. Inquisitive westerners arriving in Asia were at best humoured, rarely respected. Chinese or Japanese emperors had no desire to explore, and restrained sailors who wished to. Muslim sultans in India and the wider world of Islam typically rejected exploratory outlooks. Chinese, Indian, Arab and Turkish rulers created incredibly impressive cultures, but they produced few explorers, with consequences in the long run.

Sailing the seas

Over time, better understanding of seas and rivers brought real advantages to Europeans and would help them dominate much of the world by the nineteenth century. In 1500, though, mariners worldwide viewed the earth as a set of physically separated geographical islands, as people had for millennia. In early modern minds, the oceans constituted vast, mysterious, barely mapped bodies of water, a bewildering and fearful barrier to human movement. The thought of finding vast new lands, as in the Americas, was incomprehensible across Africa and Eurasia. Similarly, indigenous Americans could hardly have imagined worlds such as India, China, Africa or Arabia existed.

European expansion into the Atlantic derived mostly from geographical luck. From an environmental perspective, Europeans did not so much 'discover America'. They discovered how weather patterns worked, and used this knowledge. Atlantic Ocean currents and winds pushed sea-bound Europeans towards the Americas, whereas sailors from the Muslim world, Africa or Asia had no such geographical fortune. Northwest Europeans just happened to inhabit a spot of earth that would bring control of new markets and ocean shipping lanes. In the 1600s, small nations like Holland and England rose to prominence in seafaring and international trade,

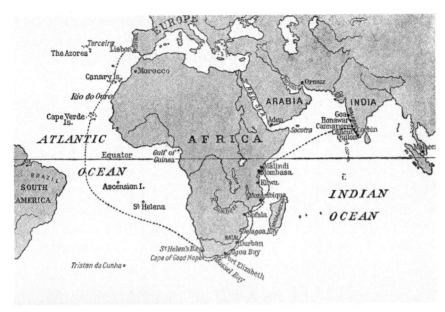

Figure 1.2 Vasco da Gama (1469–1524) Portuguese explorer and commander of the first ships to sail directly from Europe to India (1497); dotted line indicates this voyage. http://www.bbc.co.uk/history/british/tudors/vasco_da_gama_01.shtml. Accessed 22 March 2021.

ultimately dominating financial markets and conquering large areas of the globe. By 1750, the Atlantic Ocean became an intercontinental commercial crossroads, dominated by English, French, Spanish and Dutch ships (Figure 1.2).

Well into the 1800s, however, timeworn, inaccurate methods of navigation persisted. Sailors relied on cloth sails, trial and error or rule of thumb, limiting their ability to steer accurately. Sailing times were slow and navigation was hard to predict. Months, even years, could pass before a ship reached its destination. Sailing times from Mexico or North America to Europe ranged from one to three months in the 1600s:

Mexico to Spain – 12–18 weeks
Boston to England – 4–7 weeks
Chesapeake to England – 6–9 weeks
West Africa to West Indies – 9–10 weeks
West and central Africa to Brazil – 6–7 weeks[2]

The happenstance of European geography provided considerable advantages. Western Europe literally stuck out into the Atlantic, practically 'facing' the Americas. Thus, the actual physical position of England, Portugal, France, Holland and Spain facilitated movement into the Atlantic oceans and, fatefully, the Americas. The English, French and Dutch learned well from the travails of the early Spanish and Portuguese explorers, eventually moving more people and goods faster, and impacting more lands and lives. Nature and the environment often dictated the seafaring fortunes of early modern states. Success in long-distance voyaging depended on ocean currents and winds, which ultimately determined who landed where.

Yet, human attributes also mattered. Europeans' geographical curiosity, obsession with profit and impulse to convert souls to Christianity combined to push explorers well beyond their homelands. For instance, when the Portuguese sailor Vasco da Gama rounded the Cape of Good Hope in 1498 to reach India, he longed to tap into the riches of Asia and to convert souls to Catholicism. This desire – for the world's wealth and so many souls – over time created an expansive trade network on the Indian Ocean that then stretched into the Atlantic. Ambition to dominate these trade lanes further motivated shipbuilders in North-western Europe to innovate and increase ship speeds. Understanding of winds and currents improved through a slow accumulation of navigational expertise, and European technologies gradually developed to help sailors arrive at intended destinations.

There is a reason Europeans regarded adventurers as heroes. Explorers suffered great hardships to bring home gold and glory, and to deliver to God those they considered infidels. Those who dared to challenge existing accounts of earth's geography suffered immensely from existing power elites. In a seventeenth-century Europe torn by religious conflict, those who doubted the Catholic Church's view of the universe were met with the Spanish Inquisition and cruel torture.

Oceans of riches

Between 1500 and 1750 Europeans developed their knowledge of previously travelled routes, building upon other Eurasians skills. This brought increased confidence in the predictability of voyage outcomes. Along with advanced understanding of the environment, capital investment and interest from those with money – wealthy investors and the leaders of states – grew accordingly. By 1750, because of European colonization, the spread of capital markets and cultural linkages the world grew far more interconnected than it had been in 1500 (Figure 1.3).

As noted, learning about ocean currents and wind patterns was more a factor than any particular genius or individual heroism in Europe's eventual mastery of the seas. Westerlies, North-east and South-east trade winds, above and below the equator, moved people around the world regardless of origin. Europeans happened to be sailing in those lanes from continent to continent.

Still, European sailors did work out how to calculate latitudes and to grasp the angles of the sun and planets. To arrive ashore, even if in error or months later than planned, they needed a practical, almost scientific, approach to cartographic knowledge and ocean navigation. Once Western Europeans figured out how to sail open oceans with confidence, they then begin to establish ports, build factories and ultimately empires.

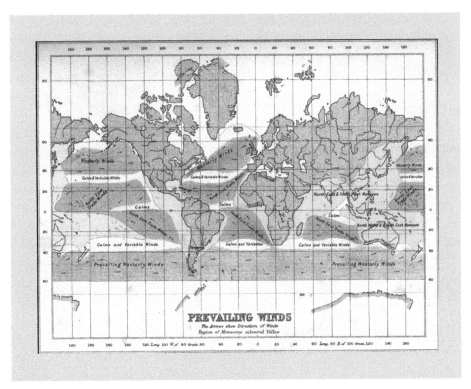

Figure 1.3 Prevailing wind patterns (© Getty Images).

They also improved immeasurably with regard to timekeeping, complex mathematics and other means of measuring time and space by the 1700s. Though many seafarers from many places had similarly mastered the seas, Europeans were both more recent in recognizing longitude and latitude, and far more modern in their approach.

By the 1800s, Europeans possessed better ships and guns with which to dominate existing traders and their states. Important cities such as Vijayanagar in modern India had long served as entrepots for traders, from China to the Middle East and Mediterranean. Europeans had been small players in this Indian Ocean trade, but once the oceans opened up, a massive global marketplace became the domain of European voyagers and merchants. In the 1800s this would provide them industrial levels of raw material extraction.

Following Spanish and Portuguese voyagers, Dutch and French explorers harnessed navigational knowledge to draw wealth from the earth and its peoples throughout the 1600s. By 1750 the English were building on these earlier precedents to dominate ocean trade, and from here this small nation began developing the world's strongest navy. Voyagers such as Francis Drake, John Cabot and others plundered Dutch and Spanish shipping, sidelining them from the global fight for economic power by the 1700s.

Even among Western European rivalries, the British were fortunate in environmental terms. Their island location brought advantages in intra-European conflict. Since winds blew from the west, English coastal mariners could defend the country easily against local rivals, the Dutch, whose ships and ports had to face eastern winds. Continental Europeans had to fend off attacks by British ships buoyed by favourable winds and currents.

Western Europeans also drew riches directly from the oceans. Though sugar, gold and silver are the most conspicuous symbols of early modern Atlantic trade, fish was the most sought-after product initially. Portuguese sailors had first ventured out into the Atlantic in the 1440s, where fishermen had searched for codfish for centuries. Deep-sea currents along the Atlantic coast of the Americas pushed up nutrients and fish that enticed Portuguese merchants. Atlantic cod in particular was abundant. In this period, hundreds of thousands of tonnes of cod caught in the eastern seaboard of the Americas fed bellies in expanding European cities, providing a major source of protein for growing populations.

Using and owning land

Although sea voyagers everywhere used similar sailing techniques in the 1500s, approaches to land usage differed considerably. Societies around the world adapted to very specific local circumstances. In the highlands of East Africa, for example, a unique agricultural system developed, suited to a high-rainfall, subtropical, elevated environment. Local Bantu-speaking peoples in this region grew bananas as their main crop, supplemented by grains, yams and beans grown around the banana plantations. Although unique to the wet highlands, this agricultural strategy shared an important characteristic with many other societies around the world: **intercropping**, where those working the land planted different crops near each other, usually so as to make optimal use of a soil's nutrients. This was not an efficient strategy since it made harvesting complex, but it was highly sustainable and commonly used from the Americas to Africa and Asia. If not as 'productive' in the short term, it proved more sustainable than how Europeans exploited the land.

Europeans took a different approach to exploiting resources. They pursued a strategy of marking out, managing, separating and ordering landscapes, seeking quicker, more productive outcomes. The polder system of the Netherlands (Holland) is one example of this strategy. The Dutch used dikes to reclaim land from the sea. They carefully planted this land with individual crops, or turned it over to livestock, with great efficiency. These two systemic approaches illustrate very different strategies of land management pursued around the world after 1500. Over the course of the early modern era, for better or worse, the European strategy expanded dramatically and became a new norm by the 1800s. It would replace customary practices in almost every place the two systems met (Figure 1.4).

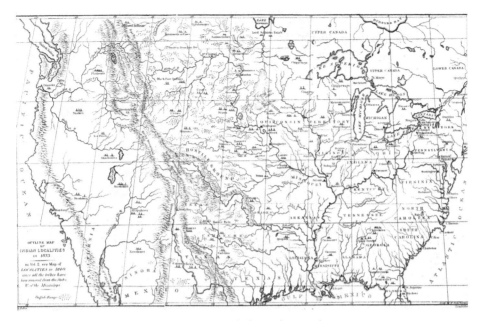

Figure 1.4 North American tribes map (© Getty Images).

Change came slowly though. For the first 200 years after Europeans arrived in the lands of Native Americans, new trade and land practices emerged slowly, with only limited environmental impact. Indians in the Americas, like most people worldwide, continued to live in small villages, employing various customary approaches towards land usage, agriculture, hunting, gathering and pastoralism. Indigenous people subsisted in diverse ways. Some populations were sedentary, some were nomadic and many combined approaches in order to survive, usually with a light touch on ecosystems. Peoples in the Americas and Africa had long exploited natural resources in their own way, but within sustainable limits, focused more on sharing than competition. A race for wealth was not the intent: indigenous social groups manipulated the natural world to extract what they needed to survive, with long-term sustainability in mind.

European intrusion steadily weakened the traditional economic and social patterns of native peoples. By 1750 household and early factory production emerged in Western Europe. At the same time, large-scale agriculture replaced subsistence land usage, as Europeans chased profits, using capital to produce more food and income. Newly developed European bureaucratic and legal institutions demanded fixed property lines for land typically owned by one legal entity, usually composed of upper-class men. After 1750, large-scale change eradicated traditional ways of life worldwide, as burgeoning industrial agriculture and an increased demand for profit – instead of careful stewardship of nature's resources – prevailed, spread worldwide by European colonizers.

In North America, once English colonists learned to plant foods (with the help of natives), hunger would afflict Indians far more than Englishmen. Europeans brought diseases and new plants and animals that upset native ecosystems. Some native populations resisted by moving away to survive. Forced migration turned sedentary populations into nomadic ones, perhaps most notably the North American Plains Indians. By 1750 most Indians in the Americas had died from disease, been killed or pushed onto marginal lands. This process only worsened after 1800, when populations of European stock spread over the whole North American continent to form the current United States of America.

Everybody *used* the land one way or another. Both the Inca and Aztec Empires practised intensive agriculture, using farmland, terracing and irrigation to produce food for survival. Some hunted and fished, some gathered and population densities remained low. But harmful effects on ecosystems were few, as populations across the Americas regarded land as sacred, something to be held in trust rather than exploited to its fullest. Likewise, most Eurasian empires considered land a collective good, to be protected for the welfare of all. Emperors technically owned all land in the Ottoman, Mughal and Qing Empires, but even here they were expected to allow broad use of the land in a way that benefitted society as a whole.

This traditional approach brought low yields, but sustained life and land. The new European approach – emphasizing productivity and profit – took as much as possible from the land and monetized agriculture, heedless of downstream consequences. Where Native Americans cycled the land so it thrived, and they moved to new pastures only if necessary. Europeans maximized farm and forest for gains, taking the best farmland and other lands from natives when they encountered them. Europeans saw 'God's green earth' as infinite; nature existed to produce capital gain.

So, when Portuguese explorers landed in South America, they saw an endless environmental bonanza to exploit. After stumbling upon modern-day Brazil in 1499, Pedro Cabral proclaimed he had found a resource to exploit for the good of himself, king and church. In a fertile land considered boundlessly productive, Europeans saw flora, fauna, ores, men and women as there for the taking. Ominously, by 1750 plantations had exhausted the soils of Brazil, leading Portuguese merchants to mine gold instead. They would soon diversify to produce tobacco, cotton, rice and coffee for global markets.

Then as now, the natural environment offered great prospects for some and terrible toil for others. For Native Americans, life after 1500 meant absorbing the impact of European advances, including deadly epidemics, labour exploitation, forced migrations and desecration of the indigenous heritage. For many West Africans, it meant enslavement in the Americas. By colonizing vast areas, Europeans gained swathes of **ghost acreage** – new lands they could exploit beyond their own, to add products like sugar, cotton and wood materials to their economies.

By 1750, particularly in North America but eventually in all continents, Europeans and other elites categorized, organized and ultimately exploited land through a transplanted system of legal land ownership. This state-supported system was draped over a patchwork of loose-knit, overlapping native ecosystems worldwide. Indians considered land as held in common from time immemorial. It was not a commodity to be valued as a constructed unit of exchange based on transactions completed in an abstract entity called the market. But eventually it would be.

Competing for land

Early modern land development and colonization went hand in hand. Indeed, burgeoning states in Western Europe, and later the United States, were shaped by colonizing and dispossessing lands, though this was hardly exceptional in world history. Competition for control over land and resources reinforced national and imperial power everywhere in these centuries. It always had, if not on quite the scale of this global expropriation.

The development of the Russian state, for example, which formed in the mid-sixteenth century, paralleled Western European economic and environmental expansionism. After 1700 the explorer Fyodor Luzhin (d. 1727) mapped, claimed and named vast eastern lands in Eurasia for the Russian state. Russians even claimed land in California and Alaska in the 1810s, and Poland and the Baltic states were consistently pursued aggressively by Moscow. Expansion south through Central Asia into the Muslim world also incorporated countless populations into the Russian state in the 1800s.

Likewise, after 1650, Chinese rulers expanded imperial borders to dominate Tibetans, Mongolians and many steppe populations. Russian and Chinese leaders agreed to grab vast swaths of land in the 1689 Treaty of Nerchinsk. Through this, the Chinese realm added vast lands to the already huge loess plateau in the north and the wetter south, bringing great population growth as a result. The huge states of China and Russia were no less averse to dominating indigenous peoples and claiming land – they just did it closer to home than Western Europeans.

As Russia and China expanded, three great Muslim empires – the Ottomans, Mughals and Safavids – grew in Eurasia, gradually controlling vast amounts of land in much of today's Middle East and North Africa by 1700. African empires such as the Mali and Songhay, for example, dominated weaker groups by conquering and expanding across the African continent, long after the slave trade began. Powerful African kings successfully exploited new ways of managing land and people, becoming slave-supplying political powerhouses to Europeans. Wealthy elite families had long derived power from herding or land ownership, but now chiefdoms fought among themselves to profit from supplying slaves to foreign merchants and world markets. Queens and kings in the powerful Kongo empire fought Europeans to end slavery in the seventeenth century, while others readily supplied captives to the transatlantic slave market.

Wider commercial linkages in the seventeenth century stimulated the rise of new African kingdoms, such as the Oyo and Asante. The Asante controlled gold, guns and slaves, centralizing regional power into one large kingdom. The Oyo empire connected the interior of Africa to the coasts, benefitting from new global trade connections. African elites gained, even as so many other people died and suffered. New geographical linkages upended traditional power structures in West Africa. But new kingdoms in West Africa emerged, exploiting access to guns and slaves to gain and solidify power.

In the Americas, indigenous empires also dominated through land management. The Inca in modern Peru controlled outlying populations for centuries from their high mountain valleys, forcing regional labourers to terrace millions of acres of land and pave roads in the name of imperial order. Incan populations grew to the high numbers Pizarro encountered in 1524 because of extraordinarily effective vertical agricultural production, land use and forced labour.

Aztec hydro-engineering demonstrated impressive capacity for gaining high yields. After initially being defeated by other groups and exiled to infertile lands, the Azteca reclaimed swamplands, creating fertile mud flats and floating isles called chinampa. These floating lake gardens intersected with aqueducts and natural springs to aid their domination of weaker peoples throughout modern Mexico. When the Spanish conquistador Hernan Cortes arrived in 1519, he drained parts of Tenochtitlan in an act of environmental warfare, emptying moats of water to defeat the Aztecs and claim the land for Spain.

Spaniards, of course, claimed and grabbed huge tracts of land in the Americas. Cortes conquered over 7,000 square miles in Central America, building castles on previously communal land. He and other officials enjoyed massive land grants from the Spanish monarchy through the *encomienda* system, defeating and enslaving Indians 'legally'. Along with gold and land, Spanish conquerors took native women at will, in a vast bounty of both opportunity and oppression. There was no rule of law in this world.

But prior to the Spanish arrival, Indians in North America used the land actively, burning fires to replenish soils and control mosquitoes. Newly scorched areas attracted bison, who fed on freshly grown grass to in turn feed natives. Amazon tribes grew into huge settlements as a result of actively enriching soil, through the construction of reservoirs and irrigation. Still, compared to the ecological consequences of silver extraction, timber felling, animal depletion, fur trapping and the dispersion of newly planted European grasses, the indigenous touch was comparably light.

Poor Europeans

Elites gained worldwide, while the majority suffered. Poor Europeans lost access to lands in this period, owing to the growing elite emphasis on productivity and profit. In emergent European nations, masses of common peasants lost power to elites. In England, the Tudor dynasty encouraged drainage of the fens, moors and marshes in the east to create new domains for the monarchy, which it then claimed and distributed to political allies in the nobility to consolidate power and sustain allies. Such acts of intimidation, and the displacement of commoners, were justified in the name of efficiency, as they often increased overall quantities of food through new agricultural practices. In Western Europe, after 1600, landowners sought to maximize wealth and land production through **enclosures**, where landowners forced peasants from customary lands they claimed were ancestral. The enclosure system made lands previously used in common – through custom, not title – legal property that elites could exploit at will.

Enclosures in Europe were just as alien to peasants as European fencing and titling of lands in the Americas were to Indians. Both were justified by claims of efficiency. The three-field rotation system of Northern Europe improved upon the earlier two-field Mediterranean system to produce an abundance of sustenance after 1600. Other parts of the world also experienced increased productivities in land usage in this period. Japanese farmers, for example, converted 1.5 million hectares of land to over 3 million cultivated hectares by 1750, and peasant rights were scant anywhere.

Nevertheless, this proto-industrial, early capitalist European approach to land was different in scale, exploitation and competition to others worldwide. Only recently have humans begun to understand the need to preserve diversity and protect nature's bounty. In the early modern period Europeans tended not to conceive of environmental damage as a problem. The loss of access to land made migrants of peasants in Western Europe, many of whom moved from the rural lives to which they were accustomed to the growing number of cities.

Cities – covering the land

Urban environments such as cities are the most obvious example of human modification of nature. Cities had existed for thousands of years all around the world, but this era brought the emergence of thousands of new conurbations worldwide. Empires that encroached on native populations were typically centred on capital cities, with adjoining agricultural populations forced to sustain urban centres. Empires, states or temple-towns depended on cereal production from adjacent hinterland regions, which they usually controlled. Hence the city was, and is, a stark illustration of a state's environmental and political control. The Spanish alone established close to a thousand urban settlements in the Americas between 1500 and 1800. Colonization was also a process of urbanization.

By 1750 England was becoming the most urban, industrialized state on earth. In 1500, Europe possessed numerous trading cities in Italy, but most of the world's principal cities were located in China. Cities like Beijing, Hangzhou and Nanjing teemed with half a million residents each, while most westerners lived in villages or smaller cities. Vijayanagar in India and Cairo in Egypt had similarly large numbers.

Constantinople in the Ottoman Empire and Edo (Tokyo) in Japan were vast bustling metropolises, with around 250,000 people competing for resources. Only after 1600 did Paris, France, reach a similar size. In the 1500s Europe still consisted mostly of smaller cities of no more than 25,000. By 1750, when London and Paris developed into major urban centres of wealth and power, few could have predicted it in 1500.

As in all cities, these large settlements often produced negative ecological consequences. By 1700 Chinese woodworkers had deforested vast hinterlands, chopping down forests to turn marginal areas into arable land for food. From Asia to the Americas, growing demand for tobacco fed the habits of city workers, and a growing need for fuel and building materials, prompted relentless land exploitation.

Cities certainly existed in the Americas before 1492. The Aztec capital of Tenochtitlan (modern-day Mexico City), for example, had a population of over 200,000 when Cortes arrived in 1519, far more than any European city at the time. With the arrival of Europeans in the Americas, however, the process of urbanization accelerated. Spanish rulers saw the founding of towns and cities in the Americas as central to their project of colonization. Places like Potosi and Mexico City became centres of Spanish power. Cities like Santa Fe and St. Augustine (the oldest city in the United States) helped Spain consolidate its power to the north. These were towns populated by the world's people, not only Europeans. By 1600 Mexico City was a mixture of diverse people from all of Eurasia, where a fast-paced life and a Wild West rush for mineral riches despoiled surrounding lands while eliminating countless lives through forced labour (Figure 1.5).

The mad rush to mine precious metals facilitated commerce across Eurasia, but native people and native soils suffered wretchedly. Potosi is perhaps the most blatant example of early modern people reshaping lands and lives to control resources. Potosi, formed from an extinct volcano, was a mountain of untapped silver – 50 per cent pure ore. The Spanish worked native labourers mercilessly, mining it to the fullest. As waste poured onto the surrounding lands, Spanish galleons guaranteed shipment of silver to China and Europe. Unimaginable human pain and forced labour excavated untold volumes of wealth and silver and gold. It made some rich and shaped global economic markets, but produced incredible suffering among native peoples and slaves.

The process of land exploitation expedited greatly between 1500 and 1750. New cities bursting with up to a million people grew to generate new desires and new diseases. Regional ecosystems were transformed for extraction, impacting millions of acres around mines and quarries. The deaths of millions of labourers served to provide wealth for a few Western states, for some elites in those states, to the detriment of the majority of humans alive. Then as now, the wealth derived from efficient capitalization of nature's goods would serve the few rather than the many. Indeed, this period of history was also subject to another very familiar component of modern life, which impacted all people, climate change.

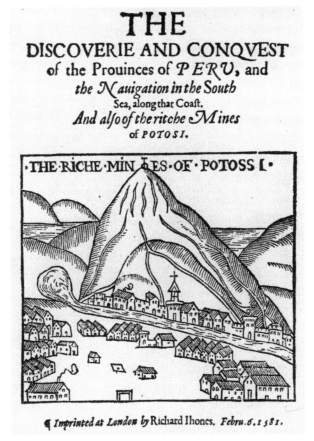

THE
DISCOVERIE AND CONQVEST
of the Prouinces of *PERV,* and
the Nauigation in the South
Sea, along that Coaſt.
And alſo of the ritche Mines
of *POTOSI.*

·THE·RICHE·MINᴇS·OF·POTOSS I·

¶ *Imprinted at London by* Richard Ihones. *Febru.6.1581.*

Figure 1.5 View of mines. *C.* 1581, a view of the silver mines of Potosi from a book by Augustin de Zarate, translated by P. Nicholas. One of the main objectives of the Spanish Conquistadores was the finding of silver (© Getty Images).

Little Ice Age

If early modern people found oceans mysterious and forests forbidding, they could barely comprehend the vast weather systems encircling the earth. For all the grandeur of human actions in sailing seas and creating cities from nature's raw materials, larger natural forces defined possibilities and shaped activities greatly in these centuries.

Modern readers, familiar as they are with stores full of products imported from around the world, can easily underappreciate the centrality of the local environment to food production. Aside from political formations, religious world views, technological aptitude and economic proclivities, humans of all shades, classes and origins ultimately depended upon the resources they could derive from their nearby natural environment. The survival of greater numbers of humans fundamentally depended on access to food, whether through traditional gathering, planned harvests or industrial agriculture. The cultivation of crops and production of dairy products produced foods for sustenance.

All of this of course depended on the weather: geography, geology and climate shaped the actions of people in all cultures, constraining some or enabling others.

It is, therefore, important to note that along with voyages and state expansion, the whole Atlantic world underwent a drastically altered climate in these centuries. Colder temperatures and longer droughts afflicted the northern hemisphere from 1500 through to the end of the eighteenth century in what is known as the **Little Ice Age**. Beyond Europe and Asia, a lack of data limits our understanding, but it is likely this global climatic event impacted societies worldwide to some degree. Sunspots appear to have cooled the earth in this era, and changes in weather systems made life harsher for millions worldwide. Some scholars estimate that between 1400 and 1800, average global temperatures dropped by 1 degree centigrade. This amount of change affected not only bodily warmth but also the productivity of agriculture. Given that survival for most people was already tenuous – famine was common worldwide, death always at the door – a shortened growing season of just a few weeks meant hunger for millions and starvation for many.

In Europe, marginal lands were no longer cultivable with the cooling of temperatures. Shorter growing seasons lowered the amount of energy available to wide populations, causing hunger, which increased competition for food. The resulting conflicts lessened lifespans and forced migrations to better lands or cities. Major droughts in North America doomed large settlements just as European settlers coincidentally arrived in growing numbers. Colder weather possibly explains why thousands felt compelled to move from England to settle in the northern part of Ireland after 1610 – one of the first outposts of the eventually vast British Empire. Settlers from England also began a new life in Jamestown in 1607, and tree rings show that ten years of horrible drought had just begun.

Then, a major volcanic eruption from Peru in 1600 devastated agriculture in many parts of the world for over a century. Its effects reached far afield, prompting famine in Russia, damaging crops as far away as France. The Russian Famine of 1601–3 may have killed up to 2 million people, with perhaps a third of the population dying of hunger. The worst cold weather occurred between 1590 and 1610, with spells returning in the 1640s and the 1690s. Glaciers increased in size in the northern hemisphere throughout this period.

Through the 1690s, Europe suffered extremely low temperatures and recurrent crop failures, bringing hunger, frozen nights and droughts. Some already barren Northern countries suffered from extensive starvation; Iceland's population declined 15 per cent between 1650 and 1750, while cold haunted much of Eurasia. Chinese peasants endured recurrent floods that ruined staple crops like rice and brought famine. While rainfall increased on the eastern coast of Africa, West and central Africa endured extreme drought between 1650 and 1750, as the edges of the African Sahara moved southward, forcing further migration and growing conflict over scarcer resources.

Nature's bounty

But just as nature took away, so it gave back. Effective exploitation of nature's resources increased significantly in the early modern period, and again, the Americas were crucial. Europeans found an extraordinary world of plenty on the newly found continent. Early European testimonies upon arriving in the Americas emphasized the diverse abundance of flora (vegetation) and fauna (wildlife). When Francisco de Orellana discovered the headwaters of the Amazon in 1541 in modern-day Ecuador, he could not believe the scope of the new lands he encountered. A copious profusion of new natural resources thus became available to Europeans after 1492.

Flora and fauna

New World plants and foods would enrich all of Eurasia, providing nutritional gains for countless humans. South and Central America were far more diverse environmentally than Eurasia – rain forests, grasslands, forests, mountains and deserts enticed rapacious Europeans like children in a candy store. Europeans voraciously mined lands, cut forests and shot animals as if they would last forever, indifferent to local life, environmental preservation or sustainability.

Plant life

Some societies lost while others gained. Europeans upended American ecosystems, overtaxed soils and introduced foreign plants and animals. Prior to their arrival, the Aztecs had enjoyed more nutritious diets than those in the 'Old World'. People in the south of the continent enjoyed many varieties of potatoes prior to industrialization. A year-round supply of food sustained South Americans, as potatoes could be freeze-dried for surplus. Llamas provided wool to keep people warm.

The cross-fertilization of plants that ensued between Eurasia and the Americas favoured Europeans and Asians. Maize (corn) spread over the fields of Europe and Africa to create new landscapes. Almost the perfect grain, maize supported a new type of global agriculture. It matured quickly and could grow in varied environments across Eurasia, sustaining millions in the Old World who may never have survived without American foods.

These diverse forms of maize and other American foods were shipped to mouths worldwide. Chia seeds provided a rich source of protein, and nutrients from chocolate supplemented meat dishes. Other gifts from the Americas included squash, string beans, pumpkins and domesticated turkey.

Foods moved around the world more than ever. Eurasians already enjoyed African items such as yams, okra, millet, watermelon, peas and rice. In turn Africans gained from the arrival of cassava, introduced from the Americas, to this day an African staple. Africans also imported Asian fruits such as oranges, bananas and coconuts, in addition to pineapples and papayas of American origin. Rice travelled to the Americas, where Africans with experience cultivating brought expertise to slave plantations.

New foods from the Americas seemed magical to those who had never known of their existence. In the sixteenth century, fruits such as bananas and pineapples excited the taste buds of the fortunate few who tried them, and scorching hot chilli peppers shocked pallets of the privileged, adding zest to bland foods. Less alluring but even more important as a source of nutrition, potatoes, tomatoes, peppers, yams and corn supported healthier Eurasian populations after 1500 – all while those who had previously enjoyed such foods in the Americas were decimated by disease, domination and starvation.

Sugar

American plants and tropical fruits nourished millions in the Old World, and demand for them grew accordingly. Perhaps no food impacted as much as the sweetest of them all – sugar. Muslims introduced it to Christian Europe in the eleventh century during the Crusades (the word 'sugar' is of Arabic origin – *al-zucar*). Christian Europeans taste for religious conflict was matched by a growing craving for the sweet substance. New lands in the Americas were well suited for growing sugar cane. By 1570, Portuguese sugar production moved from the small islands of Madeira and Sao Tome off the coast of Africa to Brazil. There, vast plantations soon produced sugar on artificially constructed plots of forest and farm estates, plantations – in essence the first industrial enterprises and modern factories. A further proliferation in sugar cultivation occurred after 1650 when West Indian production further satiated Eurasian desires.

Sugar not only tasted good, it provided crucial energy for workers to produce in European workshops and early factories. Europeans even exploited sugar for medicinal purposes, as it prevented the growth of bacterium and promoted the healing of wounds or sores. Voracious demand for sugar soon drove efforts to produce it as efficiently as possible. This resulted in a massive increase in the transatlantic slave trade to supply the sugar industry with labour, leading in turn to deforestation and erosion of American lands, particularly in the Caribbean islands.

One French commentator noted in the eighteenth century the consequences for humanity of these new cravings:

> I do not know if coffee and sugar are essential to the happiness of Europe, but I know that these two products have accounted for the unhappiness of two great regions of the world: America has been depopulated so at to have land on which to plant them; Africa has been depopulated so as to have the people to cultivate them.[3]

Potatoes

Even the poorest peasants across Eurasia gained from American foods. Corn imported from the Americas was then grown locally; the much poorer south of France saw an end to recurrent famines. Even more than corn, the potato probably saved millions from starvation. Since potatoes and sweet potatoes grew in marginal lands, families could sustain themselves even in rocky acidic soils lacking nutrients, from Ireland to Russia. Notably, after the potato arrived in Europe, few major famines of note occurred. Populations with potatoes needed only to find sources of vitamins A and D to survive, which came readily enough from milk. Supplementary carbohydrates provided by rice, nuts and potatoes stimulated population booms across Eurasia, from Ireland to China in the 1600 and 1700s.

The Americas thus sustained life across Eurasia. Asian societies gained also from the exploitation of American lands. Some of the basic components of modern Chinese food – sweet potatoes, peanuts, maize, cassava, cashews, pineapples and chilli peppers – originated in the Americas. China's population growth soared in the early modern era as a result of the Columbian Exchange. In addition, Chinese farmers brought more land into cultivation to produce higher-yield strains of rice, imported from Southeast Asia. Combined, this alleviated the hunger inflicted on Eurasian lands and peoples in the generally conflict-ridden seventeenth century.

Monoculture

While much of the world gained from the Columbian Exchange, the costs to lands in the Americas were as damaging as they were to indigenous people. As westerners began to reshape American land for agricultural profit or for ownership, the delicate ecosystems Indians had long sought to maintain deteriorated. Europeans sought to maximize profits through specialized farming of the most profitable crops, known as **monoculture**, which lessened the diversity of ecosystems in the Americas. Indeed, large-scale production for export diminished plant diversity across the Americas by the 1700s. Since plants need nitrogen to photosynthesize, crops like sugar, tobacco, rice, coffee and cotton stressed lands, depleting soil nutrients, nitrogen and phosphorus. More people only worsened soils.

Europeans in American cities exported American crops to nourish the faraway bodies of Eurasian consumers. Nitrates and guano derived from bird and bat excrement provided substitute fertilizer in Europe and Asia well into the nineteenth century, maintaining the lives of millions. Crops such as maize transformed lands from America to Southern Europe. In the Americas, however, Eurasian plants and grasses reduced the diverse mixture of plants and animals. Eurasian grasses used as bedding on ships and transplanted to the Americas choked native grasses. Farmers turned American forests and prairies into arable land, producing huge volumes of staple crops, such as tobacco, corn, wheat and rice. The land was transformed everywhere.

Deforestation

It is easy to overlook the earth's woods, which are also central to human history. Wood – and water – had for millennia constituted a ready supply of energy, long before coal or oil could be utilized. Wood, of course, came from land, and large stretches of land at that. This meant farmers or pastoralists wishing to use land functioned in tension with forests and woods and had to cut them down to subsist.

By 1500 Europe's forest cover had been depleted for centuries to provide wood for home heating and cooking. Indeed, through our period, deforestation was rampant: by 1750 the British Isles had seen over 90 per cent of its medieval tree cover chopped down. Scandinavia was heavily deforested between 1500 and 1800, and agricultural land across Northern Europe was overexploited. China altered its environment significantly through forest cutting and expansion into steppe lands across inner Asia. The removal of wood cover warmed the Chinese region as a result. Rivers flowed faster due to increased snowmelt and tree loss in the seventeenth century. Fast-paced deforestation of the Ganges region in India after the sixteenth century also degraded the environment, and the Japanese cleared most of their mountains of trees by the late seventeenth century. The rush to construct buildings and cities altered ancient landscapes considerably.

Shipbuilding, the technology that brought Europeans to America, required a great deal of wood. Rigid, straight log pines, which were generally abundant, formed ships masts. Ship hulls, however, needed flexible woods, bringing further expansion into woodlands worldwide to find more trees. Aside from its use in shipping and home construction, wood was the main source of heating in cold European and Asian climes. The eastern forests of North America were integral to the growth of the British Royal Navy and that island's growing global power. By 1750 New England colonists exported forests of timber to Europe to build ships and heat hearths and homes.

Europeans also exploited forest products for luxury items. Explorers extracted dyes for colouring textiles from Brazilian trees to produce a light red for clothing. Indigo from plants made a beautiful violet for garments, while cochineal from insects yielded an opulent red, a colour the princes and sultans of Eurasia wore with great satisfaction.

The trees of the world were thus sliced apart to warm, clothe and transport people, with little regard for nature's limits. By modern standards, though, environmental destruction was limited. Over 50 per cent of Russia was still forestland by 1750, and most people from Eurasia to the Americas still practised pre-industrial farming, living off the land in small farms. Pre-industrial handicrafts and home workshops predominated until the nineteenth century, with rural peasants the largest portion of populations anywhere. As in 1500, most people still lived in villages of less than 5,000 in 1750. Early modern exploitation of nature, though remarkable, was nothing like the scale of abuse to come after 1900. But it laid the grounds for later abuses and environmental destruction.

Animal rights

Spicy meats

Like plants and woods, animals are central to human history. Europeans initially sailed to sea in pursuit of Asian peppers of course, but they were to preserve animal meat. Subsequently, European plants and animals reshaped the Americas, bringing an environmental watershed that upended ways of life indigenous people had developed over centuries. The introduction of domesticated Eurasian animals – horses, sheep, goats, cows, cats, dogs – altered the land enormously. Native American animals, like indigenous people, made limited physical impact on land before Eurasian animals arrived. Aside from the dog in the north or the llama in the south, no domesticated animals or pack animals roamed American lands prior to Europeans' arrival. This was a comparatively pristine ecosystem compared to what was to come.

Newly introduced Eurasian animals impacted lands from South to North America from 1500. Herds of cattle, sheep and pigs escaped from colonial pens, breeding at will and modifying the environment widely. Cattle and sheep ground vegetation to shreds, inhibiting the regrowth of shrubs and trees. Pigs ran wild, ruining plants – a small number of pigs brought to Cuba in 1509 were reportedly running in numbers as high as 30,000 by 1514. Wild cattle and goats despoiled grasslands, overbreeding and turning out weaker species. Spanish horses bolted from forts, turning feral and breeding tirelessly. Horses arrived in small numbers in the 1540s. By 1750 they ranged across North America, with wild herds spreading to populate the continent. Rats emigrated on ships along with humans to devastate crops and food supplies. Cross-fertilization could also be positive: the English brought honeybees, which pollinated crops and orchards productively. European animals provided more meat in the diets of all, even for surviving natives.

Animal control

Societies worldwide had controlled animals for millennia of course. But whereas indigenous populations had conserved animal numbers with next year in mind, Europeans bred, used and owned livestock. Animals even played a role in the domination of indigenous people: Spanish soldiers used fierce dogs to attack and kill Indians in the 1500s, and horses were tantamount to modern tanks, providing strength, mobility and power for Europeans. Appreciating the advantages horses brought, Spanish colonizers did their best to keep them out of the hands of natives. Notably, during the 1680 Pueblo Revolt against Spanish rule in modern-day New Mexico, Spain abandoned Santa Fe and its hundreds of horses in defeat. These horses were the ancestors of what became many tribal herds, especially for Plains Indians.

Previously in the Americas, native peoples sourced animal furs for limited, practical uses. Europeans now sought to source and stockpile hides and furs for profit. By the eighteenth century, trappers and hunters wiped out fur-bearing species to supply voracious Eurasian demand. Furs were of immense interest to Europeans, who learned from Indian hunters how to catch animals. They then traded pelts for metal products such as guns that Indians desired to gain advantage themselves.

Indeed, the Little Ice Age meant humans needed animals more than ever. Fauna in colder regions of North America and Russia produced thicker furs, which became highly prized luxury goods through the 1600s. The ensuing boom in the global fur trade wiped out millions of animals from North America to Eurasia, while feeding wealthy patrons' aspiration for sartorial status symbols. Sable furs were common throughout northern European forests until 1700. Thereafter only Siberian sables remained, as ranges diminished to critically low levels.

In this era, animals were not treated with compassion. Concern for animals' feelings is a modern notion. Native Americans drove animals over cliffs or into dead ends to slaughter them. Animals were mostly feared – fairy tales worldwide often cite wolves and forest beasts for good reason. From India through Central Asia, tigers had long killed villagers and were hunted to low numbers. Wild elephants, requiring large forestlands for survival, were hunted to small numbers in India in this era. By the 1750s, elephants captured for Mughal elites declined to the point they were rarely seen in India. Few worried about sustaining species across Eurasia; human survival and state profits mattered far more.

Tragedy of the Commons

In the process of mapping land and sea, Europeans subjugated millions of people in the Americas and enslaved millions of Africans. Strangely then, a positive outcome of this explorative mentality was the priming of human curiosity about the world at large. Already by 1700 Europeans such as Edmond Halley had quite accurately mapped the continents. The four continents surrounding the Atlantic – Europe, Africa, North and South America – are today part of a unified, entangled commercial entity with a common oceanic world view, at least partially a result of this geographical curiosity. Significantly, Europeans would both name these oceans and gain most from them (Figure 1.6).

Like all people, Europeans did not have one mindset in this era. Even within Europe, some criticized such avarice and exploitation. Already in 1649, a group in England known as the Diggers argued exploitation of land went hand in hand with exploitation of labour. Gerrard Winstanley demonstrated how the wealthy and powerful competed with each other to grab as much land as possible from the wider, poorer population, in what he called the '**Tragedy of the Commons**'. In this real-life human tragedy, once some family or great man appropriated land by whatever means, competitors grabbed the rest in emulation, creating an interminable race to the bottom for loot in land and despoliation of nature. The poor were left poorer and the rich even richer. This tragedy was played out worldwide after 1700, and persists today.

Figure 1.6 Halley's map of 1700. World's first ever weather map. This map of the trade winds and monsoons in the seas of the tropics was drawn up by Edmond Halley (1656–1742), and is taken from 'Philosophical Transactions of the Royal Society' (1686) (© Getty Images).

Ironically, fifteenth-century decisions to end overseas Ming empire expeditions were inspired by desire on the part of some to help save the lives of common Chinese people. One court faction in particular was responsible for ending Zheng He's famed voyages, arguing for the need to focus on domestic issues instead of risky adventures. Had they not persevered, China might have found the Americas prior to Europeans! One isolationist claimed that expeditions 'wasted millions in money and grain, and moreover the people who met their deaths may be counted in the tens of thousands . . . This was merely an action of bad government of which ministers should severely disapprove'.[4]

But an addictive land grab mentality developed in Europe after the 1500s. When westerners arrived in the Americas, Asia or Africa, what had been a loosely connected system of villages and small states – either independent or under the control of one chief or emperor – were transformed into a competitive battleground. A new, broad conception of land utilization emerged after 1500, utilitarian and wasteful (Figure 1.7).

In these centuries, Europeans coincidentally came to consider non-westerners as lazy or inferior genetically. As they claimed the lands of Indians, Arabs or Africans, indigenous people were labelled apathetic or docile, even though the very goal for Europeans in taking new lands was often to acquire an easier life! Most of the coerced groups had in fact enjoyed an easier life prior to European incursions, living in a manner that did not overtax the natural environment rather than working endlessly to exploit it for monetary profit. Where Europeans proposed to extract nature's bounty, multiplying in population year-round, Native Americans purposely endured hunger in the winter, awaiting the plentiful return of spring, something their European counterparts could not fathom. Natives had rational reasons for doing this;

Figure 1.7 Zheng He, Ming voyager (© Getty Images).

why toil incessantly to produce excess amounts of food, 'profits' and disparity among peoples? Since there were no domesticable animals of note, Native Americans accepted a slower movement of goods, ideas and people, with less impact on the land – and on their own bodies.

Technology was obviously simpler in indigenous societies. Hoes were the most advanced equipment turning the land to produce food. There was no rush to produce or profit. This was a world with no ploughed fields or farming, where land was not despoiled, the animal world not depleted. American Indians did not *own* things; they shared food and tools, with each other socially, and with newcomers. This fit in with a collective, ancient understanding of plants, animals and seasons, premised upon a moderate use of environmental resources, free of an emphasis on individual gain and competition. Though the Americas were in no way unused or empty lands, indigenous peoples had not overexploited them for thousands of years the way Europeans would.

Conclusion – 'Fighting terrorism since 1492'

So, goes the notorious T-shirt worn today in the United States, whose slogan aims to expose the hypocrisies of European-descent Americans who colonized their lands through terrorism, but today express fear of foreigners. For indigenous peoples, white people were the original terrorizers who stole their lands. The swarm of Europeans into American lands over these centuries was not an unusually vicious enterprise in world context; it was neither planned nor blueprinted. Nor did it replace a peaceful, Arcadian world of indigenous harmony, relaxation and concord. Europeans simply searched for a Garden of Eden congruent with their own long-standing belief system, influenced by a biblical narrative where 'God's Green Earth' was to be used by Christians. Between 1492, when Columbus landed, and the British global defeat of French power by 1759, a New World view emerged, however. A new normal emerged, one that has persisted and spread since, of maximizing land exploitation and gaining from it.

By the 1750s, vast numbers of Europeans settled in the Americas, bringing a culture of gain, a desire for never-ending progress, and a zealous belief in productivity. By 1700, Thomas Savery had invented the Miner's Friend in England, an efficient and easily usable steam pump. In 1712, the Newcomen Engine was constructed, an early cylinder-piston machine for producing fast motion. These machines represent the early rumblings of the Industrial Revolution, which kindled a new era in human history, which has been labelled the 'Anthropocene'. Human ingenuity brought unthinking environmental devastation after this era, which still despoils the lands of the Americas and around the world.

We have explored the above ways in which some humans acted on new lands after 1500. In the next chapter, we will investigate changes in the social environment that often derived from these ecological explorations, emphasizing new types of behaviours that emerged in the centuries following the Columbian Exchange.

Keywords

Intercropping
Utilitarian
Columbian Exchange
Ghost acreage
Enclosures
Little Ice Age
Monoculture
Tragedy of the Commons

Further reading

Aguilar-Moreno, Manuel. *Handbook to Life in the Aztec World*. New York: Oxford University Press, 2006. Thorough study of all aspects of Aztec life, with sections specifically focused on attitudes to land and beliefs about nature.

Burke, Edmund, and Kenneth Pomeranz. *The Environment and World History*. Berkeley: University of California Press, 2009. In eleven essays, the contributors connect environment history to early modern world history, considering demographics, resources and natural extraction as primary motors of change.

Crosby, Alfred W. *Ecological Imperialism: The Biological Expansion of Europe, 900-1900.* New York: Cambridge University Press, 2015. Highly influential work that showed how Europeans' displacement of indigenous peoples was as much biological as military or cultural.

Grove, Richard. *Green Imperialism: Colonial Expansion, Tropical Island Edens, and the Origins of Environmentalism, 1600–1860.* Cambridge: Cambridge University Press, 1995. Grove provides a vast array of information demonstrating how different empires impacted nature and used the environment to control people.

Mann, Charles C. *1493: Uncovering the New World Columbus Created.* New York: Knopf, 2011. This is a readable, comprehensive survey of the world that changed so much after 1493, with a refreshing ecological perspective.

2

Exploiting people – The human environment

Chapter Outline

Situating the chapter

The early modern period was one of widespread violence, disease, squalor and broad environmental forces that humans could not overcome. Such traumas served as an overpowering part of everyday life for millions. In three centuries that brought the largest period of sustained, large-scale population growth in history, most people nonetheless lived lives of struggle. In any given year, millions died from hunger, disease and sickness; millions more were enslaved; and nearly all common people lived hard lives of desperate toil. Few, if any, considered this situation could or should be remedied. This was life as it had always been for most everyday people. By 1750 change was coming, however, and this chapter explores these environmental alterations.

Narrative – Human behaviour?

Demography

Demographically, more people than ever before were born in this era, and most lived lives of struggle. In 1492 only about 350 million people inhabited the planet, the same number found in the most populated fifty cities on earth today! By 1750, global population more than doubled, reaching over 800 million people.[1] As plant and animal species mixed, so too did humans. Before 1500, people had of course moved for wanderlust or trade, and indeed movement was a central component of human history for millennia. But for thousands of years prior to our period, Asians usually lived in Asia, Europeans in Europe, Africans in Africa, Americans in America and so on.

This changed forever after the Columbian connection. Newly forming, hybrid societies mixed the human gene pool more than ever before in a very short span of historical time. Some areas obviously suffered far more than others from this intermingling. The European enslavement of Africans, for example, critically damaged population balances in many regions of West and Central Africa. It was not only the removal of millions of young, healthy, productive individuals that brought disaster; the wars in which Africans were enslaved – whether by Europeans or by Africans profiting from the trade – were violent and destructive too. Entire communities sought to escape enslavement by fleeing fertile farmlands for marginal, more protected areas like marshes, mountains and forests. Fertility declined in communities under constant threat from violence and slaving. Even beyond enslavement, the impact on West African societies was catastrophic.

As the transatlantic slave trade decimated African families, and while millions of natives died in the Americas, populations boomed across East Asia, South Asia and Europe. European populations grew particularly fast. Within Europe, infectious diseases like the plague had lowered populations in the 1400s, from 80 million to 50 million. Fertility returned after 1500, however, aided both by internal agricultural productivity and by nutritious American foodstuffs that improved both the palettes and lifespans of Europeans.

European exploitation of New World resources accelerated through the sixteenth century, bringing a great population boom. There were under a million people in Portugal, and only 3 million in England, when the first explorers found the Americas. Spain was larger, with up to 7 million people, and France had as many as 15 million. All these nations would profit indelibly from the work of indigenous and slave labour.

England's population rose dramatically in the early modern period. It actually declined from 6 million to around 2.5 million in 1500 following the fourteenth-century plague. But by 1700 it had tripled, rebounding to 9 million. By the 1600s, large numbers of labourers looking for work dotted English lands, after wealthy landlords threw them off customary lands. Many proved willing to migrate overseas to secure a living, which had important consequences for the Americas and worldwide. English elites also took land in Ireland, the Caribbean and North America (and later South Africa and Australia) where millions of English settlers would thrive. By 1700 up to 350,000 English people lived in the Americas, most of them settled permanently. From 1700 to 1780, huge increases in Irish and Scottish settlers to North America contributed to the continent's growing stock of Europeans. Ireland's population grew from 2 million in 1500 to around 8 million in 1750, mainly owing to nutrition provided by the American potato. This growth turned to decline, however, with the 1848 famine, which occurred under British rule, prompting massive Irish migration to North America.

Sparsely populated Southeast Asia grew, too, from about 15 million humans in 1450 to 25 million by 1650. Japan's population increased from 10 million in 1500 to over 30 million by 1750, mostly in a few urban areas. For centuries, China had supported more people than the land could comfortably hold. Over 300 million worked the land by 1750, almost tripling from 1500. India's population soared, too, as the arrival of wet rice cultivation from Asia and American crops filled more stomachs. Even accounting for persistent famines, the population of Mughal India rose from 145 million in 1600 to over 200 million by 1800. In these centuries, world population doubled from roughly 400 to 800 million people; the previous doubling of the global population had taken 1,000 years!

Early modern peoples usually died young by today's standards. Though it may sound fatalistic today, in these centuries no one could conceive of countering nature's capacity for death. To try to improve conditions in the name of progress were alien notions to early modern humans. People didn't expect longevity or a happy life. Chinese aphorisms from the period highlight this gloomily realism, with an appreciation of the power of nature applicable to all societies:

Question: 'Do heaven-and-earth have a way of dealing with this situation? Answer: Heaven-and-earth's way of making adjustments lies in flood, drought and plagues.'[2]

Sexuality and reproduction

Like all mammals, humans naturally procreate given the opportunity. In climates of stress, however, people rarely produce at the rate they do in abundant times. The considerable population growth in this era derived partly from nature taking its course, but also from better nourishment in most societies. Higher populations, while useful for building strong states, were not necessarily good for ecosystems. More people meant more competition, crowding, disease, strains on food supplies, and damage to lands.

Indeed, in these centuries, many new cities developed, and were arguably worse places to live in than the rural village hovels of peasants worldwide. Cities inclined people towards various new types of interaction, and one of the most predictable outcomes of mixing in city quarters was sexual intercourse. Sexual interaction between peoples of different ethnic origins began to transform populations around the world, particularly in the Americas, where large populations of peoples of mixed ethnicity emerged, usually between Spanish men and Indian women.

A huge increase in European migration after 1500 shaped new hybrid populations. Colonizers brought diverse approaches to intermixing. Portuguese traders, both Christian and Jewish, partook widely in sexual relations with women in the Americas, and Portuguese families moved en masse to populate the lands of Brazil. The Dutch were typically uninhibited regarding sexual liaisons and relations with Indonesians. In North America, the English usually classified populations strictly by race and avoided intermarriage, developing a reputation for racist aloofness. In the Caribbean, where much of Britain's slaving occurred and where few European women lived, mixing was more common.

French men mixed freely with natives because of the dearth of French women. French men who moved to the Caribbean produced high numbers of mixed-descent children. Of the roughly 150,000 Spanish emigrants who moved to the Americas between 1500 and 1750, only 15–30 per cent were women. Most newcomers were men who took indigenous wives. Due to intermixing between Spaniards and natives, the population of New Spain doubled to 3 million between 1650 and 1750. It doubled again by 1810, by which time those of Spanish descent reigned supreme over subjugated natives.

In a world without contraception, innumerable casual encounters between European men and African women produced many children of mixed race. Colonizers usually discriminated against mixed-heritage individuals, gradually delineating people socially and economically. Spanish American societies established a harsh racial caste system, *las castas*, that privileged 'pure' Europeans and consigned Indians and African slaves to the lowest status. **Mestizos**, offspring born to native mothers and Spanish fathers, occupied a middling status in this system. Across European colonies, **Mulattos** were born of European fathers and African mothers. Both groups would be maltreated by lighter-skinned whites who came to dominate the continent by 1750. Europeans, thereafter, shaped a severe racist hierarchy founded on myth and hatred, in which they were supposedly superior. In time, racism became institutionalized throughout the Americas, North and South, as it did in Europe.

Marriage

Ideological racism emerged alongside institutionalized patriarchy in these centuries. Though women were treated as inferiors everywhere, legal approaches towards marriage varied worldwide. European societies were particularly stringent in using laws to thwart familial intermarriage. The Catholic Church purposely prohibited **consanguinity**, marriage between blood cousins. This was not common elsewhere: American Indians often married cousins; Middle East and North African societies long accepted first-cousin marriage, as did much of China. In North America, native peoples freely divorced and re-partnered in keeping with tradition, unimpressed with European pressure to abide by Christian understandings of sex and marriage. Though nobody understood genetics, it was, it turns out, a wise move to prevent marriage between blood relations.

Then as now, people fell in love, but no universal, 'natural' approach to love or marriage covered the planet, before or since 1500. Diverse cultural and traditional practices influenced attitudes to marriage, sexuality and reproduction. Everywhere, material circumstances encouraged or inhibited marital bonds. In Europe, Asia and the Americas, some men had children with numerous women, as long as they could afford them or possessed sufficient authority or standing. African and Mediterranean men usually married to connect extended families and strengthen economic and political ties. Marriages in India were often economic arrangements, not romantic ones. In the 1600s, northern and western Europeans in the 1600s began to settle more into what we today call a nuclear family, with husband, wife and children. This was not common anywhere else on earth in our period.

With rare exceptions, attitudes towards women around the world were exceptionally severe by modern standards, at all levels of society. England's Henry the VIII famously had six wives, murdering two in the 1540s. China's Wanli emperor had two wives, and around twenty consorts or concubines upon his death in 1620. He confined scores of women to his palace at night to ensure that any children born to them would be his offspring. The Japanese shogun Tokugawa Ieyasu (d. 1616) had similarly high numbers of wives or concubines. In most of sub-Saharan Africa polygamy was common, and men normally had more than one wife in North American societies. In the Muslim world, men could take four wives, but they could own as many concubines as their standing supported. In India, Akbar the Great (d. 1605) had one consort, or main wife, and six secondary wives. African families gained economic advantage by offering daughters to Portuguese traders, earning prestige and position in the process.

Women did enjoy some freedoms though. Unlike Muslim women elsewhere, Mughal women lived social lives outside the home. Asian and European women worked fields and possessed freedom of movement in villages, though less in cities. In more traditional rural regions, women were often less constrained than in urban ones. Of course, many women possessed great power: a Ukrainian prostitute named Roxelana (d. 1558) rose from slave to one of the most powerful women in the world in the Ottoman Empire. Elizabeth I was one of many influential women in the early modern period, and scores of powerful European queens shaped European history in this era, and noblewomen presumably influenced male decisions more than the historical record shows. Indeed, the mixed populations of the Americas could not have developed without the contributions, voluntary and otherwise, of countless native women, who thus helped shape the demographics of the New World. Still, the role of women was usually confined to the crucial matter of production and reproduction.

> Weddings in Mughal India reveal the complex conditions in which some Muslim husbands and wives arranged marriages in 1639. Women of honour and position enjoyed real power, while female slaves did not:
>
> Whereas the honourable Abdullah, son of Hajji Mubarak, sought and took in marriage as wife the chaste, virtuous lady Habiba . . . with four conditions that are commonly prevalent of Muslims. The first condition: that beside the said wife he shall not marry another. The second: that the husband shall not beat the wife, without her committing any perfidious transgression of law, in rage, and fury, so as to leave marks of the stick visible on any part of her body. The third: that the husband shall not leave the wife without her consent . . . the fourth: that if the said husband keeps a slave-girl as a concubine . . . the aforesaid wife shall the be the agent on behalf of the said husband (entitled) to sell that slave-girl and take the proceeds of her marriage-dower, and if she so desires, make that slave-girl forbidden to the aid husband by manumitting her off or by giving her in gift.[3]

Marital age differed, too, but averages everywhere appear to be very young. The average age of female matrimony was fifteen in the Americas, twenty in China and Europe, though this varied in time and place. Hernan Cortes married an Indian girl in her early teens after being presented with twenty slave women from Azteca tribal leaders. Pizarro intermarried with a native woman of a young age. Both the Aztec and Inca had long practiced marriage as soon as girls menstruated. Polygamy – not monogamy – was most common in indigenous societies and worldwide.

Across Asia and elsewhere, couples married young, though they lived under the watchful eye of extended families. In Europe, however, the Catholic Church worked to ban excessively young marriages. Also, families in northern and Western Europe frequently set up separate households, and were encouraged by late marriage to save enough to live separately. In much of Western Europe later marriages increased in this era. Some scholars argue that Christian Europe enforced a particularly patriarchal form of gender relations upon previously egalitarian native societies, though this is disputed.

Men and women interacted in many ways everywhere, through consent, open relations, marriage, cohabitation, and, of course, through violent acts of coercion and rape. Many people also fell in love mutually and women usually possessed some form or relational power. In both indigenous and complex societies, however, men tended to subordinate women.

Only toward the end of this era do more modern, critical attitudes regarding women's place in society emerge, and in perhaps the most liberal state in the world at the time. In 1697 England, Elizabeth Johnson, referring to the extraordinarily influential John Locke, wrote scornfully of Western claims about freedom and liberty given the subordinated position of women in English society:

We women think with reason, that our fundamental constitutions are destroyed . . . there are notorious violations on the liberty of freeborn English women.[4]

Johnson was one of many women who by 1750 advocated for more rights for women in England and Western Europe. Though English society proved slow to respond to these early feminist arguments, they were harbingers of new attitudes, where women would reprimand male supremacy over their public and private lives. Indeed, in Western Europe a wide debate about women's rights and the nature of women, known as the *querelle des femmes*, occurred around 1750. This debate foreshadowed what would much later become feminism in the West and was exceptional for the time.

Other reproduction patterns and inclinations mirrored modern practices. As ever, humans were born outside of marital intercourse, and many people chose not to marry. In sixteenth-century Western Europe about one in five men or women remained single, though they often had children. Remaining single had long been accepted in Europe. Most European migrants were men looking to venture out, as women could rarely travel alone. Innumerable men thus chose to remain free to take temporary wives, moving on as they deemed desirable in an environment free of church or state judgements. Homosexuality, practiced as long as monogamous or non-monogamous marriage in all societies, was rarely condemned or discussed in any culture. Though it was not encouraged, it was usually ignored as long as it was not public or overt. Countless European kings enjoyed the company of men and women before and after 1500 and homosexual practices occurred in all cultures.

Substance abuse

Of course, the environment that humans inhabit comprises more than weather, forests or home life. The early modern environment was dire and dangerous for most of humanity as we have seen, but it also brought considerable cravings for new substances some considered aberrant but most found alluring.

Indeed, sugar was possibly the first modern addiction. Millions of people acquired cravings for new foods that Atlantic trade connections brought, and almost everyone, Eurasian or American, consumed sugar. Sugar production requires unforgiving work, particularly if quick profit is the aim. Labourers, usually slaves, cut stalks that were then crushed in a mill, producing a juice to be then boiled into crystallized sugar. Keen cravings for the sweet crop, in both the Old World and New, drove efforts to produce it as efficiently as possible, ensuring greater demand for slave labour and more human exploitation.

The Portuguese began producing sugar in the decades before 1500, although Arabs had grown sugar cane for centuries. After 1640 the British became the dominant sugar traders when production began in Barbados. Around that same time the French began producing in Martinique. Both Caribbean islands were severely deforested in the process, as industrial-scale plantations replaced diverse agriculture lands to become the first modern factories (Figure 2.1).

Sugar production increased the availability of alcohol, the era's other key addictive substance. Sugar producers wasted little in the search for profit, as they transformed the molasses leftover from sugar production into rum. Alcohol dependence was a constant, if undiagnosed, social problem in many societies, the Muslim world being a notable exception. In the Americas, rum production boomed by 1650, making it affordable and ubiquitous. Rum (and brandy) decimated indigenous American communities who had no previous exposure to these intoxicants.

In Britain, city life brought appalling scenes of alcoholism, as evidenced by the growing number of babies born to alcoholic parents. The celebrated artist William Hogarth's Beer St. engraving considered beer more commendable than *Gin Lane* (given the effect of hard alcohol), and consumption of both liquors was rife in cities lacking fresh running water. Sailors in the British Navy drank rations of up to a pint of beer a day in the eighteenth century! Eastern Europeans produced vodkas from potatoes and consumed it in large quantities.

Other substances altered experiences and numbed existence for millions. Hallucinogens had long been used in many societies. Naturally occurring substances such as coca in Peru, or jimsonweed and peyote in North America, provided hallucinatory escapes from life. Andean peasants routinely drank maize beer, or chewed the coca leaf as a source of cocaine. Hashish had always been consumed in North Africa and the Muslim world, as a respite from life's hardships. Laudanum, an extract of opium, soothed the pain of struggling Europeans for much of this era.

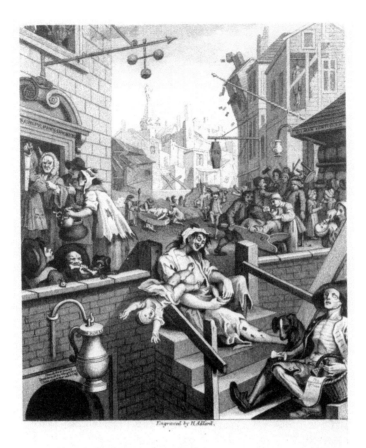

Engraved by H.Adlard.

BEER STREET AND GIN LANE.

Figure 2.1 Scenes of debauchery and drunkenness in 'Gin Lane', one of two engravings entitled 'Beer Street' and 'Gin Lane' by William Hogarth, London, 1751 (© Getty Images).

If sugar was the first addiction of the early modern era, tobacco represents perhaps the first consumer frenzy. From the Americas to Eurasia, tobacco smoking became the habit of choice, as the highly addictive attributes of nicotine stimulated vast demand, production and consumption. Tobacco was even snorted to get the nicotine into the bloodstream faster. By the 1700s tobacco use doubled in China, where users often blended it with opium. Doctors in Europe believed tobacco purified the body through the pores. Its supposed health benefits inspired teachers to whip boys at elite English schools in the seventeenth century for *not* smoking!

Along with sugar, alcohol and tobacco, coffee and cacao altered moods and eased social connections among strangers. Coffee developed into a new European craze after arriving from Turkey in the 1640s. It aided commercial relations, as traders often negotiated deals in coffee shops. Some Spanish women were so addicted to chocolate they instructed their maids to bring cups of it to church during mass in 1620s Mexico.

None of these substances attracted widespread care or social contempt. No counsels, health experts or civic leaders compelled people to consider their negative physiological effects. Given the wrenching social and economic changes of the era, many people understandably sought solace through the use of mood-altering substances.

Sense and sensibility

Indeed, such attempts to ease existence combined with a search for new experiences and sensations as the period progressed. A new appreciation for the pleasures of the imagination via music, literature and art resulted in many urban arenas. The literary and artistic world of musicians, public concerts and other cultural pleasures offered considerable joys that intoxicated the senses of many. With new global connections came new aromas, sounds and visions, to alter the world of early moderns. Previously unknown foods enriched the often-putrid smell of many cities. In an era bereft of fresh urban water, soap or even attention to hygiene, delight in new aromas and tastes stoked desires. Millions of people – usually those with privilege – were now exposed to startling new sensibilities, ingesting new tastes such as coffee, tea and chocolate, even as they absorbed new ideas and conquered new lands.

> Mexico City's first Spanish magistrate was lured to his post from Spain by a letter claiming the Americas offered all he could desire:
>
> > Good houses, good horses, beautiful women . . . and a thousand other things lacking in Spain that are, to sight and taste, delightful.[5]

A major outcome of the Columbian Exchange transatlantic linkage, therefore, was the transformation of human sensibilities. New flavours, foods, sounds, people and ideas prompted a lust for more goods and a wider range of experiences, including cultural life. Visual sources and artistic works suggest that sexuality and sentiment became more prominent features in this era.

Emotion and sound

Fiction, myth, oral traditions and storytelling represent ancient attempts to explain the human condition. Most of the world's fictional forms or narrative tropes contain a limited number of plot lines – typically tragedy, romance, comedy, rivalry or ambition. Storytelling, religious or supernatural themes dominated the arts in all cultures in this era. In Western Europe a particular vernacular style developed. At the turn of the seventeenth century, the works of William Shakespeare and other dramatists began to express human emotions in radical new ways. Shakespeare's comedies, tragedies and histories broke with the past in style and quality, presenting more secular subjects and problems than had been common prior. Shakespeare used drama to depict human reality, exploring more complex characters and personalities than medieval writers had anywhere around the globe. He dived headlong into the inescapable conflicts of human life from an everyday perspective.

In the 1700s, the printing of sheet music across Europe aided the transmission of sounds and emotions to growing numbers of people. The development of notation aided both playing and learning of music as an art. Musical knowledge and new sounds were thus diffused through printing, as more complex choral or instrumental dynamics could be expressed visually. This increased musical literacy among a broader swath of society. Writing scores in both *piano* (soft) and *forte* (loud), J. S. Bach (d. 1750) produced passionate choral and church music that reached new heights of musical emotion.

European music in this era shifted from religious themes to more secular compositions. Musical motifs, such as imitation or repetition, invited passions that moved people to tears, and new arrangements shocked the senses. The composer Gabrieli's (d. 1612) complex scores, with four or five choruses, produced more sophisticated sound, accompanied by ensemble instruments producing new resonances. Counterpoint offered contrasting voices in place of solo singing. In Europe, public concerts exposed more people to the power of Baroque and later Classical styles of music.

Cross-cultural interaction also influenced the development of new musical styles. When Spanish soldiers encountered Native Americans, both sides played music to attempt to overawe the other, in a war of brass and percussion. Europeans encountered natives playing drums, pipes and flutes. African and American societies exposed westerners to previously unheard-of forms of dance and rhythm. The banjo moved from West Africa to the Americas, where it became a beloved instrument of everyday people. In the Americas, Catholic colonists, uncomfortable with its subtle meanings, purposely suppressed native music. When in the 1690s, the Spanish tried to ban music and dance in communities inhabiting what is now the south-western United States, natives revolted (Figure 2.2).

Across Eurasia, opera emerged, combining music with drama to explore the full range of human emotions. Italian opera was perhaps most developed. Uniquely, Italian court attendees and members of the public could enjoy the new art. Chinese opera was also sophisticated, although more narrowly focused on the problems of social elites. In the Sunni Arab world, music was sometimes considered sinful and frowned upon. But from Persia to China, Sufi mystics performed for royal courts to entrance wide audiences. In Japan, Taiko drumming provided a form of martial intimidation to motivate soldierly pride. In India, musical composition was a collective enterprise, not the product of a single author as in Europe. Rather, it was a universal,

Figure 2.2 Bunraku and Kabuki Theater, 47 Ronin Story. Japan (© Getty Images).

collective symphony of sounds for all to enjoy publicly. Music was part and parcel of people's lives in all cultures though. In seventeenth-century England, common people even protested using 'rough music', in which they banged pots and pans to publicly shame men who beat their wives or others whose acts were deemed unacceptable.

In Japan, Bunraku puppet theatre and Noh drama developed, offering inward-looking and orthodox subjects, wary of offending elites. In the 1600s, however, Kabuki reacted to these staid forms of theatre, by emphasizing pleasure and aiming to shock and astonish observers. In a mostly male world of fantasy and desire, Kabuki drama and dance expressed ribald, lewd sexual and erotic intimacy, mostly to please male clientele. Men would impersonate women, who were forbidden to act. Ihara Saikaku (d. 1693) also wrote poetry and novels about erotic love and romance, brothels and dancing, Geisha girls and homosexuality. Ukiyo, or *floating world*, an urban culture of pleasure-seeking, offered excitement in Japanese cities through the eighteenth century, free of the moral censure found in Christian Europe or Islam.

In the sixteenth-century Ottoman Empire, puppet theatre grew into wildly popular forms of expression, with farcical takes on subjects such as minorities, profanity or erotica. Various types of passion plays, folk tales and shadow puppetry also developed in societies across Asia, from the Middle East to Thailand. Many of these complex societies explored human emotions, such as love and jealousy, through satire and biting wit. Everywhere people gathered, emotions were expressed through music and narrative.

Printed word

As visual and aural art forms altered people's awareness, print literature provided means to perceive the social and political environment anew. Along with the discovery of the Americas, in this era a new, more complex, repertoire of human sensibilities developed across Eurasia. A new emphasis on individual autonomy, emotion and everyday life emerged in some societies, expedited by the growth of print culture. New methods of communicating and articulating thoughts emerged in ink. Increasing accessibility to the printed word allowed broader populations to experience and even contribute to emotive art forms. Between 1500 and 1750, printed novels, like films today, created whole New Worlds of sensation and sentiment. Authors accentuated, in fictional form, new ways to behave, believe and think, replacing or challenging church, emperor or monarch as guides to attitudes and ethics.

East Asian cultures examined the human condition mostly through poetry and literature, in keeping with tradition. The Japanese Edo-era poet Basho (d. 1694) introduced the acclaimed Haiku form of poetic expression, aiming for stark emotional honesty to depict the social environment. Seventeenth-century China saw a flourishing print culture, represented in gorgeous calligraphic forms often depicted in pieces of landscape art. A celebrated novel, *Plum in the Golden Vase*, told tales of eroticism and affluence, and the eighteenth-century masterpiece *The Dream of the Red Chamber* offered complex psychological investigation, using a realistic style to explore the human spirit through literature. This story – of a powerful family and their arrogance – is an apt metaphor for the lives of both Ming and Qing imperial elites. By 1750, increasingly guarded Qing rulers only allowed artists to perform under censorious, controlled conditions, however, and hence few Chinese people, let alone peasants, experienced new art forms thereafter.

Literacy levels grew comparatively more in Western Europe than elsewhere. Journals, essays and novels were important drivers of social and cultural change. In England, after 1711, *The Spectator* periodical proved an outlet for scathing wit, humour and biting criticism, shaping a culture where almost anything could be expressed, unlike most societies at the time. Western European writers such as De Foe, Richardson, Fielding and Pope demonstrate a particularly open contempt for deference towards those in power, seeding an important new sense of rights into the minds of common people. European satire developed into a written art form through Jonathan Swift, whose *Gulliver's Travels* satirized human arrogance, inventing imaginary lands to parody human conduct.

Michel de Montaigne (d. 1592) famously defined the essay in this era. His essays were models of this written art form, expositing a clear, reflective form of argumentation, some might say to torture future students. Moliere (d. 1673) examined humanity through parody. Making use of pantomime and street theatre, his sarcastic style exposed human hypocrisies and ignorance, ridiculing aristocratic attachment to notions of hierarchy and privilege. The Jewish-Spanish author Cervantes's 1605 classic *Don Quixote* also ridiculed traditional feudal ideals, questioning power and tradition. England's William Hogarth (d. 1674) produced mass market engravings that, in works like *Gin Lane*, depicted lives of vice, pain and misery that would later influence social reform movements in England. In *A Harlot's Progress* he asks why a woman is forced to move to the city to become a prostitute and die of venereal disease – blaming society rather than the individual, a shocking notion at the time. English humourists and caricaturists, such as Thomas Rowlandson and James Gillray, by 1750 even openly insulted authority, with pornographic and highly humorous depictions of social and political life. Such portrayals pondered life through comedy and anguish, with representations of humanity we can relate to today (Figure 2.3).

Asian and Arab art forms questioned the social environment less stridently than Europeans. Orthodox Islam prohibited depictions of humans in art altogether, and literacy remained low in the Muslim world, as it did in Africa and most of South Asia. Still, it is important to note that what we call Western art, music or theatre today was not essentially superior to masterpieces of Islamic calligraphy, Asian portraiture, Indian art, Persian gardens or African sculptures and statuary. It was simply different.

Female literacy rose in China and Europe in this era, and it planted the seeds for rising female literacy in Europe. In 1811, the English novelist Jane Austen gained

Figure 2.3 'Drinking Problems'. Learning to Smoke and Drink Grog by Thomas Rowlandson, hand-coulored plate (© Getty Images).

fame across Europe for her romantic novel *Sense and Sensibility*, in which she depicted a world very changed from the 1500s. Increasing quantities and quality of literature, theatre and art foregrounded the passions, emotions and love after 1750. Though certainly not for all people, and still dominated by men in all societies, more people could now cherish the joys found in themes of romance, love and sensuality through the new environment of music, drama and art. In 1500, only elites enjoyed such sensory pleasures.

Few sources clearly reveal the deep feelings of people in the past. It is difficult, then, to tell precisely how much the performing arts and printed word shaped different societies in this period. Nonetheless, forms of expression through art, sound and word tell us as much about cultural proclivities as do political documents, speeches or other official nostrums. For most people, sensuality and sensitivity were not central to daily existence. Though it was slowly changing, sensory joys were mostly limited to the privileged few. Another part of the human environment in this era, however, was less savoury and impacted all levels of society, the spread of new diseases and an increase in violence.

Viruses and violence

Disease and death

As the ethnic mix of populations increased around the world after 1500, diseases spread more than ever before. As the past few years have shown to the whole world, viruses are near impossible to fend off without modern vaccination. Intimate human contact provided an environment for germs to spread, which triggered virulent new diseases. Of course, diseases had decimated human populations throughout history, but once Europeans crossed the Atlantic, viruses that previously thrived in isolated locations crisscrossed the world's landmasses. With increased interaction among global populations, with new hordes of animals roaming the lands, the early modern period was one in which diseases like smallpox and cholera became widespread and virulent.

Once the disease regimes of the New and Old Worlds merged, life changed for everyone. New diseases victimized indigenous Americans most. Up to 20 million indigenous people died after the Spanish and Portuguese arrived. Humans across Eurasia and Africa north of the Sahara had coexisted for thousands of years, so one large disease regime existed in the Old World of Eurasia before 1492. Europeans brought with them new disease pools that wiped out American populations lacking immunity. An array of infectious diseases tormented millions of Indians who died and those who survived. Swine flu, hepatitis, measles, encephalitis, cholera, scarlet fever and meningitis all arrived in the Americas along with smallpox, bringing agony to so many.

Diaz del Castillo's account in 1521 of smallpox sufferers in Mexico reveals the awful consequences of European oceanic curiosity:

> The streets, the squares, the houses . . . were covered with dead bodies; we could not stop without treading on them, and the stench was intolerable . . . all the causeways were full, from one end to the other, of men, women and children, so weak and sickly, squalid and dirty, and pestilential that it was a misery to behold them.[6]

The root causes of sickness, not to mention effective remedies to combat infections, continued to confound humanity. A fatalistic acceptance of death and pain was the only reasonable response in such circumstances. Since germs were not understood until the late nineteenth century, those who tried to understand illness often contrived magical explanations for bad health. Most people believed sickness emerged from divine retribution, where angry gods punished sinful humans who deserved their fate.

European and Asian thinkers theorized that imbalances within the body – such as the four humours, blood, black bile (anger), yellow bile (melancholy) and phlegm – caused illness. Healers relied on ancient ideas that supposed bodily substances interacted dynamically with the natural elements of air, water, earth and fire. Treatment might consist of purging the stomach of its contents to force vomiting. Bloodletting, a form of bleeding believed to cleanse and heal the body, was another major remedy. Both usually worsened the situation or killed patients! Worldwide, few understood contagion or provided useful remedies. Mostly male medical authorities in Europe considered exotic fruits from the Americas as unnatural, offering advice not to eat them! Inhaling the fumes of sugar was considered good for the lungs, and doctors suggested higher tobacco consumption.

More rational approaches to medicine emerged in the eighteenth century and slowly began to overcome ancient methods. By 1593 English authorities began to collect official medical statistics to study disease, and in the 1600s, Europeans practiced dissection of cadavers to understand the inner workings of the human body. Knowledge gained from then highly unusual procedures helped doctors shed light on how to cut out cancers. William Harvey's discovery of blood circulation in 1628 opened the way to an understanding of heart disease in England. These were all key discoveries for humanity.

But modern understandings of human health remained elusive. Bubonic plague, or Black Death, was the principal disease vector across Eurasia in the medieval era, and it continued with little respite through these centuries. In the 1620s and 1660s mammoth epidemics slowed population growth in England. In 1666 up to a quarter of the population of London, perhaps 100,000 people, succumbed to hideous deaths from plague. Europeans habitually attributed diseases to outsiders, and considered lepers, Jews or Muslims as sexual deviants and infidels who spread sickness. The healthy often cast the sickly, beggars and disabled people out of cities. They considered epileptics, the mentally handicapped and even those who seemed depressed to be inhabited by demons.

Nowhere on earth were the sick likely to receive good treatment by modern standards. European doctors, unaware of the significance of hygiene or dangers of contagion, increased death rates through transmission of germs to newborn babies. Well into the nineteenth century, hundreds of thousands of women died in childbirth from puerperal fever or bacterial infection.

Chinese, Muslim and Indian medical practitioners typically employed a sophisticated long-standing tradition of medicine compared to those found in Christian Europe. Doctors in the Qing Empire inoculated against smallpox by the 1700s, fighting disease through practical knowledge. Persian doctors had treated measles for centuries. Indian traditional healing through Ayurvedic methods and yoga practices worked to heal the body and improve health as they had for millennia. Native American healers, including females, used herbal cures from nature to cure, as did populations in Southeast Asia and other parts of the world where local, natural remedies had long proved useful in curing sickness.

Some Bantu societies in sub-Saharan Africa chose to focus on the communal or spiritual causes of individual disease. If a person fell sick, caretakers attributed the cause to a conflict either with another person or with some element of the spirit world. African Diviners sought out the cause of illness by interacting with the spirit world to resolve ill health. Many doctors, such as the *nganga* of Kongo or the Yoruba *babaalawo*, entered the Atlantic world as slaves, and brought their healing practices with them. These medical rituals became central to cross-Atlantic sacred creeds such as Santeria and Voudon in the Caribbean and Candomblé in Brazil, merging with Catholicism to shape Latin American faith and salvation (Figure 2.4).

In these centuries, though, influenza epidemics were as ordinary as bad weather, killing millions in Eurasia and the Americas. Viral diseases like smallpox and measles spread widely, and parasitic diseases like malaria increased in ferocity. Well-intentioned acts such as the drainage of the eastern English fens by Tudor rulers actually boosted malarial vectors. Even though England's population grew overall, it lagged for two centuries in the east of the country due to malarial epidemics. This strain of malaria probably travelled to North America and killed hundreds of thousands of European settlers.

Numerically, the populations of the Americas declined more than anywhere else on earth. Soon after Columbus arrived, Taino and Caribe populations were wiped out by smallpox, and the hunter-gatherer way of life began a global decline after tens of thousands of years. We can only imagine the shock of natives facing the sudden presence of Europeans, perhaps feeling ill soon thereafter, and then experiencing the decimation of villages from disease. In the Caribbean sugar islands, African and

Decimò, corporis alicui parti, modo huic, modo illi, Caracte-
F   rem

Figure 2.4 Compendium Maleficarum Woodcut Illustration from a 1626 Edition of 'Compendium Maleficarum', by Francesco Maria Guazzo. 'Compendium Maleficarum' was a witch-hunter's manual written in Latin, and published in Milan, Italy in 1608 (© Bridgeman Images).

indigenous labourers had few options for escape. With nowhere to run on small islands, higher percentages were killed than on the mainland. By 1600, repeated disease epidemics had devastated the Americas for over a century to deplete numbers.

In the Potosi mine in Bolivia, the source of so much Eurasian bullion, disease sickened and killed countless natives. Cakes of mercury were mixed with silver and heated to produce gold and silver, bringing painful and poisonous deaths as the Manila Galleons moved currency to global markets. Of course, once natives died off in large numbers, Europeans imported African slaves to be worked to death in their place. Most captive Africans came from the malarial west of Africa, so the enslaved population was immune to malarial strains. It was this immunity that made Africans so effective as labourers in the Americas – which in turn encouraged further enslavement. Africans died from other diseases, too. Abused bodies already debilitated from the stress of capture and undernourishment succumbed to yellow fever, which likely arrived in the Americas along with sugar cane. Though they did not suffer the same disease regime as indigenous people, slaves were whipped, beaten and abused by the million, as they produced crops like sugar and tobacco. A life of hell awaited those packed into ships as human cargo. Mercifully, many died on the passage over, avoiding their terrible fate in the Americas.

This was a world of widespread suffering. Poor Europeans suffered, too, in the voyages to the Americas. Indentured European servants were packed into awful conditions below ships' decks – vomit, faeces and desperate water shortages prompted the onset of fever, dysentery and heat exhaustion. If measurably negligible compared to Indian or African anguish, up to half of European sailors nonetheless died on slaving ships. Sailors endured miserable conditions. Diets lacking in nutrition caused scurvy (until citrus fruits were found to counter it in the seventeenth century). Perhaps 2 million sailors died from this gruesome disease, and gastrointestinal disease killed countless low-class ship workers. While natives and slaves died from smallpox, influenza, diphtheria and typhus, Europeans were cursed with a new sexually transmitted disease from the Americas, syphilis (Figure 2.5).

Life was ghastly for all subjugated groups, but misery also awaited European colonists in the Americas. The first English settlers to Virginia in the 1600s suffered up to a 75 per cent death rate, owing largely to disease. The majority of those who moved to a New World of religious freedom and opportunity died within a decade. All who arrived – elites, middling, or indentured labourers – had to be 'seasoned' to become accustomed to strains of diseases such as malaria, yellow fever and smallpox that flourished in the swampy environs of coastal

Figure 2.5 Pontiac, an Ottawa Indian, confronts Colonel Henry Bouquet, who authorized his officers to spread smallpox among Native Americans, 1764 (© Getty Images).

Virginia. This was a painful process of biological acclimatization that all had to withstand. Newcomers could expect deathly fevers and only hope to survive the first few years in their new American climate. After the journey over, some settlers were forced to eat dead bodies to survive. Such gruesome scenes in fact appalled natives, who often took pity on these baffling pale-skinned strangers in tight clothes.

While native populations were particularly helpless against European oppressors and their bodily germs, all were vulnerable to disease in the early modern era. Amidst repeated epidemics, Europeans could do next to nothing to counter death or infection. Daniel Defoe's 1722 *Journal of the Plague Year* illustrated the desperate plight many felt when faced with epidemics in Europe, to the point some began to lose faith in the heavens above:

> But here again the Misery of that Time lay upon the poor who, being infected, had neither Food or Physick, neither Physician or Appothecary to assist them, or Nurse to attend them. Many of those died calling for help, and even for Sustenance, out at their Windows in a most miserable and deplorable manner; but it must be added that whenever the Cases of such Persons or Families were represented to my Lord Mayor they always were relieved. It is true, in some Houses where the People were not very poor, yet where they had sent perhaps their Wives and Children away, and if they had any Servants they had been dismissed; – I say it is true that to save the Expences, many such as these shut themselves in, and not having help, dy'd alone.[7]

By 1750, understanding of the human body remained crude everywhere, and the majority of humans continued to struggle with everyday maladies. Likely the healthiest people were those in more isolated populations such as Southeast Asian islands or tribal groups unencumbered by Eurasian 'civilization'. Though all humans suffered from disease, indigenous populations were generally healthier than those in Eurasia prior to contact. Indeed, all these diseases remained untreatable until the nineteenth or twentieth centuries. Many continue to wipe out millions of people around the globe in less developed countries.

Accustomed to violence

New global connections also brought greater large-scale violence. From poor peasants to privileged princes, people suffered from mundane levels of physical cruelty unimaginable today. Silver shipped from the Americas to Eurasia increased conflict in the 1600s. Its influx into the markets of Eurasia prompted wild fluctuations in the economy and instability. Those who lost out met impoverishment while the connected

Figure 2.6 Tudor period hand-crushers (© Getty Images).

and successful were enriched. The indebted spent pitiless days or months in freezing prisons for the crime of owing small sums in Europe. Some around the world were enslaved for life as a result of bad economic fortune or poor decisions (Figure 2.6).

The slave trade was, of course, a business of endless violence. Shipboard deaths killed hundreds of thousands of African slaves before they even arrived in the Americas. Though not all ships were death traps, those with crueller masters lost high percentages of slaves as well as employed hands on deck. Death rates were up to 25 per cent in the mid-seventeenth century, falling gradually to 14 per cent by the mid-eighteenth. Sailors as well as slaves had their skin flayed by whips for minor offences. Strict disciplinary violence often stood in for management in this period.

Governed by violence

Greater violence derived in part from better governance as well as from a related higher availability of guns. The strong arm of new-formed states, with their organized militaries and legal systems, reached more people after 1500. As Spanish, Portuguese, Dutch or English military expansion encroached upon American and Asian populations, warfare became more professionalized and prevalent in Europe. Governments often conscripted common men, forcing them to join armies to defend royal causes or fight regional enemies. Each increase in violence provoked aggressive responses in turn.

In this era, centralized complex states from Eurasia committed massive political violence in comparison to simpler societies. Robust governments intent on pursuing prosperity claimed a monopoly on domestic violence through soldiers and militias, spreading violence globally. Strong states – and more alcohol, more people and more disease – punished people everywhere. Put together, the possibility of physical abuse increased in a world already plagued by persistent aggression.

Fight or flight is a universal physiological human response to fear, and in this era, fight seemed to be a more common response than flight. But the first interactions between Europeans and others brought a certain curiosity, which only gradually turned to conflict. In 1455, when Venetians arrived in the Senegal River region, Africans were fascinated by the arrival of early European voyagers:

> Little by little the blacks drew nearer, gaining confidence in us, until at last they drew alongside my caravel; and one of them who could understand my interpreter boarded the ship, marveling greatly at her; and at our method of navigating by means of sails, for they know of no method except by rowing with oars. . . . He was overcome with astonishment at the sight of us white men and marveled no less at our clothing.[8]

European states were obsessed with producing more soldiers to fight enemies within Europe or abroad. As the scale of armies grew, violence became endemic, bringing a more ruthless efficiency in slaughtering defenceless victims and combatants in villages. The widespread dispersion of gun technology in the sixteenth century meant that people were not only killed more easily, they could now be injured from distance. Rulers from Africa to China to Europe to the Americas expanded militarily with guns at hand.

Once Christendom split into Catholic and Protestant factions after 1517, religious and political violence grew in Europe. The zealous Spanish state that encouraged sailors to find lands for God and country in the Americas proselytized worldwide through the 1600s. Predictably, this invited defiant responses from disgruntled states with their own armies. Spanish Catholics had long persecuted *Moriscos* (Muslims forced to convert to Christianity). One civil war in 1568 prompted the wholesale slaughter of Muslims, and other Muslims naturally retaliated. The Protestant Dutch too fought to gain independence from the Spanish for almost a century, ending only in 1648 after hundreds of thousands of deaths.

Europe's Thirty Years' War (1618–48) combined dynastic rivalry with religious violence to bring two generations of uninterrupted large-scale conflict to the continent. Up to 10 million people lost their lives in a cycle of hatred where princes and their armies despoiled lands and lives for decades. The Catholic Irish peasantry suffered for their refusal to convert to the Protestantism of their more powerful English neighbours, inviting English and Scottish incursions, and centuries of domination. A massacre of Catholic Irish at Drogheda in 1649 prompted ensuing retaliations and recurrent hostility. British soldiers' vicious treatment of Irish peasants saw thousands of innocents and civilians slaughtered. Between 1648 and 1653, a terrible civil war in France known as The Fronde prompted violence that continued for decades.

In Eastern Europe, Russia's Time of Troubles (1598–1613) spread disorder owing to a succession crisis which brought famine and political violence. This culminated in the founding of the autocratic Romanov dynasty, who ruled Russia from 1613 to 1917.

Even without the fuel of religious zeal, political rivalries brought violence everywhere. For much of the sixteenth-century Sengoku period, Japan endured a bloody civil war, with the Tokugawa military shogunate taking control of the whole country in the early 1600s. For decades, thereafter, Ronin (embittered samurai warriors) roamed the country fighting one another and terrorizing innocent peasants. In the seventeenth century, Japanese leaders renounced European guns, but social violence continued in an established culture of aristocratic sword attacks upon warriors and those who dared defy them.

In the mid-seventeenth century, the collapse of the Ming dynasty brought decades of violence. The Manchu conquest of China stemmed from broader economic global interactions, as American silver brought inflation which undermined the economy. Since the Ming could no longer pay for defences, greater regional fragmentation led to violence and millions of deaths in a dynastic battle. In 1645 the Manchu Qing dynasty (1644–1911) proclaimed the Queue Edict, forcing Han Chinese to submit and shave their foreheads, a humiliation that persisted into the twentieth century. Civil war brought misery, economic instability and death as the Chinese population endured three centuries of Manchu domination.

Aristocratic values

Everywhere, from Asia to Europe, during this period, the violent principles of aristocrats brought conflict to all members of society. Inheritance wars, aroused by landed elites' desire for power, ruined the lands and lives of common people, as a culture of retribution worsened religious and political conflict. The ambitions of aristocrats and monarchs killed countless soldiers, even while eradicating millions of Indians and Africans. In Europe, sword fights, duelling or physical attacks were considered perfectly acceptable behaviour towards equals or inferiors. Monarchs had people executed for the slightest caprice. Rotting corpses in towns were a familiar sight, warning the masses of dissent or the consequences of disrespect. Impaled heads were as common to Londoners as police sirens today. Much-revered monarchs like Elizabeth I hung, drew and quartered hundreds of priests over religious differences.

If life across the Old World of Eurasia appears cruel, the Americas before the arrival of Europeans was no paradise either. Torture and cruelty were part of daily life everywhere. The Aztec sacrificed human captives as freely as a butcher kills animals. Azteca religious beliefs decreed that the earth's fertility required the spilling of human blood. Hundreds of thousands of defeated victims died tortuous deaths even before the Spaniards set foot in the Americas. Aztec and Inca society were harshly hierarchical, with religious violence a central part of daily life. Incan emperors gathered virgins for sacrifice in a royal cult of blood sacrifice, and superstition sat in for reason. A volcanic eruption in 1600 provoked the immediate sacrifice of hundreds of young Incan girls and animals in an attempt to appease the gods. Europeans found American and African societies as replete with interpersonal violence as at home. Portuguese explorers reported cannibalism among some societies after 1500 in Africa, although modern scholars protest such claims.

Of course, men committed most of the violence, and brutality towards women was barely worthy of note. Columbus's first crew of sailors began engaging in a practice of routine European rape of indigenous women, accompanied by the regular sexual assault of female African slaves in the Americas. Indeed, the rise of the Aztec, in the century before Columbus, pushed women out of public life compared to earlier practices. As in Eurasia, warfare masculinized society, marginalized women and ensured Aztec control of weaker societies. Muslim and Asian princes and nobles enjoyed vast harems, locations of at-will sexual domination. Under the Qing, men expected female obedience and idealized women as quiet, docile, and homebound. For thousands of Chinese women, the painful cultural practice of foot binding indicated high class and provided visual eroticism for elite males. Indian women recognized male domination: hundreds of thousands burned themselves on funeral pyres to depart with their husband to the afterlife. The British met harsh resistance when they tried to abolish the practice of Sati in the nineteenth century.

The powerful lived in fear also, both of each other and of lesser peoples. Because of increased interaction and competition, European aristocrats feared their cultures might face ruination if mixed with the impure blood of those they considered inferior races. The modern conception of **racism** emerged in this era, developed by Spanish elites to maintain distinction from and control over newfound populations and Jews and Muslims in Iberia. The *casta* system that emerged in the Americas ranked people according to their supposed moral value, and over time, connected this to skin colour. Millennia of conflict based upon cultural differences or religious preferences morphed now into loathing based upon melanin levels. The British and French would take Spanish prejudice to new levels when they colonized people of colour in coming centuries, institutionalizing racism in Western European and then American culture.

It did not escape the attention of white merchants that those they fought and conquered had darker skin. This led to increasingly harsher views founded on race, bringing an easier capacity for violence. One captain indeed wrote guiltily:

I have been inform'd that some commanders have cut off the legs or arms of the most wilful, to terrify the rest, for they believe if they lose a member, they cannot return home again: I was advis'd by some of my officers to do the same, but I could not be perswaded to entertain the least thoughts of it, much less to put in practice such barbarity and cruelty to poor creatures, who, excepting their want of Christianity and true religion, (their misfortune more than fault) are as much the works of God's hands, and no doubt as dear to him as ourselves; nor can I imagine why they should be despis'd for their colour, being what they cannot help, and the effect of the climate it has pleas'd God to appoint them. I can't think there is any intrinsick value in one colour more than another, nor that white is better than black, only we think it so because we are so, and are proneto judge favourably in our own case, as well as the blacks, who in odium of the colour, say, the devil is white, and so paint him.[9]

Europeans eased their consciences by convincing themselves that dying Indians were inferior beings. Subsequently, a long-term consequence of early modern international intermingling and aristocratic violence was the newfound ideology – premised upon the supposed purity of the blood of certain races – that purity was linked to skin colour. Here emerged a racist philosophy with profound global consequences.

Forced labour

Forced labour has always been a form of social and economic violence. Involuntary toil was a central, almost defining, feature of the work environment in this period, justified by elites' deep-seated belief in inequality and the widespread view that violence was acceptable. At root, power differences fuelled envy or disdain. This also empowered some to make others work for them. To worsen things, connected global markets demanded increases in labour productivity and human servitude. With its emphasis on profits, the unquestioned accrual of material wealth easily disregarded actual human beings involved in the production of goods.

Hierarchies have always existed, but were usually premised on religion, ethnicity or class. This type of distinction endured through this era, but difference now became premised upon skin colour. New types of labour organization were created, where people of colour did the dirty work. Such ideologies were facilitated by disparities in different societies' technological expertise, differing control of environmental resources, competing religious beliefs and a desire for political expansion.

In 1500, most of the energy that produced goods still came from the muscles of animals or labourers. Wind and water power delivered the major source of natural energy to supplement muscle. Since up to 80 per cent of the people on earth were peasants, and since land was not movable, the portability of cheap labour was an easy source of wealth for the powerful. Oligarchs, aristocrats, wealthy merchants and landowners could work peasants hard, holding a carrot to their nose by offering scraps such as bodily security, national pride or possible freedom (Figure 2.7).

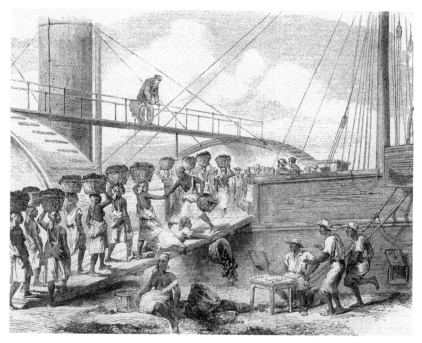

Figure 2.7 Loading coal in Morant Bay, Jamaica, eighteenth century (© Getty Images).

The exploitation of American lands made luxury goods more available to many Europeans, nurturing an insatiable demand that further justified enslavement. New market items such as dyed clothing, trinkets, furniture or jewellery motivated ordinary people to work harder, to buy objects, ownership of which increased their status in turn. Commoners emulated the wealthy to gain social mobility, and a new early modern concept of **consumerism** slowly emerged.

By the 1560s, as epidemics wiped out Indians, the need for African slave labour increased. The benighted economic institution of slavery was thus driven by a new desire for riches, as African sellers, European monarchs and traders all accrued returns from the subjection of people. Horrific though it was, when the modern transatlantic slave trade began in the 1440s such servitude was deemed normal enough. Serfdom was standard everywhere east of France in Europe. Bonded workers were bought and sold throughout the Mediterranean, Africa, Europe and the Muslim world. An ordinary part of everyday life, enslavement moved in all directions. Tens of thousands of European Christians were enslaved by Muslims in the early modern era, often to collect ransom or for cheap labour. Hundreds of thousands of desperate white indentured servants also moved to the Americas along with slaves.

In most places, owning property meant owning people and their labour. This had long been true in parts of the Americas and Africa, where most could not freely move around. In much of Africa, unfree people worked the fields or in the home alongside family members of their masters in a somewhat benign relationship. Owners accrued status by dominating unfree dependents, using them as concubines, soldiers, scribes and in other serving roles.[2] Usually, however, lower-class villagers did not constitute a separate class of labourers, such as slaves or factory workers.

All societies around the world accepted forms of coerced labour, including slavery. Religious leaders, political rulers and economic elites all benefitted from and used the force of law or custom to justify coercion. People in indentured servitude worked off debts across West Africa, Asia or Western Europe through these centuries; serfs were forced to work the land of aristocrats in Central and Eastern Europe for next to nothing well into the late nineteenth century. In South Asia, people were, and still are, confined to particular types of labour through low-class status or family background. Across India, subjugated landless individuals could survive pandemics or famines by agreeing to become slaves for the wealthy.

Arab and African elites in northern and coastal East Africa had long enslaved locals for labour. Arab elites developed a specialized, long-distance slave trade in sub-Saharan Africa in the medieval era. Arab traders had enslaved millions of Africans in the preceding thousand years. In the Americas, Indian societies like the Algonquian practiced slavery, and American Indians in the Southeast used slaves as gifts or property for sale. In colonial North America, enslavement was not wholly restricted to Africans. Between 1670 and 1720, Carolina traders bought up to 50,000 Indian captives, even as African slavery began to escalate.

Of the roughly 500,000 contracted workers who moved from Europe to the Americas in this era, up to half were initially **indentured**, sent for seven years to pay off debts. At least, for them, freedom beckoned if they survived the seven years of their indenture. Still, factories conceivably made conditions worse for Western workers towards the end of the eighteenth century, as industrialization loomed in Europe. Most humans, free, enslaved or somewhere in between, obeyed the orders of higher-class masters in this era. Few could do anything about it.

'Women's work'?

Women worldwide were, by today's standards, certainly subject to coercion into all forms of forced labour. In most societies, females were commonly treated as sexual slaves or for offerings to men of power. Women worked the fields from Asia to Africa, considered as units of profit or sources of sexual pleasure. They had little public voice in the Muslim or Indian world, and all cultures expected labouring women to accept submissive lives. Indentured European female servants were commonplace across the Atlantic and Eurasia.

Though the idea of women's rights did not exist yet, women protested nonetheless. In Mexico the famed part-Spanish poet Sor Juana Ines de la Cruz (d. 1695) bravely spoke out regarding the folly of male attitudes to war but even advocated gender equality. A nun and poet who chose the convent over marriage, she wrote scathingly in 'Arraignment of the Men':

> Males perverse, schooled to condemn
> Women by your witless laws,
> Though forsooth you are prime cause
> Of that which you blame in them:
>
> If with unexampled care
> You solicit their disdain,
> Will your fair words ease their pain,
> When you ruthless set the snare?
> . . .
> Scorn and favor, favor, scorn,
> What you will, result the same,
> Treat you ill, and earn your blame,
> Love you well, be left forlorn.
>
> Scant regard will she possess
> Who with caution wends her way,
> Is held thankless for her 'nay',
> And as wanton for her 'yes'.[10]

There's slavery and there's slavery

Of course, women were enslaved along with men in the Atlantic slave trade. It does nothing to diminish the horrors of the slave trade to point out that other forms of forced or coerced labour were customary worldwide. Indeed, the sheer numbers of African slave victims defy comprehension. Between 10 million and 20 million humans lost their lives, with several millions more dying from shipping or overwork. Already by 1650 the Spanish and Portuguese had shipped over 650,000 slaves. In the eighteenth century England became the dominant trading nation, and the majority of slaves were in fact shipped after 1700.

Though human subjugation had long existed, the impact on the family structures of enchained Africans and the resultant social destruction was immeasurable. Unlike past forms of slavery, sex ratios were sharply skewed in the Atlantic trade. Enslaved males, desired for their physical strength, outnumbered females by two-to-one; women remained in Africa to work for masters there. Most cruelly, the anonymity of what is called **chattel slavery** counted people as economic units of labour, mere factors of production rather than feeling humans with lower status. Capital-intensive land uses, such as large-scale plantation agriculture in the Americas, required more forced labour for more profits. Indeed, over 75 per cent of slaves worked on sugar plantations.

But enslavement was not an exclusively African horror. It was a global curse, justified and spread by religious, political and economic elites for their own enrichment. Slavery uprooted populations around the world and forced them to leave familiar farms and villages. As in the Americas, natives in the Philippines laboured on farms run by Spanish priests, forced to pay taxes or tribute to subsist. From the Eurasian steppes to Southeast Asia, marginalized peoples were pressured into joining more powerful state systems as indentured workers. Asian labourers endured horrific conditions to work in the Americas after the 1500s; both Mexico City and Potosi abused large Chinese workforces, where cosmopolitan labour pools provided the muscle for plantations and mines. South American mines were scoured by the hands of Asian, African and native peasants, sending 16,000 tons of silver into global markets to lubricate Eurasian and Atlantic economies.

Resistance – weapons of the weak

Though the severity of the early modern environment is indisputable, we should not assume that the beleaguered millions were incapable of protest or agency. Oppressed people, male or female, always engaged in some form of resistance to power abuses. Humans did what they could to retain their dignity, difficult as it was in this period. Women often stood up to men if they could. Women of all social standing influenced male decisions and behaviour, even at the risk of retribution.

Native peoples fought against colonizing Europeans through these centuries, losing ground once and for all only in the nineteenth century. North American societies, and their counterparts in Central and South America, fought European-Americans for centuries. In the 1650s, the Iroquois Confederation responded to disease and incursion by merging five societies into that one new powerful nation. In the 1690s south-western natives revolted against Spanish colonists, refusing to cease dancing or practicing traditional rituals that conflicted with the Catholic worldview. The Yaqui revolt against Jesuits in 1740s Arizona affirmed their irritation at Christian attempts to evangelize, culminating in the expulsion of the Jesuits from Spanish America in 1767. Some societies, like the Charrua of Uruguay, remained independent well into the nineteenth century.

Resistance to oppression is a continuity in world history. Southeast Asian and Central Asian peoples persisted in opposing Chinese domination; Central Asian and Arab societies constantly fought back against the gunpowder Islamic empires of the Mughals, Safavid and Ottomans; Philippine natives regularly resisted Spanish overlords; the Irish defied English domination into the twentieth century.

Even with the savagery of slavery, Africans were not merely wretched beings. They resisted to the extent they could. Africans were in fact enslaved in relatively small numbers until around 1650, and rebelled at every turn. The first slave revolts occurred as early as 1512. On board ships, Africans worked to develop capoeira, a weapons-free method of martial defence and defiance, disguised through dance. Like oppressed farmworkers across Eurasia, African and Indian labourers would simply refuse to work. They would vanish, work slowly, break equipment or purposely ruin crops and products to protest. Across the Americas, free blacks and mulattos also fought for freedom to work for themselves. Many slaves and ex-slaves eventually became managers, craftsmen, smiths and cowboys in the Americas.

> Many Africans fought their misfortune to alter their environment, even to the point of departing life on earth to avoid a dark fate. One slave trader ship sailing from West Africa to the Caribbean island of Barbados in 1693–4 recorded this fearful ship log:
>
> > We had about 12 negroes who did wilfully drown themselves, and others starv'd themselves to death, for 'tis their belief that when they die they return home to their own country and friends again.[11]

The Inca in Peru also fought through the sixteenth century, persevering in rebellion against the Spanish even while populations mingled. Even the factionalism of native societies illustrates resistance. Those groups who allied with the English sailor Francis Drake against the Spanish were actively taking sides, participating in multidirectional conflicts with tribal agency. Those societies who sided with Cortes against the Azteca were acting in their own interests against an imperial ruler. Though the famed La Malinche is accused of betraying American peoples, she too resisted in her own way. Aztec-born, offered to Cortes as a sign of conciliation, she bore a child with him, demonstrating her own survival skills by interpreting for various societies through her linguistic capabilities. Indians and Africans used Spanish and colonial courts to fight injustice, if perhaps in biased circumstances, for centuries (Figure 2.8).

Just as weaker societies fought more powerful ones, peasants and serfs within states fought their superiors or owners. That the historical record does not leave many details of such dissenters does not mean they accepted a life of discrimination and despair. In these centuries, thousands of food riots occurred across Eurasia, often with women at the fore owing to their central role in managing households. When crops failed, food riots often resulted. Famines through the 1700s met powerful peasant protests. European court records are replete with acts of defiance towards unjust tax and legal officials, including physical attacks. Like native Africans and Indians, Asian, European, Muslim and Indian peasants revolted in these centuries against encroaching dynastic states, even if historical sources don't tell their side of the story.

Limited power

For most of this period, elites in Europe and elsewhere actually possessed limited power. Most people could live free of state intervention, given transportation

Figure 2.8 La Malinche (Dona Marina) acting as interpreter during the presentation of women and gold by Montezuma (1466–1520) to Hernando Cortes (1485–1547) illustration, 1892 (© Bridgeman Images).

technologies and the vastness of the natural environment. Local rulers, political and religious, were the main source of contact for everyday people. Most were not in towns or cities at this point, so they lived lives of tradition and convention, in an environment they found familiar and natural. The reach of most state rulers, a common focus of historical attention, was relatively weak.

But this was changing slowly. By 1750 European states were imposing more centralized power upon common people across Europe, particularly in the West of the continent. They also slowly dominated the seas and many coastal lands, though inland control remained elusive through the eighteenth century. Real power and control would come in the late nineteenth century. In many colonies, Indians and Africans easily fled to resist in the hundreds of thousands, often creating new societies further inland. **Maroons** (slaves in the Americas who succeeded in fleeing captivity) formed new communities and worked in concord with natives. Thousands of such settlements existed from the south to the north in the Americas.

Since these new groupings sought security in huge forests or mountain regions, it is easy to ignore them historically. But they demonstrate the limited reach of European power in the early modern era. In these centuries, Europeans possessed only tiny footholds on Indian, African and Asian coastlines. Small numbers of Europeans lived in places charted and claimed on maps, although local collaborators gained by interacting, allying and usually westernizing over time.

Indeed, European traders arriving in the vast continent of Africa did not simply steal gold or people – many Africans gained from the interactions. Elite Africans willingly sold people from other chiefdoms into slavery. African elites and traders benefitted from the slave trade, too. By shipping, loading, furnishing crews and sending supplies along with slavers, they made great profits. One African trader in the eighteenth century claimed he sold 18,000 slaves and other profitable commodities, proudly enriching himself as much as any Eurasian monarch.

Conclusion

In 1500, Europe was barely worth noting to people in societies across Eurasia and the Americas. But in these centuries New World foods, derived from the Columbian Exchange, benefitted Europeans, as well as Asians, immensely by enriching diets and increasing populations. Europeans in particular gained from ghost acreage, agricultural resources taken from the lands of colonized societies. They also increased their fertility rates, through enhanced agricultural techniques, such as the use of fodder crops, improved animal husbandry and greater understanding of biology and medicine. Within Europe itself, ratio yields per seed and per acre increased considerably in the seventeenth and eighteenth centuries. Northwest Europeans made use of turnips and clover to the point they were self-sufficient by 1700, enjoying insurance against winter hunger and ending historically normal famine cycles. They increasingly relied on science to understand the land and exploit it as efficiently as possible, which sustained European population growth and eventual global expansion.

In the centuries after 1750 world history was increasingly shaped by the norms and values of colonizing European countries. Europeans spread to the Americas, Africa, India and Asia, dominating ancient societies, subjugating countless people and despoiling their lands in the process. Europeans colonized, influenced or controlled almost all regions of the world by 1900.

This proved ominous for non-Europeans around the globe after 1750. Once new lands were mapped and claimed, a feverish print culture of guidebooks stoked interest in foreign lands and stimulated additional emigration, expansion and ascendancy. In the 1700s, outlandish travel narratives enticed readers with exotic stories of foreign lands, pressing Europeans to venture further afar. Inspired by flowers, herbs, plants and ideas from the Americas, European and Asian royal gardens were planted with thousands of species gathered overseas.

In the early modern era, then, some human populations managed to exploit the environment more profitably than others. The consequences were generally baleful for most people, the land itself, and for the world's flora and fauna. This change in uses of the land put in motion a system of political exploitation that persists, driven primarily by centralized, bureaucratic early-modern military-political states, the formation of which we shall explore in the next chapter.

Keywords

Mestizos
Mulattos
Consanguinity
Racism
Consumerism
Indentured
Chattel Slavery
Maroons

Further reading

Brewer, John. *The Pleasures of the Imagination: English Culture in the Eighteenth Century*. London: Routledge, 2013. Exploration of the high culture of eighteenth-century England, focusing on the morals of literary and artistic life of theatre-goers, artists and pleasure seekers.

Cronon, William. *Changes in the Land: Indians, Colonists, and the Ecology of New England*. New York: Hill and Wang, 2003. This is a unique history using extensive sources to analyse the impact of utilitarian attitudes to land in colonial North America.

Greene, Jack P., and Philip D. Morgan, eds. *Atlantic History: A Critical Appraisal. Reinterpreting History*. Oxford: Oxford University Press, 2009. Thirteen deeply researched essays appraising the history of the ocean by transcending national borders with an eye to connecting indigenous histories with European histories.

Patel, Raj, and Jason W. Moore. *A History of the World in Seven Cheap Things: A Guide to Capitalism, Nature, and the Future of the Planet*. Berkeley: University of California Press, 2018. Short, readable and succinct study of the connection between consumerism, economic growth and the despoiling of nature.

Richards, John F. *The Unending Frontier: An Environmental History of the Early Modern World*. Berkeley: University of California Press, 2003. Identifies four components of early modern world history; intense land use, biological encroachment, hunting and energy deficiencies from Japan and China to Europe and the Americas.

Interlude 1 – Population problems

What can the early modern environment tell us about our world today? Most obviously, along with considerable violence, genocide, enslavement and disease, more people were born to endure or enjoy life on earth. These births propagated our species, planting seeds for the billions that would come to live in the past century. With only around 450–500 million people on the planet in 1500, the early modern era would bring a steady increase in population, though not on the scale of recent decades. In the twentieth century alone, world population grew from roughly 1.5 billion to over 7 billion (Figure I.1.1).

A set of new changed behaviours helped boost populations: the bounty of the New World, improved understandings of agriculture and innovative food production technologies all fed bellies and prolonged lives. Greater extraction of calories and nutrition through exploiting forced labour and new lands in the Americas meant that between 1500 and 1750 populations expanded from Ireland to the Middle East, from India to China. In this era, the planet's population had almost doubled, approaching a billion people for the first time in history as the eighteenth century ended.

Though we might consider population growth as a positive change for *Homo sapiens* in this period, it might be our downfall in the present era. Concerned astrobiologists from the American Geophysical Union recently declared that unchecked population growth, and accelerated climate change resulting from it, is *the* major challenge humans face in sustaining life on earth today. They contend we are now at a crossroads that could lead to either natural extinction or some form of technology-induced immortality. Present-day anxieties concerning climate change and large-scale environmental alteration stem from a quite recently formed appreciation that all human life relies upon soils, air and water for its existence. Ironically, then, our current environmental predicament stems from early modern accomplishments in sailing the seas, using the land and subsequent population growth.[1]

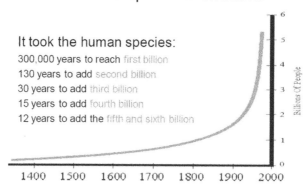

Figure I.1.1 Population issues. https://bixby.berkeley.edu/what-we-do/core-researc h/population/. Accessed 15 May 2021.

Strength in numbers

Population growth in the last century imitated the events of the early modern period, only in far larger scale. In the 1500s, the actions and ideas of a small number of barely literate men such as Cortes and Pizarro caused the eradication of millions of American natives, while the economic interests of a relatively small number of slavers and plantation owners annihilated millions of Africans. In the twentieth century, massive wars prompted by a small number of political elites and their cronies slaughtered well over 100 million people. But, as in the early modern period, global population in absolute numbers escalated nonetheless – particularly after 1945: from roughly 2 billion to 8 billion. In both periods, millions of lives were senselessly destroyed, even while millions more were born (Figure I.1.2).

Lone actors can, and do, influence history. The likes of Genghis Khan, Columbus or Hitler come to mind. But just as the decimation of native peoples after 1500 derived from the actions of a few men, in recent decades, one man in particular contributed to huge population growth. Descended from Europeans who landed in North America in the 1850s, the relatively unknown Norman Borlaug changed the world. Borlaug received the Nobel Peace Prize in 1970 for helping end famine and malnutrition in poor countries that had suffered from Western encroachment in recent centuries. His scientific approach to agricultural improvement helped develop new strains of wheat and rice, saving up to a billion people from starvation in developing countries, in the process helping Indian, African and Latin American populations sustain millions of lives.

Population growth or technology such as this was inconceivable in the early modern period. Throughout the sixteenth, seventeenth and eighteenth centuries, famines and changing weather patterns ravaged populations worldwide. Indeed, by

Figure I.1.2 Agriculture Nobel laureate Norman E. Borlaug, 87, visits Green Revolution farms in India (© Getty Images).

1750 we might have expected widespread global population collapse, as occurred in both the third and fourteenth centuries CE. Throughout the seventeenth century this seemed probable, as hungry peasants raided storerooms worldwide, bandits fought for survival and conflict over food persisted across continents. To counter desperate peasant protests in 1642 China, the Ming governor foolishly destroyed the Yellow River's dikes, prompting decades of floods, famine and smallpox epidemics, and drowning up to 300,000 people. In the decades prior to 1670 a massive agrarian crisis led to misery throughout Mughal India. The Gujarat region in India suffered repeated famines thereafter. From 1630 rains failed four years in a row. Mice and locusts attacked food supplies causing disastrous effects and vast suffering. Such events were commonplace in this era everywhere – people died from famine and other environmental challenges and nobody knew what to do about it.

As in the last century, cross-cultural interaction prompted both the eradication of millions in some societies and population booms for others. Access to fresh foods from the Americas helped Eurasian populations explode, while disease, enslavement and war killed off indigenous peoples. Intensified use of land produced larger quantities of food; by 1800, Eurasians had colonized marginal lands and extended control over hunter-gatherer cultures worldwide. This ended millennia in which societies lived off the land lightly, introducing constant population growth that in the twentieth century would necessitate the type of nutritional science Borlaug accomplished (Figure I.1.3).

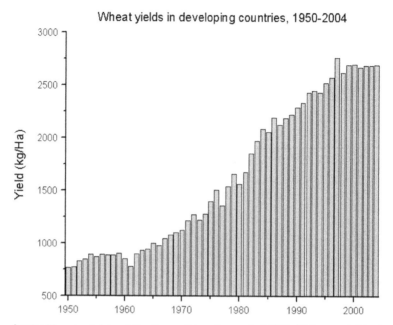

Figure I.1.3 Wheat yields. http://en.wikipedia.org/wiki/File:Wheat_yields_in_devel oping_countries_1951-2004.png. Accessed 15 May 2021.

From 1500 to 1750 humans migrated just as they always had, but over far vaster distances. Subsequently plants, animals and germs modified bodies and minds in far greater ways. Previously separated landmasses in the Americas were connected to Eurasia through a process of migration and enslavement. The Americas were ecologically reshaped with plants and humans from Europe, Asia and Africa. Sugar grown on large plantations recreated ecosystems and devastated millions of lives.

In these centuries, people from Eurasia – and Europe in particular – began to migrate and exploit nature more extensively than ever before in history. As the eighteenth century passed into the nineteenth, natural population checks occurred as they always had around the globe, except in Europe. Along with increased agricultural yields at home, Europeans occupied the lands of populations that were in decline worldwide. In the same centuries that saw widespread famine in Asia, vast numbers of Africans and Indians murdered, European populations increased, doubling from around 75 million in 1500 to 150 million in 1750. This was the beginning of Western domination that lasted well into the present and was no small contributor to the racist ideology many white people would commit to in the nineteenth century and after.

Humans today seem unable to alter well-worn habits developed in this era. Surging population pressure on the planet combines with relentless material desires for goods, hurting the planet and many of the people producing those goods. The following four chapters will explore other types of human behaviours that impacted humans, animals, nations and societies in the early modern era – from daring voyagers to innovative thinkers to murderous fanatics, who along with everyday people shaped the early modern political, economic, religious and technological worlds we have inherited.

3

State-building with gunpowder and gunpower

Chapter Outline

In the early modern era centralized states and government became increasingly influential, and invasive, in the lives of people across the world. In this era new, huge empires stretched across vast areas of land and sea, while in many regions small-scale states and loosely governed societies continued to predominate. In some regions, the era witnessed sweeping innovations in relations between state and society. It was also an age of state-led colonial exploitation which resulted in the destruction of societies and the imperial subjugation of people globally. Though there was considerable diversity in forms of governance, certainly one of the most important political stories of this era was the rise of vast, centralized states across much of Eurasia – and the related expansion overseas of mainly European maritime empires. This imposition of political power on the lives of so many is the central narrative of this chapter, although we will also explore the limits of state power in this period also.

This chapter is partly about the actions of states and of state relations with each other. It is also, however, a story about transformations in **governance** – the strategies by which elites in societies created, managed and implemented laws and regulations. Governance involves the operation of state institutions – armies, police, tax collectors, royal courts, even education and hospital systems, as well as individual politicians, ministers and monarchs. This chapter is also a story about **political culture** – the ways in which individuals and groups of people participated in decision-making. In most places and periods, political culture was the preserve of a small group of aristocrats or courtiers. In societies today, many sources influence political culture, with large groups participating as voters, lobbyists, political consumers and even elected officials. However, in our period, while there was some experimentation and innovation in political equality, this emerged only slowly and in only a few places. Elites made the rules. Democracy was barely a dream (Figure 3.1).

We will define a number of important terms that help us to understand early modern politics and the rise of the centralized state: **centralization, rationalization, expansionism, sovereignty, legitimacy, enclosure** and **state** itself. Other terms are descriptors of types of political organization, such as **acephalous** societies, **chieftaincies, confederations** and **chartered companies**. Still others, such as **governance, political culture, sumptuary laws** and **diplomatic system**, are terms that help us to understand the nature of politics more broadly, and last, some are specific to a single state: **millets, durbar** and **viceroy.**

By the end of this chapter, readers should be able to

- Synthesize historical narratives from different parts of the world to explain the spread of the centralized state political model.
- Explain changes in political transformations in Eurasia, Africa, the Americas and the Pacific.

Figure 3.1 Brueghel, Pieter the Younger (1564–1636) The Tax Collector. Tax collectors were some of the most visible – and disliked! – representatives of the increasingly centralized and bureaucratic state in the early modern period in many parts of the world (© Getty Images).

- Appraise the ways in which the early modern state affected – or did not affect – everyday life for most people.
- Analyse the means by which states expanded their authority, in terms of both formal institutions and cultural changes like rituals and sumptuary laws.

States and sovereignty

We live in a world of **states**. Most human beings on the planet today live in territories governed by centralized governments, with systems of laws, highly developed bureaucracies of state officials, and defined borders. These governments collect taxes, implement law and order, and claim **sovereignty**: the authority to govern. We are so used to this system of states that it is hard for us to conceive of an era when many, if not most, people lived outside of states.

This chapter explains the development of a centralized, state-focused model of governance from the fifteenth century onwards. This model brought forth more efficient and larger states, which were able to expand, first across large regions of Eurasia and then around the world. In the process, they overcame or destroyed many alternate political systems that could not compete with them and were weakened by conquest, disease and slavery. Most societies worldwide thus had to embrace this centralized state model – partly in order to survive in the onslaught.

Political diversity in 1500

In 1500, when this volume begins, most people did not live in a centralized state. Many lived in **acephalous**, often roughly egalitarian, societies without a single ruler or clear government. Such societies existed in areas like northern Siberia, parts of southern and central Africa, Australia and parts of North America. They were usually organized along family lines, with decisions largely made by family collectively or by elders. Still other societies took the form of **chieftaincies**, where larger groups of people were ruled by elected or hereditary leaders, but without the professional bureaucrats or rigid set borders of a state. Some nomadic peoples in Central Asia and many African, American, and Polynesian societies were chieftaincies of one form or another.

Of course, states did exist in every region of the world. Some were very large, with powerful central governments. Others, however, were governed through more diffuse political models. Many states were **confederations**, in which power was balanced among several different families or regional governments. Large regions of North America – from Massachusetts to Arizona – were governed as confederations made up of several chieftaincies. Indeed, the modern names of many of the states of this region are drawn from political terms used by earlier confederations as geographically distant as Connecticut (the Land beside the Long Tidal River) to Colorado (Red Lands). Similar confederations held sway in West and Central Africa, and tribes across the Middle East and Southeast Asia functioned likewise.

In 1500, we see examples of centralized states in every region of the world, from American empires like the Inca to the hundreds of small kingdoms and republics in Europe, to Indian Ocean trading states, strung along the coast from East Africa to southern India. Yet most of these regions included large populations free of centralized rule. Over the next several centuries, these societies would be overwhelmed or incorporated into more centralized states with more rigid borders, more formal laws and highly organized bureaucracies. The expansion of the centralized state between 1500 and 1750, both through the diffusion of the state as a political concept and through violence and warfare, is the main story of this chapter.

A system of empires and kingdoms in Eurasia and North Africa

The great diversity of political systems in the fifteenth century, however, was in decline. A great shift was beginning to take place with the expansion of the number and size of highly centralized, well-organized states across the world, beginning in Eurasia and North Africa. Around 1330, much of Eurasia had been under the control of the vast Mongol Khanate – geographically perhaps the largest empire in human history. Smaller states had revolved around the fringes of this massive central polity, which controlled long-distance trade routes between them. In the mid-fourteenth century, the Black Death plague spread from China into Central Asia, Europe and parts of Africa, breaking this system apart. In the process, it weakened states from England to Japan, Scandinavia to Morocco. Following the break-up of the Mongol-centred network, hundreds of smaller states emerged, until by around 1380 CE, more than 500 states existed in Europe alone, with thirty or so in Central Asia and more than twenty in Southeast Asia. This was a period of fragmentation.

By 1490, however, this disintegration across Eurasia began to reverse, as societies recovered from the collapse caused by the plague. Large, unified states re-emerged in regions the Mongols had once controlled. Two patterns appeared: first, societies around the outer edges of the Eurasian landmass formed into dozens of relatively compact kingdoms, sultanates and other centralized states. The easternmost of these was Japan, which unified under Tokugawa Ieyasu in 1600 after he defeated a number of rival feuding clans to take control of the island nation. Nearby, the ruling Korean Joseon dynasty expanded the area under its rule in the fifteenth and early sixteenth centuries by fending off outside rivals to the north. In Southeast Asia, the rise of the Burmese Kingdom in the sixteenth century under the Toungoo dynasty provided a balance of power alongside the Le kings of Vietnam. After 1563, a largely unified Thailand under the Ayutthaya kings emerged, and numerous other small kingdoms also formed, including small trading city-states like Melaka and Aceh. Trade and cultural links grew among states across Southeast Asia and India, with both Hindu states like Vijayanagar and, in the sixteenth century, a number of Muslim-led kingdoms in northern India.

In Europe, too, a constellation of small states slowly stabilized in the fifteenth and sixteenth centuries. The Scandinavian Peninsula in Northern Europe alternated between a single unified state and regional kingdoms, before definitively dividing into three strong states of Denmark, Norway and Sweden in the seventeenth century. France began to consolidate in the sixteenth century into its current octagonal shape, as powerful kings gradually defeated or incorporated nobles like the Dukes of Burgundy, ethnic minorities such as the Celts of Brittany, and Protestant religious minorities. Across the English Channel, the Tudor and Stuart dynasties of England forced the separate parts of Britain – England, Scotland and Wales – into a unified state against the wishes of most minorities. This was symbolized by the union of the Kings of England and Scotland in a single person, James I, in 1603. English kings also occupied Ireland, suppressing Catholics to initiate a global Protestant empire. On the Iberian Peninsula the Christian Kings of Portugal established full control of their territory by the early fifteenth century, and Spain became unified by 1500 under devout Catholic rule. Across the Mediterranean in Morocco, the Sa-Idi family brought together urban Arabs and rural Berbers in a single, strong kingdom in the same period.

While these mid-sized centralized kingdoms sat on the edges of Eurasia, several large empires gradually came to stretch across the middle of the vast landmass. China was the easternmost of these. Fragmented by the Mongols into several weak states, the Ming dynasty reunified China in 1368. The Ming emperors ruled a stable empire until 1644, when their dynasty fell to an invasion of Manchus from the northeast, who established the Qing dynasty. Both Ming and Qing Emperors interacted with another fast-growing state in their north and west: the Russian Empire. This vast realm grew out of the tiny Duchy of Muscovy, which had thrown off Mongol rule in the late fifteenth century. In the 1500s, Muscovy Dukes asserted their authority over both Muslim and Christian states at the point where Europe and Asia joined. Styling themselves tsars, or emperors, of Russia, they conquered eastward across Siberia and southward to the Caspian Sea. Their main rivals here were the Sultans of the Ottoman Empire, also former tributaries of the Mongols in Southwest Asia (Anatolia), who had by 1500 taken over the Balkan Peninsula of Europe, much of North Africa and chunks of Asia up connecting to Russia.

To the East the Ottomans encountered the Persian Safavi kings, who had defeated the last of the descendants of the Mongol rulers of Central Asia. Beyond the domains of the Safavi, a remnant of the Mongols built a new, smaller, Sunni empire. The great conqueror Zahir-ud-din Muhammad Babur brought followers from Central Asia to conquer the Ganges and Indus river valleys. His Sunni Muslim successors called themselves the Mughal dynasty, and they would occupy most of the Hindu Indian subcontinent and large territories in Central Asia.

In the far west, much of Europe came under the rule of the Habsburg dynasty. This family empire was centred in the fragmented territories of Germany. The Habsburg family were important dukes in this ramshackle collective of polities and through a series of fortuitous marriages, they acquired Bohemia, Hungary, Poland, most of Spain and large parts of Northern Europe. Spread over many mountains and peninsula, however, this empire proved hard to hold together under a single, centralized government. In 1555, it split into a western and an eastern half and over time, these became the Spanish Empire and the Austro-Hungarian Empire.

The two types of centralized states that emerged in Eurasia and North Africa in this period – the relatively compact kingdoms of the Eurasian periphery and the sprawling empires of the core – differed in more than just size. Gradually, the smaller kingdoms would develop a sense of themselves as homogenous 'nations' – with one set of laws and one shared identity. For example, the British kings and queens promoted a sense of British identity for their Scots, Welsh and English subjects – although they excluded the nearby Irish, whom they had conquered. The expansive empires of the core, by contrast, had to deal with many more different communities over whom they ruled. Rather than constructing a single national identity, they tended to invent complex systems of law and cultural practice that acknowledged multiple identities. A good example is the Ottoman Empire, which had Jewish,

Armenian Christian, Orthodox Christian, Catholic and, of course, both Sunni and Shi'ite Muslim subjects. As we will discuss herein, this diversity led the sultans to allow many communities broad autonomy, so long as they remained loyal to the throne. Yet, the more ideologically uniform kingdoms, like the British, French and Spanish, would prove more powerful in the long run.

Centralization, rationalization and expansionism

Together, the small states of the periphery and large empires of the interior of Eurasia shaped a world of relatively stable states in the fifteenth and sixteenth centuries. Most would survive the entire period to 1750 and well after. Some still exist, often within approximately the borders they assumed during this period. Their resiliency is partly a result of the strategies they developed in the early modern period to make the state – government and its methods – an extremely powerful institution in society. These strategies can be described as *centralization, rationalization* and *expansionism*.

The key distinguishing feature of the emerging Eurasian states was greater **centralization**, where both power and authority tended to consolidate, over several

Figure 3.2 The Tosho-Gu shrine at Nikko, Japan. These shrines were dedicated to Tokugawa Ieyasu by his son and successor, who sought to elevate his father as a national hero in order to strengthen the shogunate and continue the unification of the state. Built 1615–36 (© Getty Images).

generations, under a single state authority. Usually this central power was a ruling monarch or dynastic family surrounded by a loyal royal or imperial court. In some instances, or for a period of time, the monarch might be a weak figurehead and real power lay in the hands of a body of aristocrats or wealthy landholders. A good example of this is Japan, which in 1490 was in political disarray, as regional lords, or *daimyo*, battled for supremacy across the Japanese islands. These wars exacerbated the suffering of Japanese peasants, who rose up in armed groups, sometimes with the help of organized religious sects. But this chaotic situation slowly reversed in the sixteenth and seventeenth centuries through the actions of a series of military leaders, the shoguns. These men hailed from old, established families and a few talented commoners. Together, and with the nominal authority of the Japanese imperial family always in the background, they defeated the various *daimyo* and imposed the apparatus of the centralized state. In 1603, Tokugawa Ieyasu became shogun (r. 1603–16) – his successors would rule Japan until 1867. The shoguns were military leaders who ruled in place of the emperor who was a god to his people largely uninvolved in day-to-day political affairs. Appointed by the emperor, the shoguns used their political authority and their own military forces to restrict the power of the regional *daimyo* and dominate Japan (Figure 3.2).

As well as centralizing authority, state elites implemented policies focused on **rationalization**, by which authority and power in the state became increasingly organized through a permanent bureaucracy. This process took several centuries to develop in most places, often punctuated by periods of dramatic reforms. One such

Figure 3.3 Rationalization: Provost and Municipal Magistrates of Paris, 1689 (© Getty Images).

transformative period occurred in France under King Louis XIV (d. 1715). Louis expanded the army while placing under the control of loyal professional soldiers, conveniently demoting many of the old aristocrats. He replaced the many different regional laws of France with a single new body of law that applied throughout the country. To administer this new legal code, Louis also appointed a large group of well-educated middle-class officials who now received government salaries. Further, he expanded the system of roads crossing the country, partly to more effectively maintain its unity. To pay for new projects like roads and salaries, he established a series of taxes on customs, salt and land. He also tried to stimulate trade by encouraging artisans from across Europe to settle in France. Altogether these policies tended to result in a much stronger, rationally organized and centralized France (Figure 3.3).

Figure 3.4 Russian Empire by 1900 (Wikimedia Commons).

Over time, such policies of centralization and rationalization spread from one Eurasian or African state to another, as their advantages became obvious to rulers. Powerful monarchs soon undertook policies of **expansion**, by which they sought to increase the territory they controlled and then over time develop imperial institutions and power structures. One of the most successfully expansive states in this period was Russia, which grew from tiny domains to a vast, continent-spanning empire across Eurasia. The most dramatic example of this expansion took place under the rule of Mikhail Romanov (d. 1645). In the west, Russia under the Christian Orthodox Romanov tsars conquered territories in Europe on the Baltic Sea. To the south, the Romanovs claimed large areas of the Caucasus Mountains and parts of Central Asia. It was in the east, though, that the greatest expansion took place as Russian fur merchants supported by troops and tax collectors built an empire stretching across Siberia all the way to the Pacific Ocean (Figure 3.4).

Other states expanded in this era. The Sunni Ottoman Empire, for example, grew over the course of two centuries to include parts of three continents – North Africa, Central Asia and Arabian, and the Balkan Peninsula of Europe. Sometimes, expanding states like the Russian and Ottoman empires fought each other. Usually, these conflicts broke out along religious lines. Catholic Spanish states fought to 'reconquer' the Iberian Peninsula from Muslims in the late fifteenth century, while the Catholic Pope organized a 'Holy League' in the sixteenth century to oppose the Muslim Ottoman Empire in the Mediterranean. Protestants built alliances with their co-religionists to oppose the Catholic Habsburgs in Europe, while Hindus in South Asia united against the Muslim-ruled Mughal Empire. Alliances crossed religious lines, however, when they suited rulers. Catholic France allied with Protestants to oppose the more powerful Catholic Habsburg Spain in Europe, and Safavid Muslims even fought against the Ottoman Muslims in coalition with Christian Europeans at times. In the short term, such conflict brought chaos and instability, but the victors usually went on to maintain their hold on power, and, in doing so, shaped future states and the dominant faiths within them.

During the early modern era, major wars between large states occurred frequently. But even more common were smaller-scale internal conflicts resulting from state centralization. The main obstacle facing rulers engaged in power centralization was the power of aristocrats and landowners who feared losing their traditional privileges. Often, they aspired to rule themselves, so monarchs fought to subdue these regional nobles or warlords and strengthen the power of the state. Kings and queens had several advantages in these kinds of fights, as we'll see in the next section.

Accounting for the Eurasian centralized state

In the early modern era, several factors, acting in concert, made possible the development of new centralized, rationalized and expansionist states. Most of these are discussed in other chapters, but warrant mention here. The first factor was rising population densities. As discussed in Chapter 2, the late-fourteenth-century recovery from the Black Death plague was followed by innovations in agriculture that gradually spread across Africa and Eurasia. Increased food yields helped sustain the population growth that followed the recovery. Rising populations stimulated trade and provided centralizing governments with new taxes, labour and resources.

Another factor encouraging expansion and centralization was the increasing availability of cash. Metal bullion, from the mines of Japan, Austria and – crucially, by the mid-sixteenth century – the Americas made this growth of cash possible. Specie currency stocks grew as bullion arrived in Europe and China on board Spanish caravels and galleons, then dispersed across Eurasia. By the 1650s, gold from the Americas in the form of pieces of eight was so widespread that it formed a sort of common Eurasian currency. This money, and taxes made from increasing trade, became available to governments to pay for wars, infrastructure projects and other needs of state.

Perhaps most importantly, these funds helped states develop large armies supplied with gunpowder weapons. Firearms – personal guns and cannon – gave a huge advantage to those rulers who possessed them. Unlike bows and swords, guns could be used by comparatively untrained soldiers, and proved effective against previously invincible regional warlords and their armoured knights, sipahis or samurai. Cannon could breach the walls of ancient castles and forts. Rulers and states with these weapons, then, gained formidable advantages against domestic rivals for power, like aristocrats and knights, who used older, less effective forms of military technology.

Other technologies played a role in developing state power also. In more open societies with growing print cultures, rulers could use the printing press to publish government edicts and publish new laws across a large state that increasingly literate populations could read. Better roads sped administrators and armies across widespread empires. The printed word also spread new ideologies that legitimized the emerging centralized state. We should not underestimate the role of 'technologies of thought' and administration, discussed in a later section, in creating new mental and political worlds.

The 1648 Treaty of Westphalia was a key sea change for Europe. European states thereafter sought to resolve religious differences, fighting less over Catholicism or Protestantism. Together the major states agreed to recognize a large number of diverse nation-states of Europe and focus instead on growth and centralization. Perhaps the best example of a rationalized, centralized and expansionist state was the Netherlands. The Dutch people were ruled by group of merchants, not one ruler. Through supreme administrative efficiency, Dutch cities retained a high degree of sovereignty, with Amsterdam the central hub of goods, shipping and trans-shipping for profits worldwide. The Dutch political state was small and sleek, yet soon expanded globally.

The Eurasian model goes to sea

The drive by these influential leaders to expand their states – and their own authority – was a common trend across Eurasia and North Africa in this era. China's Ming dynasty employed a sophisticated bureaucracy to deepen its penetration into everyday life. To the west of China, states like the Mughal Sultanate, Romanov Russia and the Ottoman Empire expanded rapidly into Central Asia, annexing countless minor societies. By contrast, states on the very west of the Eurasian landmass (namely Western Europe) were not particularly large or powerful. Nor did they have nearby territory that would allow for easy expansion. Moreover, they faced financial limitations. Unlike the large states of East Asia, they did not have access to great stretches of land and large population from which they could raise tax revenue. Unlike states in central Eurasia like the Ottoman Empire they could not easily act as middlemen, taxing trade as it moved its way across the supercontinent. Boxed out of the lucrative landed trade to the east, the smaller states on the Atlantic seaboard – including Portugal, Spain, France and England (unified in 1707 with Scotland and Wales as Great Britain) – had to look to the oceans to find opportunities for lucrative trade and political expansion. This they did with fervour, shaping much of the world in ensuing centuries.

The chartered company system

This mutually convenient alliance between merchants and monarchs would ultimately accomplish the overseas expansion of Western European states in the early modern period. In Portugal, this alliance took the shape of the *Estado da India*, a merchant company that boasted the Portuguese king as a major investor. As they spread across the world, the *Estado's* merchant ships could be ensured of the king's support in the form of Portuguese warships and troops. In return, the king received a share of the company's profits. Towards the end of the fifteenth century, Portuguese began establishing trading stations on islands off the coast of Europe and then along the West Coast of Africa. In the early 1500s, Portuguese admirals held the Swahili city-states of East Africa for ransom, threatening to bombard them if they did not pay. Soon Portuguese stations dotted coastal South Asia and the islands of the Indian Ocean. Through this coercion, they came to control the rich trade in silver and silk between Japan and continental Asia which provided Portugal with its main source of income.

For several reasons, Spanish monarchs controlled overseas expansion even more tightly than their Portuguese neighbours. First, Spain had a surplus of soldiers and warships after long wars fighting to expel Muslim states like Cordoba from the

Iberian Peninsula, and soon set soldiers to work on imperial expansion. Second, committed Catholic Spanish monarchs could pay for their military expeditions by confiscating the wealth of Jews and Muslims, many of whom had been citizens of Cordoba before its conquest. Finally, the massive amounts of gold and silver Spanish extracted from the Americas financed the further growth of the Spanish power in Europe under the Habsburg Empire.

In general, the rulers of the Atlantic states of Europe relied heavily on groups of independent merchants to begin building overseas empires. Several of Spain's rivals – the Netherlands, England and France – initiated their ventures in the Atlantic by granting independent pirates official support to prey on Spanish treasure fleets. This mutually beneficial agreement gradually morphed into more organized trading companies in which governments often invested. Some were immensely successful: the Dutch East India Company soon became a rival to the Portuguese in Africa and Asia. Meanwhile, the British East and West India Companies funded settlements in the Americas and trade to India. These companies were more independent from the Crown than their Portuguese counterparts, but they still relied upon their governments for some support, which often came in the form of monopoly on trading rights between homeland and distant regions of the world. Because governments granted these companies rights and privileges through a written grant called a 'charter', the new trading groups became known as **chartered companies**. Piracy turned out to be profitable for Western states.

But not only merchants and governments committed to the outcome of European expansion into the Americas, Africa and Asia. Christian missionaries played an important role. Catholic priests settled in West Africa, East Asia and ports across the Americas in the sixteenth century and were soon joined by rival Protestant missionaries. Both groups of competing Christians provided valuable support and information for their governments and affiliated trading companies, in return receiving protection and funding (Figure 3.5).

Overall, though, a desire for wealth on the part of elites and their mercantile partners drove the growth of these maritime empires. The generation of wealth depended, however, on a growing army of labourers. As we saw in Chapter 2, the populations of Atlantic and Caribbean Islands and later the Americas quickly collapsed from diseases that arrived on board European ships. Merchants grew desperate for labourers to work the silver mines, tobacco farms, logging camps and sugar plantations of the Americas, and to staff the ships and forts that serviced the strings of settlements built by the chartered companies. At first, this meant marginalized European peoples like the Basques of Spain, the Irish or unemployed English. These groups were typically poor and politically powerless, and so were easily coerced into indentured servitude. Soon, however, the unceasing demand for labour stimulated an emerging trade in enslaved humans that became central to the growth of overseas empires.

Figure 3.5 French allegory about the founding of the East India Company (1717). Merchants and missionaries with Indians at the mouth of the Mississippi River (© Getty Images).

Conflict in sub-Saharan Africa in the Atlantic age

By the late fifteenth century, Europeans turned to sub-Saharan Africans in search of a larger pool of labourers. Within a century, Africans would form the bulk of the labour that drove transatlantic empire economies. The earliest victims of this system of forced labour were individuals kidnapped or acquired from trading partners near the European forts in Africa. Demand soon increased, so prices paid for captives did too. Hence the steady arrival of slaving ships increased pressures on African societies as profiteers filled the holds of ships for gain. Often, this required the political reorganization of African societies, like the Oyo or Asante as noted in Chapter 1.

Perhaps most significantly, the Atlantic slave trade broke down the complex balances of power by which politics worked within the acephalous societies, confederations, chieftaincies and states of West and Central Africa. Europeans who arrived in Africa seeking captives for American slave plantations brought with them guns and sometimes horses. In certain African regions, they found individuals and groups willing to trade with them. These Africans acquired new weapons and used them to become armed warrior elites and even kings. Those who resisted the trade, by contrast, were unable to acquire weapons and lost out. The rising warlords and warrior elite quickly transformed politics in several regions of Africa. In some areas, the competition for captives destroyed large states. For example, slave-raiding warriors known as *tyeddo* destroyed the unity of the Jolof Confederation of Senegambia. In other regions, armed elites completely reoriented their states towards the slave trade, failing to develop productive or diversified economies. These 'vampire' states weakened entire regions of West Africa. Most commonly, wars broke out across West and West-Central Africa as large states set out to conquer and enslave their neighbours to feed the demands of the European merchants and American plantations – now in a global market dominated by Atlantic states.

The Atlantic slave trade deeply affected the West-Central African state of Kongo. In the early sixteenth century, Kongo was both a kingdom and a confederation. Its ruler, the *Mani*, presided over a court of ruling families from the many provinces. As in many regions of the world, ruling families no longer actually governed their provinces, preferring to enjoy their time at court. The king would temporarily dispatch nobles to rural areas to act as governors, but they didn't often interfere with the rural communities that produced goods the state needed. This allowed provinces to govern themselves through elected groups of local elders. The Kongolese royal court held back from extracting too much in the form of taxes from these small communities, partly in fear of rebellion, but partly because of a complex code of morality that connected greed with witchcraft.

> With the advent of the slave trade, however, this code collapsed. Now nobles anxious for new manufactured goods introduced by Portuguese and other European slaveholders began to raid rural communities, searching for people to exchange for high-status goods. In 1526, *Mani* (King) Affonso I of Kongo even wrote to the King of Portugal saying:
>
> > many of our people, keenly desirous as they are of the wares and things of your Kingdoms, which are brought here by your people, and in order to satisfy their voracious appetite, seize many of our people, freed and exempt men; and very often it happens that they kidnap even noblemen and the sons of noblemen, and our relatives, and take them to be sold to the white men who are in our Kingdoms; and for this purpose they have concealed them; and others are brought during the night so that they might not be recognized.[1]

In an attempt to limit the new trade, King Affonso instituted a set of laws intended to protect nobles and productive peasants from enslavement, but these proved largely ineffectual. Over time, the pressures of the slave trade caused a series of wars. The nobles drifted away from the royal court back to their provinces, where they mobilized their populations to attack rival provinces and acquire captives. The entire purpose of these conflicts was to capture slaves and, thereby, enrich provincial nobles. The Kongolese kingdom broke apart as a result of outside pressures.

The slave trade may have played a role in the emergence of a greater threat: the Jaga, an invading force that almost brought about the end of the Kingdom in 1568. Historians studying Kongo only know of the invasion of the Jaga from a single source, which tells of an army invading Kongo and defeating the royal forces. The Jaga burned the capital and took thousands of prisoners as slaves before the king, aided by Portuguese soldiers, drove them back.

Most historians accept that the Jaga were an invading ethnic group from outside Kongo. A number, however, have suggested that they were local rebels. Some of them may have been rebels seeking to overthrow the king. They may also have been opportunistic nobles hoping to take slaves to sell to the Europeans. Certainly, the conflict resulted in a huge glut of captives and the famine that followed kept the flow of slaves at high volume. However, some scholars believe they were survivors of rural communities that had suffered from years of slave raiding. Having had their children torn from them and their homes burned, they had nothing left to lose. Thus, they began to wander the countryside, taking what they could find and destroying everything else. By raiding the capital, especially, they could show their anger at the architects of their suffering – the nobles who ran the slave trade.

Still, the impact of Atlantic slaving on African political entities in this period did not mean Europeans easily conquered African societies. In fact, it was the resilience of African societies that forced slave traders to rely on other Africans as partners. There were direct attempts at European rule in Africa in the early modern period. As early as the fifteenth century, the Portuguese sought to control parts of Africa. They sacked several of the wealthy Swahili-speaking ports of East Africa, but could not control them. They did build a small colony in the 1530s along the Zambezi River, where they constructed plantations and several small towns. But this fledgling colony was weak and relied for its survival on alliances with local leaders and slave traders. In West-Central Africa, the Portuguese controlled several ports from which they dominated the slave trade. Here, too though, they survived by allying with locals, including later kings of Kongo, though their ability to carve out a territory for themselves was limited by powerful rulers who resisted them, including Queen Nzinga (1583–1663) of the Ndongo Kingdom. Nzinga began a policy of allying with Portugal's rivals, including the Dutch, and increasing the bureaucracy and centralization of her own state to command the resources necessary to fight off the Portuguese (Figure 3.6).

It was only at the very southern tip of Africa that Europeans successfully carved out an African state in this era. Here, the local Khoisan population proved highly susceptible to diseases brought by European traders, particularly smallpox. Moreover, the local climate was much like that of southern Europe and hence favourable to both Europeans and their crops. The Dutch East India Company, therefore, established a small colony in this region in 1652. Built around the town of Kaapstad (Cape Town), it served as a way-station for ships en route to new colonies in Asia. The company

During their long wars of invasion, the Portuguese met a
formidable adversary in Queen Nzinga of Matamba

Figure 3.6 Engraving showing Queen Nzinga of Matamba, sometimes known as Dona Anna De Souza, sitting on a kneeling man to receive a group of Portuguese, *c.* 1626 (© Getty Images).

populated the colony with Dutch indentured servants, slaves and war captives from East Africa and South-East Asia, who quickly mixed with the native Khoisan population. The colony gradually spread outward from the growing town as the colonists used their superiority in horses and firearms to carve out large ranches and farms for themselves.

Cape Town would develop into one of many 'creole' societies to emerge in coastal Africa during this era. In ports and surrounding regions, European and African communities mixed, sometimes with Asian immigrants also. Their offspring became traders, officials and managers of small merchant firms as well as large chartered companies and state governments. As in other parts of the Atlantic, these were borderland zones, places where cultures mixed and fused. Many of them were essentially self-governing, since government or company officials sent from Europe were usually only temporarily in residence. In the West African island-port of Gorée, for example, a small class of Euro-Africans known as *habitants* set rules and judged cases within their own community, often with little interference from the French governor of the town. Slavery and the arrival of Europeans thus destabilized parts of Africa and mixed the populations of other parts.

Disease in American and Pacific political entities

By building overseas empires in the Americas, men from states like Spain, Portugal, the Netherlands, France and Britain relied on violence to colonize. The first European overseas state-builders, Portugal and Spain, were well practised in political and religious violence. The reconquest of the Iberian Peninsula had created a large militarized class of young men used to fighting, many of whom became the 'conquistadors' or conquerors who went abroad. Portuguese troops first gained overseas experience in attempts to colonize the nearby Canary Islands in the mid-fifteenth century. They also served as mercenaries in conflicts between African states and societies, eventually building their own armed states in Angola and along the Zambezi River.

Spanish troops were the first Europeans to establish permanent fortified settlements on the American mainland in the 1500s. Many of the indigenous American communities they encountered were already suffering from epidemics spread by early European explorers. Soon these epidemics roiled across the American continents. Within a few years of Christopher Columbus's 1492 arrival on Hispaniola in the Caribbean, the native populations of Carib and Taino peoples had dropped by half. These epidemics eased the way for Spanish conquest.

Hernando Cortés's conquest of the Aztec state was likewise advanced by dual epidemics of smallpox and measles, two Eurasian diseases that swept through central Mexico in 1518. These epidemics, which may have killed a third of the population, were followed over the next few decades by plague, influenza and repeated smallpox outbreaks. Similar diseases killed the Inca emperor as well as many members of the royal family, making it vulnerable to Pizarro's conquest in 1532. In the seventeenth century, hepatitis swept through North America, emptying communities along the Atlantic coastline and then spreading inland. Ongoing epidemics demoralized natives, making them easy prey for Spanish and Portuguese forces. Having defeated each community, the conquerors then forced local populations to labour for Spain, often alongside enslaved Africans.

The Spanish also allied with dissatisfied or subjugated groups of locals willing to assist them in their campaigns. They relied on such indigenous allies to complete their conquests of large states like the Inca and Aztec Empires. Their allies, of course, believed they were using the Spanish to achieve their independence from the greater local powers. By the mid-sixteenth century the Spanish had used superior firepower to conquer both of these empires, including their erstwhile allies. A series of overland expeditions into Paraguay (1537), Nicaragua (1523–4) and the south-western interior of North America (1529–50) extended the borders of a new Spanish Empire. As in Africa, divided tribal conflicts assisted incoming European powers.

Around the same time, Portuguese adventurers and soldiers slowly brought the coast of Brazil under their control through a series of bloody wars that devastated local populations in South America. Communities in South-eastern Brazil – the

Tupinamba groups – resisted fiercely, even allying with French privateers. However, the Portuguese countered by forging an alliance with a confederation of chieftaincies opposed to the Tupinamba. The conflict that followed reflected a common pattern in this period: as European states came to blows in their rivalries to colonize the Americas, the overall trend saw Europeans advancing at the expense of native peoples. Especially in Spanish and English settler colonies, European populations grew as native populations declined. Spanish and English settlers flowed into the Americas while natives suffered dispossession of their traditional lands. Some became subjugated populations in conquered societies. In others, they were pushed out entirely and replaced by European settlers, along with enslaved Africans they brought with them.

Throughout this period, other European states joined Portugal and Spain in a scramble for spoils. British and French adventurers supported by royal elites especially had pushed deep into the interior of North America by 1750. Outside of the Americas, European overseas imperialists and merchants spread their influence across the Pacific Ocean. Several Spanish expeditions left South America to traverse the Pacific in the late sixteenth and early seventeenth centuries. Beginning in 1565,

Figure 3.7 Official badge (Mandarin Square) of a high-ranking civil servant. Chinese, late seventeenth century (Qing dynasty) (© Getty Images).

they established a base in the Philippines, and gradually began to conquer this strategically important archipelago. Although the conquest was never fully completed, most of the locals found themselves living under Spanish rule. The cosmopolitan population of this colony included Chinese and Japanese merchants, Muslim principalities and many local chieftaincies. In 1695, Spanish forces landed in the Mariana Islands. Finding a great deal of local opposition, they nonetheless exterminated much of the native population, resettling the rest in concentrated villages under Spanish forts (Figure 3.7).

At first, Spanish troops and forts controlled much of the trade that crossed the Pacific Ocean along a chain of forts and island possessions. By 1650, however, other European states were sending expeditions to the Pacific. Soon after, English and French privateers entered the Pacific Ocean, and the Spanish rushed to keep control all of their strategic positions. Their rivalry spread even into the distant South Pacific. Towards the end of the early modern period, Europeans had also extinguished the independence of many Polynesian and other Pacific Island societies.

Ruling the early modern state

This widespread state expansion, centralization and rationalization inevitably meant that governmental politics began to have a greater impact on everyday life for most people in this era. The decisions and operations of the governing class – from tax collection to census-taking, building of infrastructure, law and order – became a more present reality for many worldwide. This was true in well-organized, long-standing states like China and the Ottoman Empire, but increasingly it was the case for emerging North-western European states like the Netherlands and England. Still, despite the growing importance of politics in these societies, most people could do little other than adapt to the decisions made by others. Small groups of elites such as aristocrats (members of the nobility), merchants and bureaucrats dominated the emerging early modern political culture. Many of the ceremonies and displays of power, as well as rituals of governance and diplomacy, that characterized the emerging system of early modern states took place in central settings populated by a society's elites.

Growing infiltration of bureaucracy in everyday life

The development of efficient, centralized states across Eurasia – which then expanded their reach around the world – had a long-lasting impact on the relationship between people and governments. The rise of larger and larger bureaucracies often meant the creation of whole classes of bureaucrats and officials. These classes included military officers, administrators, scribes and tax collectors. Over time, such groups developed specific, shared interests in keeping governments active and involved in the daily affairs of the people. Their interests also included diminishing the power of groups outside of the central government – especially aristocrats with competing bases of political power. Conflicts between nobles and government officials broke out in many states, and were especially intense in France, Thailand (Siam) and Japan in the 1700s.

Stronger central governments also affected people who didn't work for the state, including urban workers and rural peasants. One region where rationalization and centralization were especially significant was East Asia, where the long-standing Chinese model of professional, well-trained bureaucrats had been adopted by neighbouring states like Japan and Korea. As often, this change had both negative and positive consequences for common people.

On the one hand, government sought to control social life in ways that could seem overbearing. In Japan, for example, the Tokugawa shoguns issued regulations about farm labour that included the following:

> Farmers must be told that they must take good care of their wet and dry fields, and weed them attentively and conscientiously. If there are insolent farmers who are negligent, the matter will be investigated and the offenders duly punished. If a single farmer is unmistakably overburdened, and cannot carry on his share of farm work, not only his five-man group but also the entire village must . . . help, assist in his rice planting, and otherwise enable him to pay his annual taxes.[2]

However, highly interventionist governments like those in East Asia also brought benefits to the population. These improvements included hospitals, roads, services and law and order. European visitors to East Asia in the sixteenth century often commented favourably on the ways that governments in this region offered services. The observations of several Catholic visitors to China, for example, were cited by Juan Gonzalez de Mendoza in 1585:

> If [a disabled person] has no parents, or they be so poor that they cannot contribute nor supply any part thereof; then the king maintains them in very ample manner of his own cost in hospitals, very sumptuous, that he has in every city throughout his kingdom for the same effect and purpose. In the same hospitals are likewise maintained the needy and old men as have spent all their youth in the wars, and are not able to maintain themselves.[3]

The expansion of the state into everyday life was, therefore, a balancing act between providing positive services and laws on the one hand, and restrictions of ancient freedoms on the other. Highly interventionist governments like Ming China rose –

and later fell – on their ability to provide better services that outweighed the high cost of government, the sacrifices of military conscription and the labour expectations of Chinese elites. In fact, the Ming collapse to the invading Manchus who established the Qing Empire in the 1640s had much to do with its failure to provide expected government services.

Law and order

The problem of law and order provides a good example of both the positive and negative effects of new interventionist governments on their populations. Governments everywhere performed the functions of keeping the peace and enforcing laws, and they used a number of strategies to carry out such responsibilities. Laws could be written or spoken, and spread by government officials or, sometimes, religious or spiritual functionaries. Individuals charged with breaking those laws could be prosecuted in a variety of ways. Sometimes they were forced to swear a sacred oath before a god or shrine. In other cases, they were exposed to a typically superstitious ordeal like swimming a dangerous river or drinking poison in order to determine guilt or innocence. Sometimes they were tried by a council of elders, local officials or an aristocrat. In some societies, governments employed a mix of these strategies. All societies, in one way or another, took measures that we would today regard as excessive or barbaric. But the government's goal in all places was ensuring security, order and stability.

The maintenance of law and order for the most part remained a local affair in this period. Sheriffs, mandarins, elders and other community or local officials took care of most problems. Yet centralizing governments played an increasing role in investigating crimes, spreading behavioural norms, and upholding laws. European countries probably witnessed the most noticeable increases in central government interventions to promote and maintain stability. Previous to our period these governments had few investigative methods and punishments were mostly physical torture or death! Informal thief-takers were paid by victims of crimes to handle investigations into theft. By the eighteenth century, however, Western European states had developed prison systems for imprisoning criminals – and frequently debtors. Some, like Britain, also began to develop police systems to keep society safer. London's Bow Street runners – the first modern police force – were a group of six men formed in London in 1749 who were paid by city magistrates to keep the peace. This was a major shift in how governments imposed social control, for better or worse.

Still, most governments found it difficult to fully implement a centrally controlled system of law and order. This was especially true in vast states like the Spanish Empire in the Americas. The Spanish kings and queens often passed laws governing their colonies, but then generally had to trust local governors in Mexico City, Quito, Cartagena and other imperial cities to execute them. These governors reported to two **viceroys**, the super-governors of New Spain (Central America) and Peru (South America). These viceroys managed the governors, and each governor managed a series of local officials in smaller and smaller regions across the empire. Such local officials had a great deal of leeway and enforced imperial laws according to their views on local conditions. Even in enforcing imperial law, therefore, the function of government was often very local and quite different across provinces.

The same was true in the Ottoman Empire, where different religious groups and provinces negotiated unique rights with the sultan's administrators. Some religious groups, like Jews and Armenian Christians, were acknowledged as **millets**: groups beholden largely to their own community's laws so long as they paid taxes. Entire provinces in North Africa were also essentially self-ruling. For most Ottoman subjects, however, law and order derived from the local Muslim judge, or *kadi*, who doubled as representative of Allah (God) and the Ottoman sultan. Power was both near and far for most people on earth, but the central power of states was encroaching steadily by 1750.

Legitimacy, ceremony and display

The power of the state depended on more than the size of its military or the reach of its judiciary. The population had also to accept the **legitimacy** – the right to rule – of a ruler and government. States employed various methods for establishing legitimacy. This usually involved invoking religious or spiritual alliances. The Russian Imperial families identified closely with the Orthodox Church, for example, while the Ottoman sultans claimed to be the rightful Sunni successors to the Prophet Muhammad. Persian kings likewise claimed to be the Shiite descendants of the prophet. Other monarchs claimed to have inherited their authority from past rulers – often fraudulently. The first Ming emperor, for example, claimed without evidence his descent from the last Song dynasty emperor several centuries earlier.

Ceremonial displays of power and authority also helped states reinforce legitimacy. For example, the Mughal Empire under Akbar built an imperial court of such renowned opulence and ritualism that that European rulers studied it and tried to emulate it (Figure 3.8).

Akbar built his rituals around an imperial ideology – an invented tradition – that asserted he was heir to the great fourteenth-century conqueror of Central Asia, Timur. Declaring himself infallible, Akbar turned his generals and lords into disciples who competed to serve him in solemn ceremonies where they pledged eternal loyalty. He also borrowed from his Safavid Persian rivals the concept of the **durbar**, official

Figure 3.8 A detail of the so-called Royal Suite of Grand Mogul Aureng Zeb at the Green Vault in Dresden's Residence Castle. Johann Melchior Dinglinger created the art work made from gold and silver from 1701 to 1708 with fourteen assistants. Rulers and governments around Eurasia were learning from each other, and seeking to emulate the different strategies in use to increase a ruler's legitimacy (© Getty Images).

consultations with court members that were increasingly opulent and public and were widely celebrated in stories and poems. Later British imperialists would in turn emulate such practices to reinforce the public's understanding of where the ultimate source of political power lay, even in the case of colonizing Britons.

Other regimes sought to establish legitimacy by creating a formal system of ranks and privileges for government officials. Often, **sumptuary laws** defined the ways people of different rank could dress or act. For example, Tokugawa Iemitsu of Japan limited the housing style and dress of different groups in the mid-seventeenth century. Village headmen could wear silk, but not dyed purple or crimson, while other village officials could only wear linen. The Dutch East India Company, a chartered company that functioned much like a state in Southeast Asia (Batavia) and southern Africa (Cape Colony), operated under similar rules limiting which officials could own carriages or wear items like silver or gold shoe buckles.

Such displays played an important role in the ongoing process of state rationalization in this period. It also demonstrates the way that decoration of the body can reflect the authority, power or wealth of officials and rulers. These displays were not restricted to large states. Throughout the early modern period, for example, Polynesian societies continued to use tattoos to mark the status of chiefs and nobles in a complex pattern that was readable to any member of the society. Such rewards also enticed many members of society to devote a lifelong loyalty and deference to the state in return for opportunity of social advancement.

Sectoral alliances

Early modern rulers maintained their hold on power through alliances with other important groups within society. These **sectoral alliances** included a wide range of groups such as aristocrats, clergy and merchants. These alliances were not always consistent or happy ones, however, as both government and its partners frequently interacted warily with one and other.

The rulers of centralizing states often had an especially tortured relationship with landowning aristocrats. On the one hand, aristocrats like the Japanese *daimyo* and European nobility, with their armed retainers and castles, were an abiding threat to the state's monopoly on power. On the other hand, rulers needed aristocrats to help in military campaigns, to tax and govern the peasants, and their sons and (sometimes) daughters frequently became members of the court and served as its diplomats. Many governments tried to manage aristocrats by tying them as closely as possible to the central government. The Mughal emperor Akbar, for example, gave land and aristocratic ranks to his most loyal generals, but also required them to attend often at court. The French king Louis XIV similarly required the barons of his realm to keep their families at court and to spend most of their time in his presence, often at great expense. The Ottoman sultans tried the opposite strategy. They built a class of soldiers to rival the aristocracy. Initially relying on aristocratic clan-heads for expansion, the sultans soon built a large state army – the famous Janissaries – in order to keep these powerful men from having too much power and independence.

Many rulers of this period also turned to religious institutions for support. The Spanish and Portuguese rulers, for example, relied on Catholic priests to stir up sentiment in favour of the wars to expel Muslims from the Iberian Peninsula and, later, expeditions overseas. The Ottoman sultans relied on religious judges, the *kadi*, to administer justice and inspire soldiers. They also generally empowered priests and rabbis of minority religious community to serve as their representatives to government, and held them responsible for collecting taxes and maintaining order in their communities. The Russian tsars, too, allowed different laws for Muslims, Catholics and Orthodox Christians, so long as these groups remained loyal. Not every ruler was as tolerant. While the Mughal sultan Akbar patronized all religions, his successors allied with Muslim clergy to persecute Sikhs, Hindus and other non-Muslims. The Habsburg emperor Rudolf II (1576–1612) similarly persecuted Protestants with the support of Catholic clergy.

To deal with the high costs of the early modern state, many rulers forged close relationships with mercantile elites, thereby gaining access to sources of finance. Both Jewish and Catholic bankers supported the Spanish reconquest of Iberia. The

Ottoman sultans relied on carefully regulated mercantile guilds for taxes. Meanwhile, Russian tsars allied themselves with companies like the Stroganov firm that dominated the fur trade in Siberia.

Not all states saw tight bonds forged between rulers and commercial elites, though. Ming dynasty China generally relied on agricultural taxation for its funds, so emperors did not feel the need to empower merchants, who occupied a lowly status in Confucian culture, especially if they engaged in overseas trade. For a long time, this lack of integration wasn't a problem, but as economic yields from agriculture fell in the seventeenth century, the Ming decision to not carefully tax, regulate or support overseas trade helped to bankrupt the government. The Ming collapse in 1644 brought foreign Manchu rule under the Qing dynasty, whose conservatism dampened China's economic development for centuries until its own fall in 1912.

The emerging middle class: Political power brokers

In Western Europe, a unique stratum emerged in this era, a wealthy, middling group with growing opportunity, means and political voice. Increasingly, governments tied their fortunes closely to such people, usually bankers and investors with access to money the rulers needed. Leaders of small Italian city-states like Genoa and Venice, who made most of their money from trade, were the first among Europeans to forge alliances with a growing merchant-banker, middle class. Later, some larger, urbanized states, including the Netherlands and Britain, followed suit. These countries shared in common a large urban population, and an emphasis on trade and taxation of trade as their main means of financing government. Because of their reliance on commerce, governments in these European states had no choice but to enter deep alliances with merchants. These relationships, however, had an unintended consequence – they allowed non-aristocratic but wealthy, middling groups the ability to enter government as decision-makers.

Of course, some large states, like China, had for centuries relied on an official, non-aristocratic class of scholar-bureaucrats. But political changes in Europe were different, because the government's partners were not trained bureaucrats but rather wealthy merchants who, because of their financial influence over the state, often protested official policies. In some parts of Western Europe, the political decline of the aristocracy and its replacement by a 'middle class' was quite dramatic. In Protestant Netherlands, a long war against Spanish Catholic Habsburg rule helped to catalyse the development of the status of the *burgher*, the citizen with political and legal rights. Not everyone could be a burgher – it took some wealth and status – but burghers had specific rights to vote, to trade, and to serve in positions of authority. They gained these rights largely by channelling their wealth – gained through commerce, often global trade – to support the Dutch state in its bid for independence from Spain.

Similarly, the power of the middle class in England (and later all of Britain) stemmed largely from the ability of merchants and financiers to provide funds for the monarch. Britain's kings and queens wanted money for wars, overseas expansion and lavish court splendour. By the sixteenth century, the English parliament – a body of commoners and aristocrats that at first merely advised the monarch – gained considerable power through this process, producing a relatively democratic nation for this era.

In the Elizabethan period ending in 1603, Shakespeare used merchants and moneylenders as stock characters, in part, because wealthy merchants were a developing stratum of English society. They partnered with royal representatives to profit from overseas trade, adventures and privacy. As early as 1522, Coventry boasted about sixty merchants in a city of 1300 households. In the sixteenth century, English cities became centres of wealth creation just as in the Netherlands.

By the seventeenth century, however, England's parliament frequently found itself at odds with the Crown over religion, policies and particularly economics. These tensions led to a break in the 1640s between King Charles I (of the Scottish Stuart Dynasty) and parliament. The resulting civil war in England ended, for the first time in modern European history, not only in the execution of the king but also in the formation of a new state without a monarch at all. Following a brief military dictatorship under Oliver Cromwell, the English restored their monarchy and a bloodless political revolution in 1688 decisively ended Stuart rule in England. A compromise in which Charles's grandniece Mary and her husband William of the Netherlands acceded to the throne finally ended the crisis. In return for the throne, the new monarchs agreed to a Bill of Rights, guaranteeing religious freedom and codifying the legitimate power of parliament. This was the most 'modern' and democratic government on earth at the time, which conceded that competing centres of power could check monarchs. This development, as early as 1688, proved an important forerunner of the American Revolution and future democracies.

This new agreement ushered in a dramatic change in how people in England experienced political power. The middle class now had the ability to make laws that benefitted themselves, including those that protected private property and stimulated trade. Partly as a result, England became a nation of 'tradesman', with many small businesses emerging and the search for profit spreading widely in society. Political power remained limited to small groups; this was not a modern democracy. People without wealth, women and children could not serve in parliament or vote, and rural peasants found few advantages in the new situation. Indeed, they suffered over time, as parliament passed new laws allowing wealthy men to turn small farms into vast ranges for growing sheep to feed the wool trade. This noteworthy **enclosure** movement, which gradually turned small open farmlands into more modern agricultural businesses, converted much of an unwilling rural peasantry into an urban working class. A fundamental transformation in social and economic relations that helped fuel the coming Industrial Revolution was the result. Such peasants would be required to work in cities as desperate labourers looking for wages.

International relations

The rationalization, centralization and expansion of states in the early modern period created more potential for unceasing wars among competing powers. Anxiety over even the possibility of war compelled states to increase communication between neighbouring governments to either forestall wars or form alliances to prevent them. These contacts unintentionally stimulated the development of a **diplomatic system** of professional, official negotiations between states, designed ostensibly to prevent conflict. Nowhere did the diplomatic system develop as rapidly and extensively as in Europe, where relations among hundreds of small closely connected states close to the borders of two great empires – the Habsburg and the Ottoman – required a constant balancing act. Certain long-term alliances arose in this context – for example, France allied with Scotland to outflank England, while the English reached out to small continental states to balance the power of France. The enemies of the Habsburg Empire sought support from the Ottoman sultans, from Italian city-states and from rival German princes. These partners sometimes included the Catholic popes, who had to negotiate their conflicting interests in reducing the political power of the Catholic Habsburgs and yet securing their support against the rising Protestant threat in Europe. In these ways a bewildering array of diplomatic relationships produced an increasingly complex European international system from among the increasingly complex European nation-states (Figure 3.9).

In this world of shifting alliances, a sophisticated network of embassies and representations emerged among states, especially in Europe. This system first developed in fifteenth-century Italy, where small, but well-organized, rival states – Milan, Florence, Naples, Venice, Genoa and the Papacy – squabbled with each other and sought alliances with larger, better integrated states in Europe. The diplomats who negotiated on behalf of their states were at first just conveniently placed merchants or mercenaries, but soon full-time, permanent bureaucrats replaced these amateurs. States began to formally recognize each other's diplomats' and indeed to recognize, through documents and treaties, each other's sovereignty and right to exist as a matter of international law. In major capitals, diplomats meet regularly and often socialized, sometimes forming expatriate communities and international friendships. A new diplomatic 'class' began to emerge. In the process, ceremonies meant to mark their

Figure 3.9 The Sultan granting an audience to Venetian ambassador Jacopo Soranzo at Ottoman court in Constantinople for peace negotiations in the mid-sixteenth century. Miniature from Turkish Memories, Arabic manuscript, Cicogna Codex, Turkey, seventeenth century (© Getty Images).

authority and the sanctity of their mission adorned the work of diplomats. Diplomatic negotiations often began with prayers, public oaths accompanied the signing of treaties and even the official recognition of a diplomat in a capital came to involve gifts, displays of wealth and parades.

By the eighteenth century, the diplomatic system in Europe had reached a formal, sophisticated eminence. Diplomats now enjoyed special status, clearly serving the interests of the state from which they came. They were immune to prosecution under the laws of the country in which they resided. They communicated by couriers and secret codes sent along the slowly improving roads of the continent. Diplomats now received salaries and kept staffs of clerks, advisers and housekeepers. More and more of them were professionals – rather than favoured cronies or aristocrats – and usually trained carefully to represent their government.

These new professionals represented the first real international order in Europe. They also set a precedent for later international practices: the emergence of a system of nation-states who mutually recognized each other's sovereignty, who could negotiate to avoid conflict, but whose alliances – ironically – meant that wars often quickly spread across the continent. This state system did not abolish rivalries between states on the European continent, but it did help deflect them abroad, helping facilitate European overseas expansion at a crucial moment.

War and violence

Then as now, everyday people rarely took part in the diplomatic system, but then as now, they were intensely affected by the breakdown of the diplomatic order and resulting wars. One of the principal ways that people encountered the military was through service –by way of either conscription or volunteering – in dynastic or imperial wars. Across Eurasia, countries began to rationalize their armies in the same way they did other institutions of the government in the eighteenth century. Militaries equipped soldiers with uniforms and organized them into clearly defined units lead by ranks of officers. Being a soldier changed one's life, as a soldier's time was no longer his to control and he was subject to strict regimentation. In the Ottoman Empire, the building of the janissary corps of lifetime soldiers entailed an even greater change than most. This corps comprised enslaved young men or boys, often Christians from the Balkans. Upon induction, they were taught that the janissary corps was their new family, and entered an entirely new life of drilling, the companionship of the barracks and often strict discipline.

Being a soldier on campaign was unpleasant no matter which army one enlisted in. Common soldiers frequently starved, froze or fell sick on long campaigns, even before facing the possibility of death or dismemberment in combat. The diplomat Ogier de Busbecq, for example, described the life of common soldiers on an Ottoman campaign:

The rest of the army is badly off, unless they have provided some supplies at their own expense . . . On such occasions they take out a few spoonfuls of flour and put them into water, adding some butter, and seasoning the mess with salt and spices; these ingredients are boiled, and a large bowl of gruel is thus obtained. Of this they eat once or twice a day, according to the quantity they have, without any bread, unless they have brought some biscuit with them. . . . Sometimes they have recourse to horseflesh; dead horses are of course plentiful in their great hosts, and such beasts as are in good condition when they die furnish a meal not to be despised by famished soldiers.[4]

If life as a common soldier proved arduous, the fate of civilians in the path of battle was often worse. This was true in conflicts across Eurasia and Africa, where wars frequently involved the burning of towns or large-scale slaughter. Yet such conflicts were in many cases restrained compared to European campaigns against indigenous peoples of the Americas, who Europeans often considered pagan savages.

The Spanish monk Bartolome de las Casas wrote of this conquest in stark detail, stating:

> The pattern established at the outset has remained unchanged to this day, and the Spaniards still do nothing save tear the natives to shreds, murder them and inflict upon them untold misery, suffering and distress, tormenting, harrying and persecuting them mercilessly.[5]

Similarly, because the Atlantic slave trade worked to enslave entire populations, it provoked devastating wars in parts of West and West-Central Africa. These wars caused a vast transformation in parts of coastal Africa, where entire communities relocated from fertile plains into dense forests, deep swamps or rocky mountains in search of safety.

> Venture Smith, an enslaved African who later won his freedom, described a raid on one of these towns:
>
>> We were then come to a place called Malagasco. When we entered the place, we could not see the least appearance of either houses or inhabitants, but on stricter search found that instead of houses above ground they had dens in the sides of hillocks, contiguous to ponds and streams of water. In these we perceived they had all hid themselves, as I suppose they usually did on such occasions. In order to compel them to surrender, the enemy contrived to smoke them out with faggots. These they put to the entrance of the caves and set them on fire.[6]

Political philosophy

Two historical paradoxes of this era bear close scrutiny. First, while European states began to eradicate whole societies in the Americas and Africa, their reach was limited until the early nineteenth century, and they failed to settle most areas in the hinterlands of Africa and the Americas. Europeans had only limited global political power in this era. As we have seen, even the mighty Spanish Empire struggled to establish its power in outlying areas. Imperial power proved limited over such great distances. Family-run dynasties such as Habsburg Spain possessed little control over faraway continents in this period of slow communication and inefficient guns. Though bullion had enriched Spain and made it a powerful empire, Madrid often had to persist in its efforts to bring political elites in the Americas to heel. In Holland, and England too, while colonies brought new material wealth to urban metropoles, political control over new lands often proved precarious until the late eighteenth century.

New wealth created by the colonies went almost exclusively to those already in power, increasing their influence over already impoverished masses. Though common people did not invest in overseas ventures, they too suffered the negative consequences of international events. The influx of Spanish bullion into Europe created inflation leading to a prolonged decline in real wages for the peasantry. As we have seen, chronic poverty forced many in Europe into service on ships and in new lands. This prompted Western European peasants to demand more political representation in this era, with limited results.

A second paradox is that these same centralized states – the chief source of greater global violence and suffering – were also the cradle of new ideas that would become the basis of political democracy around the world in ensuing centuries. English political philosophers, mostly from the middling realm, began to publicize tracts arguing for the practicality, and the morality, of a fairer political system. Some, such as James Harrington, proved influential among Americans during their revolution and in later democratic reform movements. These 'commonwealth' philosophers argued against the tyranny of absolute power, providing an opening for commoners, such as the mid-seventeenth-century proto-socialist Levellers in England, who began arguing for full representation in the nation. From such rumblings would come the later seeds of individual rights, arguments about freedom and growing tolerance for a wider swathe of political views, incorporating dissent of all types within reason. Commonwealth philosophers like Harrington built on the works of other well-known Western political theorists, including Machiavelli, Hobbes, Locke and Montesquieu, all of whom differed on questions of good governance, but all of whom participated in a vigorous public debate about political ideas that in a later era posed a powerful challenge to absolutist forms of government.

In his Commonwealth of Oceana of 1656, Harrington (d. 1677) theorized a perfect republic – mixing monarchy, aristocracy and democracy. The idyllic constitution, aspiring to Utopia, or at least a better society, thus could be contemplated. If nothing else, constitutions could be considered. Property remained sacred as did wealth, but at least questions of justice and democracy were forming in embryo.

But seeing they that make the laws in commonwealths are but men, the main question seems to be, how a commonwealth comes to be an empire of laws, and not of men? or how the debate or result of a commonwealth is so sure to be according to reason; seeing they who debate, and they who resolve, be but men? 'And as often as reason is against a man, so often will a man be against reason.'[7]

Conclusion

In the 1500s, a diverse range of political systems and governments characterized the early modern world. Today, almost everyone on earth lives under the authority of a centralized, bureaucratized state. The process by which many different models became one started in the early modern period, beginning in Eurasia and spreading in recent centuries. New early modern technologies and techniques made these more efficient states possible, and this efficiency spread as societies learned ruling strategies from each other. At the same time, alternate political systems – most of which had existed and functioned for centuries or millennia – gave way over time as a consequence of conflict, conquest or slaving. This process was far from complete in 1750, but certainly the political shape of the world had dramatically changed in 250 years, and would continue to do so into recent times.

The centralized, rationalized early modern state transformed peoples' experiences – gradually rather than rapidly, but irrefutably. The state – and those elites in the various sectors of power who collaborated with elites – increasingly intervened in the daily life of most people. A few previously excluded groups managed to become players in state power politics, especially merchants, landowners and financiers in Western Europe who would in ensuing centuries become leaders of European nations.

Even in Europe, however, most people remained excluded from politics. Not only rural peasants, but also working people considered 'outsiders', and, of course, women were bereft of any political power until the twentieth century. Internationally, this was an era when rulers of complex states and their cronies – a very small proportion of the world's population, quantifiably in the tens of thousands – imposed their particular world views about authority, power and justice on the vast majority of people alive, roughly 750 million people by 1750! The world historical consequence of this was colonial subjugation and massive population losses among peoples of West Africa, the Pacific and the Americas.

The political effects of the Atlantic slaving system and increasing expansion of complex – mostly European – states brought the destruction of societies in Africa, the Americas and the Pacific. This was an era of often violent and hierarchical politics, in which many people on earth suffered losses. Political power was the province of a tiny number of people, mainly men. This political power was subsequently reinforced by growing economic power, to which we shall turn to in the next chapter.

Keywords

acephalous
centralization
chartered companies
chieftaincies
confederations

diplomatic system
expansion
governance
legitimacy
millets
political culture
rationalization
sovereignty
state
viceroy

Further reading

Benjamin, Thomas. *The Atlantic World: Europeans, Africans, Indians and their Shared History 1400–1900*. New York: Cambridge University Press, 2009. This highly recommended volume is full of meaningful explorations of the Atlantic world of the early modern era, including a great deal of information on governance and politics.

Hodgson, Marshall. *The Venture of Islam, Volume III: Gunpowder Empires and Modern Times*. Chicago: University of Chicago Press: 1977. This was one of the first books to advance the thesis of the early modern 'gunpowder' revolution. Although it concentrates on Islamic states in particular, it also takes a global view.

Morgan, Kenneth. *Slavery and the British Empire: From Africa to America*. Oxford: Oxford University Press, 2008. The most thorough recent study of slavery and British imperial power, demonstrating the negative impact on African cultures while noting the limited inputs in eventual British industrial power.

Thornton, John K. *The Kongolese Saint Anthony: Dona Beatriz Kimpa Vita and the Antonian Movement, 1684–1706*. Cambridge: Cambridge University Press, 1998. This superb account of early modern Kongo deftly illuminates the breakdown in the social order that resulted from the Atlantic slave trade.

Wong, R. Bin. *China Transformed: Historical Change and the Limits of European Experience*. New York: Cornell University Press, [2018], 2000. A sophisticated comparison of Chinese and European development over the centuries, demonstrating no one political path is normal or predestined, while examining how state power extends into imperial expansion.

Interlude 2 – Various power centres

Chapter Outline

Political power in 1600: European envy, Asian riches and world rulers

For most of our period, strong political rule was most pronounced in the Islamic world and Asia. Though by 1750 Europeans began to dominate many parts of the world, this was not the case through most of the early modern period. We can observe this shift in power by considering the immense reach and splendour of Asian monarchs and emperors compared to often better-known Western kings and queens. A comparison of the world's most powerful rulers in this era sheds light on why Europeans were so desperate to reach what they considered 'the East' and all its riches, and also the incredible historical fortune that came to Europeans after they 'discovered' the Americas (Figure I.2.1).

As her long reign came to an end around 1600, Queen Elizabeth I of England had overseen a period of economic growth for her small country, while holding what appeared to be immense political power within her family, the Tudors. Yet she had to regularly ask taxpayers for support in maintaining her lifestyle and did not, in fact, hold much power in what was not quite yet a centralized, rationalized state. Of thirteen parliamentary sessions called in her name, she pled for money in all but one, demonstrating that the power of the purse lay in parliament, and thus in the people – or at least in their upper-class representatives. Elizabeth's only method of generating revenue was by selling royal lands to loyal supporters. Expected to pay for governmental administration, she needed to pressure wealthy nobles for loans to maintain power.

Persistent conflict with Catholic Spain in this era was costly, but victory over Spain in 1588 set the island of England on a path to global riches and political influence.

Figure I.2.1 Queen Elizabeth (1558–1603) (Wikimedia Commons).

The advice of economically and politically savvy advisers helped secure Elizabeth's position; her ministers created a stable state that reaped rewards from lucrative international trade, and the power it bequeathed what would become a firmly Protestant English nation, in opposition to Catholic European powers. Though landed aristocrats continued to be the main source of capital in early Western Europe, an expanding middle class began to use their growing wealth from trade to challenge the power of ruling families, marking an early step in the gradual development of democratic government and pro-business capitalism.

By 1750, as the British Empire expanded, the Ottoman Empire, the dominant power in much of the Middle East and North Africa, entered a long slow decline that would leave it ridiculed in the 1800s as the 'sick man of Europe'. This led to its final disintegration after the First World War, with major consequences for Middle Eastern Muslim societies to the present (Figure I.2.2).

In 1600, though, the notion that Western states like England might gain wealth and power comparable to the Sunni Ottomans would have seemed preposterous to most informed people in Eurasia. The ruling sultan Mehmed the Third (1595–1603) was extremely wealthy and powerful, ruling the vast Muslim world with a

Figure I.2.2 Mehmed III of the Ottoman Empire (1566–1603) (Wikimedia Commons).

firm hand – at one point executing nineteen of his siblings to maintain supremacy. Mehmet and Elizabeth in fact were aware of one another and exchanged gifts, as they vied to impress each other in an early modern game of political one-upmanship.

But Mehmed's fate was the opposite of Elizabeth's: hers was a rising state with global political influence; his was in slow decline and fragmenting. Mehmet's empire was often at war too, with enemies on all borders. The loyalty of middling classes and the wider population to the Ottoman state was tenuous. Ongoing tax problems and a badly run state meant that Ottoman wealth declined under Mehmet's rule. He managed the economy and military so poorly that his mother Safiyye Sultan became regent. The sultans who ruled after Mehmet fared no better. As inheritors of an unstable state, they had to fend off threats on both borders, with the Austrian Habsburgs to the west and the Shiite Safavids to the East (Figure I.2.3).

Mehmed's equally powerful contemporary in India, Akbar the Great (1556–1605), lived in immense splendour also. A highly celebrated Moghul emperor, Akbar

Figure I.2.3 Akbar the Great. Third Mughal emperor. (1542–1605) (© Alamy).

fostered wide commercial expansion, developing relationships through Central Asia and Persia. He, too, would surely have laughed at the suggestion that Britain could dominate India in the centuries after 1750. In this era, India's huge cotton industry invited European envy, owing to its sizeable production of high-quality silk and cotton. Although growth continued for decades following Akbar's rule, many of his successors were so anti-intellectual, anti-business and religiously intolerant that the empire began to fragment politically, with great consequences, as Elizabeth's successors invaded in the 1700s and began rule in India that lasted until 1947 (Figure I.2.4).

In 1600, following decades of civil war, Japan began settling into political stability. After Tokugawa Ieyasu (1543–1616) became Japan's first shogun, his absolutist shogunate would hold power continuously until 1868. Tokugawa ended decades of political instability, pacified powerful samurai and improved agricultural infrastructure. The period following his rule, known as the Edo Period, was one of peace, stability and growth. Similar in size to England, the key difference between the two island nations was Japan's self-imposed isolation, which blocked most international trade to Japan for centuries. This held back Japanese development until

Figure I.2.4 Tokugawa Ieyasu, First shogun of Tokugawa Japan (1543–1616) (Wikimedia Commons).

the late nineteenth century, when a rapid modernization programme transformed the country into a world power.

Japan's great rival and neighbour, China, was ruled by the Wanli Emperor (1563–1620) in 1600. China was the largest economy on earth, so logically Chinese rulers were unimpressed by Japan, and barely aware of the distant polity of England. In stark contrast to England's anxious monarchs, taxation in the Ming court came in the form of loyal tribute from those paying dues to the elite in China and in the wider region. Most considered taxation levels relatively fair because of the vast size of China's economy, so they met little resistance, as was so often the case in both Europe and the Ottoman Empire. With Chinese factories paying regular wage labour centuries before Europeans did, China seemed set to dominate the global economy for centuries to come.

Yet gradually after 1600, there was a rapid decline in Ming power, as China had to fend off both Mongol and Japanese threats at different times. The Wanli Emperor spent his last two decades alive tending to his private tomb, focusing on his own needs rather than the nations, gaining immense weight and squandering imperial wealth. His family-run economy dragged on the government's budget, as he had to

Figure I.2.5 Court portrait of the Wanli Emperor, who reigned over Ming China from 1572 to 1620 AD (Wikimedia Commons).

support 100,000 eunuchs and a similarly high number of extended family members. With little economic innovation China, like Japan, India and the Ottomans, soon stagnated politically, just as Dutch and English financiers and merchants modernized and approached coastlines (Figure I.2.5).

By 1750, small states like Holland and England could still not impose their political influence on the great Eurasian empires, but the conditions were in place for them to do so, and by the early 1800s they were interfering with and influencing societies across the worlds of Islam, India and Asia. By 1900 European powers were far mightier politically and controlled many of these ancient societies, hindering their path towards modernity and political stability.

4

Commerce without conscience – Early modern economics

Chapter Outline

Situating the chapter

At the dawn of the sixteenth century, most people on earth continued to experience economic life as they always had. Most economies remained household-based and small. Most people's socio-economic status derived from kinship bonds, relations with family or community position. Paid labour, wage-earning or working for an enterprise was rare anywhere. Forced labour was common everywhere, as we have seen.

By 1750, however, early forms of what we now call capitalism emerged. What had been numerous, separate, global commercial centres across Eurasia slowly merged into a connected world economy – centred on the Atlantic and dominated by a small number of men. A steep decline in the cost of transactions would lower long-standing barriers to commerce, and would increase the volume of trade worldwide exponentially – to the detriment of much of the world's population (Figure 4.1).

Shifting economic norms in this era become apparent even in art, which became embedded in a world of commercial priorities. Even in the 1600s, Dutch masters like Brueghel had to sell their genius to make a living, having to work part-time jobs and entice wealthy patrons to support them. By the late seventeenth century Dutch artists, such as the famous Rembrandt, introduced a new kind of artistic representation that

Figure 4.1 Rembrandt self-portrait, 1629 (© Getty Images).

mirrored economic changes: the self-portrait, where individual subjects stared straight at the viewer. At this time too, Dutch traders normalized a new type of competitive commerce that swept the world over the centuries. Both artistic representation and the pursuit of profit were premised upon the new, unusual notion of individualism. The work of Dutch portraitists exemplified this increasingly individualist strain in Western culture, one that would soon arrive on the shores of others worldwide, for better or worse.

By the end of this chapter, readers should be able to:

- Understand how commerce transformed human life in the early modern era.
- Reflect upon the human and social costs of economic growth.
- Consider how different societies engaged in trade and commerce.
- Explain the consequences of increased economic interaction among societies.
- Appraise the effects of new connections on different populations worldwide.
- Analyse the degree to which these connections were positive or negative for different societies, or for humanity as a whole.

Narrative

The previous chapter explored how political elites organized societies into states to maintain stability or control people, which anticipated modern nation-states and empires. In the next two chapters, we investigate the seeds of modern economic life, in particular consumer and industrial capitalism. This includes the exhilaration people felt towards new wares and goods, and the enormous rewards some enjoyed, particularly those well-connected or imbued with the entrepreneurial spirit. We will see the gradual standardization of economic exchange, through both voluntary and forced means.

We will also learn of the gradual replacement of predatory traditional practices – such as tribute, extortion, theft or barter – by global commercial practices that were similarly exploitative. We will consider the emergence of a middling class of people who, in some states, developed more egalitarian attitudes about rights and opportunities. We will explore the intense competition small European merchant states compelled upon societies worldwide, as well as their domination of great Eurasian imperial powers, who had themselves traded via predation and inducement for centuries. Perhaps most importantly, we will consider the economic violence, forced labour, incessant conflict and decimation of whole cultures that usually accompanied moneymaking practices between 1500 and 1750.

Some people, and states, became very rich from international commerce, while many, (like Rembrandt), lost possessions, savings or security. Indeed, financial pressures likely ended Rembrandts life, owing to stress and the worry of monetary hardship. This, in micro, is typical of what many societies worldwide would endure, once foreigners imbued with the spirit of capitalism arrived.

This was not yet modern industrial capitalism; we might call it merchant capitalism. Traders, rather than large factories or enterprises, drove the process, as they did all over the world. Traders all over the world, Europe included, acted in much the same way through these centuries. Nonetheless, new economic practices that more efficiently exploited land, labour and capital emerged by 1750, in Western Europe. Militarized, centralized, rationalized, bureaucratic European states such as Holland and England now aspired towards sustained **economic growth**, aiming for a long-term, continuous increase in production of goods and provision of services. This idea, of promoting economic growth over social stability, was new in human history. When made manifest it would raise the standards of living in some countries, but ruin the lives of millions in others.

The Eurasian commercial core: Africa to Asia

Trading with Africa

As Europeans expanded and exploited the **Atlantic economy** in this era, Islamic empires, Indian dynasties, Asian emperors all coincidentally turned inwards, away from global trading. Small numbers of male elites outside of Europe chose to focus economic energy on sustaining steady control over their domains, to provide stability and security, in what amounted to small-scale, personal state economies. After 1492, as the Atlantic and Pacific oceans opened up to commerce, societies of the vast steppes faded in global importance, after more than a thousand years at the centre of cross-cultural trade spanning the Eurasian landmass. The economic habits and practices of north-western Europeans, developed by the Dutch, spread by the English, took precedence after the eighteenth century. The consequences of these differing approaches – Western expansion and non-Western inwardness – would be considerable.

Europeans did not just find slaves waiting for them when they stumbled upon the African coast. They entered complex, long-standing networks connecting states across the north and centre of the continent. Also, long-distance trade systems had linked the north and east of Africa to Europe and Central Asia since the ninth century. Sub-Saharan African kingdoms, on the other hand, were separated from Eurasian trade networks by North African Muslim traders, who, as middlemen, dominated commerce in the region. Trade across the rest of the continent in the South and through the Sahara Desert of North Africa was expensive and slow, limiting the number and type of goods that could be exchanged.

A great change came once European ships connected the coasts of Africa to the Americas. Portuguese merchants arrived first in the 1400s, searching for a fabled 'river of gold'. By working with African rulers, they gained access to internal commodities like gold, ivory and, of course, slaves. African merchants were active players in this trade; African rulers dictated trade with Europeans well beyond 1750. Local nobles and traders prospered through these new global connections with

Europeans. The horrors of slavery are indisputable, but this was an economic partnership among collaborating equals.

Privileged partners

The most dramatic consequence of West Africa's linkage to early modern Atlantic trade was clearly the growth in slaving. At first, trade in humans was directed more towards European destinations than the Americas. Tens of thousands of African captives ended up in European cities like Lisbon and Bristol in the 1600s. Over the course of the seventeenth century, however, the slave trade grew dramatically and became oriented towards developing European colonies in the Americas on the backs of slave labour. The search for commercial sugar profits induced great demand for labour to replace diminishing Native American populations. So many African slaves moved that by 1800 North America's population comprised roughly three times more Africans than Europeans.

Slavery did not first appear on earth, or in Africa, with the arrival of European traders. As we saw in Chapter 3, prosperous or powerful families in many parts of Africa owned people as sources of wealth and status. African elites had supplied the Arab world in North and East Africa with forced labour for centuries prior to this era. As elsewhere worldwide, servitude and slave trading were simply a form of commerce. Arab slavers continued to run large trading posts on the east coast of Africa to ship enslaved workers to Iran or India for centuries after 1500.

This was a system of elite collaboration. Europeans were not powerful enough to take African slaves freely. Commercial and political elites along the Atlantic coast of Africa gained from the slave trade by working with Spanish, Portuguese and later other European traders. African kings expected gifts before they gave up slaves for shipment. They negotiated hard, charging taxes and duties to maximize from each deal. African princes, kings and rulers controlled the African slave trade initially, not European traders and explorers. African leaders set contract terms more than Europeans, who were usually desperate to get to sea. Indeed, even in 1750 African kings and merchants likely had more control over the slave trade than they had in the 1500s.

African markets

Vast, complex trade systems crisscrossed the African continent in 1500, developed over centuries. The Muslim Songhai Empire dominated West and Central Africa from the city of Gao in the 1500s, controlling a huge trading centre on the Niger River. The city of Timbuktu teemed with up to 100,000 people, at a time when most European cities were far smaller. The Songhai had supplanted the remarkable Mali Empire, whose gold supplies first piqued European curiosity. West and Central African traders and elites relied heavily on slave networks and markets: Gao's markets sold adults for twice the price of little children. The Bight of Biafra was a fragmented region of warlord-merchants, where trade in people and goods were fundamental to commerce. The slaves at the centre of these transactions were usually prisoners of war but could also be victims of kidnapping or raids. Some unfortunates were considered witches or had simply offended elites.

Slave labour existed throughout Africa. With plenty of land and a limited labour supply, elites in places like the Niger Valley worked slaves on plantations, though it was a far more benign, household form, of slavery compared to the type Europeans later employed. Most inland male warrior societies held slaves as status symbols, and weaker tribes were easy sources of captives. Inland states often bartered kidnapped children and women during periods of war. Sudanese regional kings owned agricultural estates almost akin to the plantations of the American South, as did the Kingdom of Kongo. Slaves produced goods for domestic markets or helped owners maintain noble status, not to export global products, which would become the norm later.

Away from the coasts, African kingdoms traded with each other in diverse ways. At the heart of most central and southern African economies was a household system of small-scale barter. Most of the vast African continent was disconnected from the growing Atlantic slave trade. Across much of the continent, smaller societies traded in various agricultural products or metals such as copper, iron or gold. They continued to barter locally through traditional exchanges as they long had. Smaller regional chieftains remained decentralized, with **big men**, traditional African chiefs, aspiring to control self-sufficient households, pushing back on the economic power of central rulers who aspired to build large empires.

In South Africa, the arrival of Dutch settlers at the Cape of Good Hope after 1652 introduced a different economic system. A new type of enterprise, the Dutch East India Company, brought indentured servants, who made up the great majority of settlers. These white settlers and their servants increasingly relied on slaves from Asia or Africa. Local African populations served as middlemen, connecting Dutch settlers with peoples to the north. During the early modern period, no large merchant class arose in sub-Saharan Africa, however, at least partly as a result of European incursions. Wider trade linkages beyond the Americas were marginal or non-existent, leaving the region relatively isolated.

African agency

Existing forms of servitude prevailed across Africa, but the new Atlantic system of 'chattel slavery' was different, and in terrible ways. After 1600, Atlantic slave traders bought and sold human beings as if they were products, like pots or pans – counted, bought and shipped for profit. The sheer number of humans shipped was far higher than in the past, and the economic intention and level of organization were more 'efficient'. Slave sellers and owners considered African captives as items of commerce, used and exploited for profit until they expired. Around 35,000 slave voyages took place overall, displacing at least 10 million people from Africa to America. Slaving vessels were loaded with a wide array of merchandise, aside from people. Various stocks took up half or more of the space on board, with human beings filling the rest.

Europeans came to Africa as independent merchants, usually with royal support. But increasingly after 1600 they organized joint stock-chartered companies, forerunners of modern corporations. In the Americas, landowners preferred African over natives because they proved more skilled in Old World agricultural practices. Also, they proved easier to keep captive, as indigenous people could more successfully escape into the backcountry since they knew the land.

Europeans justified chattel slavery morally, practically and intellectually. Monarchs, merchants and priests all talked of charity and benevolence. In their minds they were relieving slaves of forlorn ignorance. Like African merchants and chiefs, Europeans saw this form of forced labour as no more depraved than any other in the early modern world. Only in the 1700s did some Europeans begin to speak of the immorality of human slaving, as Enlightenment thought and more modern sensibilities altered attitudes. Attitudes today still differ towards the effects of the slave trade: some scholars argue that in the wider context of African societies and centuries of trade, its effect was minimal. Others counter that the slave trade stifled African development for the benefit of the West. But the demographic effects on the continent were certainly devastating, with Africa having far fewer people today than it would have otherwise.

But just as Europeans debated and differed on the morality of enslavement, so too did African rulers. Chief-kings like Afonso of Kongo willingly partnered with Portuguese soldiers to defeat or enslave regional rivals, gladly offering enemy soldiers as slaves to the Portuguese. Other leaders like the kings of Benin made it state policy to forgo participation in slave trading, preferring to trade in hides, beeswax and gold to access horses from Iberia and new kinds of clothing and foods.

Though the institution of slavery damaged coastal African societies and ruined countless lives, African commerce did not collapse when Europeans arrived. Like any other region, Africans adapted to new trade patterns on their own terms. The participation of African traders made the Atlantic slaving system possible. Their decisions to enslave others were pragmatically driven by power politics and economic gain. African merchants profited from stocking provisions on outbound slave ships or providing services for the slave trade. African chiefs on the Atlantic coast traded huge quantities of cowrie shells to be used as ballast in European ships. These shells became local currency, as they were portable, durable and hard to counterfeit. African kings willingly sold captives to acquire the much-desired shells, considered highly exotic as they were sourced in the Maldives (Figure 4.2).

Once in the Americas, slaves developed new internal economies through their own labour. Slaves built the plantations and ports, grew most of the food and were an

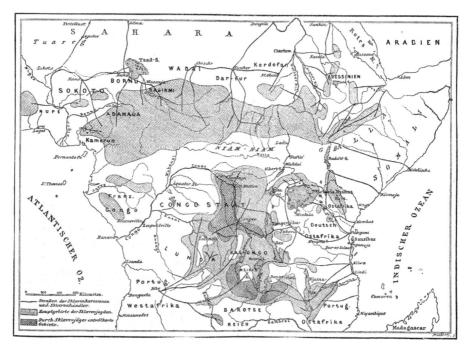

Figure 4.2 The territories of the African slave trade. Illustration from the nineteenth century (© Getty Images).

integral part of the growing global trade in this era. They traded with other slaves, produced foodstuffs and provided for one other within the broader transatlantic system. African slaves contributed greatly to growing markets, providing goods for trade and managing projects, working all manner of jobs, unskilled or technical. Slaves manufactured clothes and tools, moved goods, and worked to herd cattle and horses. One unintended, and less terrible, consequence of the new global commercial connections was the introduction of new foods such as maize and manioc to Africa, providing new sources of nourishment for millions. Over time such new foods became staples of African diets.

Islamic empires – Ottoman, Safavid and Mughal economies

Global slave trading numbers increased terribly between 1600 and 1750. Some of the more powerful Islamic states in Africa helped fuel the slave trade by creating more hostages or captives. The Asante kingdom of the Gold Coast, for instance, thrived on enslaving weaker tribes and kingdoms, using European guns to hold power. Arab merchants had long moved goods and people across North and East Africa, the Mediterranean and the Middle East. Arab slavers also captured thousands of Christian Europeans in these centuries, having developed long-distance slaving networks for a thousand years prior to 1500 to move people from Africa and Europe into Asia. Between 1580 and 1680, close to a million Christians were captured in the Mediterranean and adjoining seas by Arab slavers, a practice which continued well into the eighteenth century. In the thousand years prior to 1900, several million captives were taken from European lands and enslaved in the Islamic world.

Islamic traders moved various kinds of merchandise around a fragmented region of myriad small markets. As Christian nations began to enter global trade in 1500, Islam remained the major trading religion it had been since its seventh-century origin. Muslim traders functioned as middlemen across networks of merchants, connecting the Ottoman Empire in the Mediterranean to Indonesia and Asia. Diverse practices developed in different regions, unlike the unified economic capitalist system that European traders would develop. Internal trading in bazaars was vast in scale across the Middle East, though it did not generate great wealth or capital for reinvestment.

Many of the best craftsmen, merchants or artists in the Middle East and Central Asia were minorities in large states. Their interests lay more with their own communities than imperial or dynastic rulers: Hindus in the Mughal Empire, Armenians and Jews in the Safavid Empire, Greeks and Jews in the Ottoman Empire all greased the wheels of trade, arranging shipping and utilizing diaspora networks to make profits. Sephardic Jews, for instance, traded all across the Mediterranean, making a living wherever they could.

Similarly, Armenian family networks moved vast amounts of goods across Asia. Though this trade was not necessarily merchant capitalism in the guise of European traders at this time, it was nonetheless a lubricant for global trade and a major part of growing connections among merchants across Eurasia. Armenian traders served as cross-cultural brokers and transmitters of goods, moving products from Europe into Turkey, then over the Iranian plateau towards the old Silk Road and Asia. Persecuted at times, particularly by Iran's Safavids, they nonetheless became successful silk traders, running trade centres in Muslim towns into the eighteenth century. Armenian tax collectors and silk traders formed large merchant houses, connecting Muslims from Iran and Hindus from India to northern Russian trade routes.

For centuries prior to 1500, Muslims dominated trade across much of Eurasia. Traders practised economic coercion and profiteered, just as Spanish and other Christians would later. From Persia to India, into China and Southeast Asia, Islamic merchants moved vast amounts of product to which Europeans at the far west of Eurasia had only limited access. But after 1600, when the Atlantic Ocean developed into the key global trade circuit, the world of Islam, so central to medieval commerce, began a period of commercial decline. While Chinese and Japanese imperial officials expelled trade-seeking foreigners because of either an unquestioned belief in their own cultural superiority or a fear of European influence, Muslim rulers had no doubt that the world would eventually transform into one Islamic community, the *umma*. Such unreal expectations were perhaps understandable given the previous centuries, in which complex Muslim societies dominated massive sections of Eurasia, and Asian states were more powerful than any others of which they were aware.

Rulers in Muslim empires, like those in Asia, were disinterested in innovating on earlier financial institutions they had themselves developed. Economies remained local, premised usually upon Turkic practices of land taxation and resource extraction – to the gain of rulers and their cronies. Tight control of peasants and merchants prevented the expansion of trade networks. Though minority groups such as Jews and Armenians encouraged transnational commerce as they always had, religious and political elites in Muslim empires generally frowned upon profit-seeking commercial practices, preferring to maintain lavish lifestyles and colossal extravagance. Thus, Islamic states in the Middle East did not expand commercially in this era. Economies in many kingdoms, tribes and chiefdoms remained fragmented, trading locally or at best regionally.

Understandably, such rulers pursued stability over potentially disruptive trade expansion and exploration. Ongoing tensions between merchants and elites thwarted commercial growth in parts of the Muslim world. Diverse in ethnic make-up, traders and regional elites often lacked loyalty to faraway sultans, shahs or imams, catering instead to local needs. As elsewhere in Eurasia, merchant populations resisted payment of expected or anticipated dues to rulers. Like French kings or Russian emperors who suffered similarly disdainful subjects, Muslim sultans and shahs received inadequate sources of revenue from disloyal, irritated populations. The imperial habit of parcelling out land to tribal favourites generated only limited internal customs fees and revenues, so by 1750 – at the very point European states became more economically aggressive, efficient and expansionist – Islamic empires were weaker, poorer and more fragmented than they had been in the seventeenth century.

Just when Europeans became ravenous for global resources then, emperors and sultans across Eurasia expressed increasingly contemptuous attitudes towards commerce. Evidence for disinterest towards overseas ventures or the establishment of ocean empires can be seen in proud comments by the Ottoman sultan Bayezid II (d. 1512):

Mecca and Medina and this Old World are enough to conquer, we don't need to cross the ocean and go tremendous distances.[1]

Clear similarities existed across the three major Muslim empires of this era. Ottoman, Safavid and Mughal elites all dominated diverse surrounding populations; all created large empires founded on armed power; all were gunpowder empires with a martial ethos and all had roots in the nomadic tribal regions of Central Asia. But over time rulers in these diverse empires struggled to raise taxes, so they had to dominate commerce through firearms and cannon. A central component of Muslim economies in this era was the horse, an essential war machine, often exchanged for slaves and given to rulers or warriors. But this was not fluid currency, which was becoming the norm in the Atlantic.

Rather than practising exchange, reinvestment, economies of scale or lower transactional prices which were becoming common in Northwest European states, Central Asian Muslim empires retained traditional economic customs and practices.

Ottoman Empire – Taxing and tribute

The longest functioning state in the past thousand years, the Ottoman Empire, was formed in 1299, and conquered Constantinople from Christians in 1453. With an economy based mainly on patronage, this Sunni empire lasted until 1922, but never traded on the scale of European states. The Ottomans initially outmanoeuvred Italian city-states in the 1500s to monopolize the Asian luxury trade. They then conquered Egypt and Syria in 1516. The empire reached its zenith in the 1560s, when nations such as Armenia, Algeria and Tunisia obediently sent tribute to central coffers. Tribute also arrived from the centre of Europe with payment from the Austrian Habsburgs until 1571, when the Ottomans lost the Battle of Lepanto to the Spanish Habsburgs, a turning point in the ascendancy of the Turks.

The sultan's family held centralized power. The royal household owned all land, and state institutions were considered the private domain of the sultan. In 1520 the state claimed ownership of 87 per cent of all arable land, though in practice it was parcelled out to nobles. Most of the population had little to no stake in the economy. Privileged tax farmers controlled the mining of precious metals, sending most of the proceeds to the sultan. From the 1550s insatiable court demand for silk, muslin and furs to adorn imperial clothing hindered the economy by taking cash specie out of markets. Regional subsistence economies remained the norm. Small agrarian markets satisfied internal demand, producing locally instead of for international markets.

The Ottoman economic system centred upon the *timar*, in which the sultan granted large plots of land to regional potentates, who in turn collected rents from their territories under the auspices of imperial authority. Regional elites provided soldiers to the sultan in return for land and security. The empire's security relied a full-time, well-paid elite infantry military force called *janissaries*, combined with cavalry troops known as *sipahi*. Most tax revenues went to supplying these elite troops rather than investing overseas. For instance, Suleiman the Great in 1527 had up to 28,000 janissaries, sharing massive land grants with them to support imperial military might. Janissaries received cash salaries and shares of booty from battles and border raiding. The sultan brought in more income by enforcing tribute payments on most of the Arab world. Sultans were not only political rulers, they also exercised religious authority as *caliphs*.

The economy was diverse. Guilds regulated the production of goods and the provision of services, as in medieval Europe. Though they were not allowed to join guilds, women worked in cottage industries or on farms. Coffee houses also spread throughout Ottoman cities in this era. Coffee had arrived from Yemen and Ethiopia and soon spread to Europe. Across the Muslim world, the yearly pilgrimage to Mecca, the Haj, also created an annual economic boom, as pilgrims brought spices, foods, incense and clothing to pay for their trip.

Merchants could trade freely in the empire, and in periods of expansion generally many gained from low taxation. They usually enjoyed freedom to trade, though they could be ruined at the will of the sultan, having less legal protection than those in Holland or England. Economic growth depended on militarism. In times of military victories, sultans could afford to be benevolent, enjoying the riches gained from conquering. Once they weakened in the 1600s, though, the wealth dried up. As would be the case with the Mughals and the Safavids, in the seventeenth century military conquests no longer provided rulers with sufficient plunder. Since booty was the basis of the imperial economy the empire could no longer support itself.

Compared to previous Muslim rulers, Ottoman elites were disinclined to innovate. They resisted market economics and the crucial print technology which did so much to facilitate global trade. After 1648 the actions of one sultan, Ibrahim the Crazy, ignited fifty years of conflict in the empire, which hindered commerce greatly. Ottoman economic life depended on the sultan maintaining control. Regional fragmentation and power grabs were rampant. Since centralized economic governance served the vast imperial household, rulers intervened freely in economic life, undermining the autonomy of traders who knew better understood changing economic realities.

By the late seventeenth century more and more lands were lost through defeats to the Habsburgs and Russia, while coincidentally imports of precious metals from the Americas lowered the value of Ottoman silver mines in the Balkans. By 1750, Ottoman commerce was declining markedly, while sultans continued to live in splendour. Elite decisions erected barriers to growth, while constant military conflict with neighbours prevented commercial relationships.

Safavid Empire – Luxury and farms

The Ottomans clashed frequently with Egyptians, Syrians and Europeans. Most often they fought their great Shia Muslim rivals, the Persian Safavids, from whom they had initially taken Baghdad in 1534. For a century between 1534 and 1639, the Ottomans and Safavids skirmished, ultimately sapping the economies of both empires.

The powerful and wealthy Safavid dynasty (1501–1722) initially benefitted from Persia's location as a trade hub, where merchants sold silks, carpets and other wares to the region. Their power peaked in the 1620s under Shah Abba I, whose strong rule and military victories enriched the state and brought loyalty from elites in the region. This was a wise ruler who traded with the outside world. He connected with wider cultures, collected Chinese ceramics, exported to Europe and hired foreigners freely without disclination. The shah also created a vibrant Persian capital in Isfahan in 1598, a newly built city of vast squares and glorious architectural monuments, with countless bazaars and markets thriving in its heyday.

Blessed with gifted artists, bureaucrats and pastoralists, the Safavid dynasty did not prioritize trade. Persian peasants worked under harsh labour conditions in localized subsistence agriculture economies. Cultivation of fruits and vegetables proliferated instead of commercial innovation or investment. Religious difference and ethnic strife also prevented economic growth. By 1700 Armenians controlled almost all long-distance commerce, while being treated as marginal minorities. Like Muslim Sufis and Sunnis, Armenian Christians had to worry about intolerance and suppression from Shiite Persian elites. Tribal Sunni Afghans sacked Isfahan in 1722, and defeat followed at the hands of Afghan warriors in 1736. The Shia Safavid Empire went into terminal decline thereafter.

Hence, just as Persian elites turned inwards, the empire weakened, and Europeans dominated new ocean trade routes. As Atlantic trade had earlier brought the decline of Italian city-states in the 1500s, so too it later punished Persia, which became isolated from global trade after 1600 when the Silk Road declined in importance.

Mughal Empire – Increasing instability

India had been a central hub of Eurasian trade for a thousand years before 1500. Its power and wealth too slowly diminished in this period. The Mughal dynasty began in 1536 when an Afghan warrior, Babur of Kabul, took power by suppressing regional Indian Hindu princes. His successor, Akbar the Great (d. 1605), extended Mughal power further into the south of the Indian subcontinent by 1600.

This third Islamic gunpowder empire combined Central Asian, Indian and Persian qualities. It prospered from connections to the Silk Routes through Kandahar and from tribute yielded by Central Asian tribes. Akbar maintained prosperity and stability by using skilled Persian record-keepers to manage taxation and administered order throughout his extensive realms. The Mughals bureaucratic reach was far more thorough than the Safavids, although as in Persia, high land taxes dampened economic growth. Like the Safavids, Mughal India was in essence one giant landed estate, where the royal court controlled or influenced financial activity (Figure 4.3).

Akbar divided his realm into twelve provinces, each with a regional governor who strove to imitate the emperor's lavish court in his fiefdom. These preferred office holders, known as *mansabdari*, lived in regal splendour. Such notables enjoyed luxury imports – Arabian horses, African dancing girls, regional slave women and other exotica added to a life of luxury in chambers resplendent with foreign jewels. Since

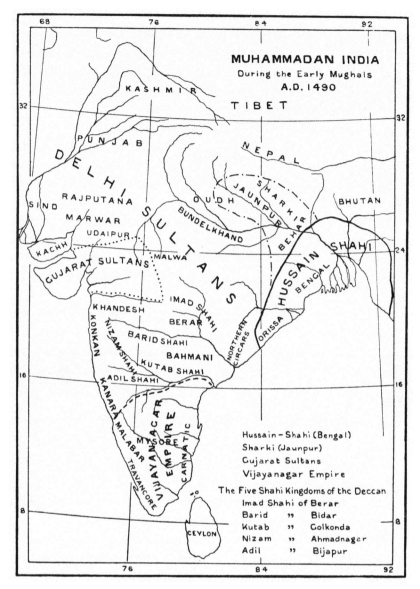

Figure 4.3 Map of Muhammadan India at the beginning of the Mughal Empire. Published 1915 (© Bridgeman Images).

wealth from these privileged estates went to the emperor upon the death of a regional ruler, they had little incentive to invest for the future. Office-holding elites took what they could for themselves while they could. This prompted the Frenchman Francois Bernier to claim in the 1660s there was no sense of private property in India.

Like all elites, Mughal rulers exploited the rural peasantry. As in the other Islamic empires, no equivalent of a middle class emerged. Mughal India had two categories of workers: individually employed workers such as artisans or peasants, and factory wage-labourers. Craftsmen lacked purchasing power and typically made products for princes rather than for markets. Land revenues transferred directly from local elites, known as *zamindars*, to royal courts, whose paid retainers and servants exploited peasants mercilessly.

Mughal nobles generally respected traders more than their counterparts in Japan or China for instance, but tax revenues merely fed military expansion or funded the building of extravagant palaces. Though some rural merchants prospered, the economy mainly leeched off the peasant masses. Zamindars became a hereditary revenue-collecting class who controlled a network of debt collection. Outside of the major temple and palace towns, they enjoyed autonomy running a village-based fragmented economy, with low-productivity agriculture at subsistence levels and peasants in constant debt to landowners. Though men dominated trade, women sometimes became notable economic advisers at court. Still, social norms compelled most women to fulfil family duties in the home or working in fields.

India had been a major trading region for centuries, so by 1700 a huge textile production system existed in the eastern Bengal region connecting Madras in the south to the Gujarat region in the west. Armenian traders linked India to Chinese markets via Tibet, which helped the Mughals extend their power beyond Babur and Akbar's earlier efforts. Under Shah Jahangir (d. 1627) and Jahan (d. 1658) the Mughals developed a booming textile industry that sent woven goods to Southeast Asia and China. World-famous cottons and Bengali silks found eager buyers in the Muslim world and Europe.

This growth ended in the eighteenth century, though, as chaos and instability emerged under the more authoritative rule of Aurangzeb (d. 1707). Though Aurangzeb incorporated southern land via expansion, he was a committed Muslim who undid Akbar's work. Intentionally or not, he inflamed religious differences in the empire. He raised taxes on non-Muslims, redirected the economy towards the raising of mosques and away from trade, even urging the razing of Hindu temples – in a Hindu-majority society. His rule brought economic fragmentation, as regional Hindu elites pulled away from their Mughal overlords, thereby avoiding payments and taxes. The Mughal Empire hence went into steep decline in the 1700s. Failed harvests, typhoons and food crises had exacerbated volatility after 1670, adding to economic woes wrought by Aurangzeb's extremism.

Also, by 1700, Indian economies began to enter wider trading networks. British traders arrived with the aim of exporting large amounts of cotton out of India, soon profiting from military supremacy and exploitative intentions. Harbouring no loyalty to Muslim overlords, many Indian merchants freely allied with Europeans. Business relations formed initially between a small number of British adventurers and local Indian traders, who offered a ready environment in which to buy and sell. The *banian* class of agents indeed helped British merchants set up in India, charging fees and partnering with them for personal profit.

Assisted by Indian traders, the British East India Company provided the foundation for British aspirations on the subcontinent, in time bringing the expanding empire exorbitant profits and power in South Asia. While British power tiptoed into India, after 1720, the Mughals entered a terminal decline. Huge palaces came down in favour of foreign-owned warehouses, factories and ports, where merchants exported India's wealth to Europe and the world. Little opposition met powerful European soldier-merchants; Mughal fighters proved undisciplined and no match for European armies with better weapons and training.

By the 1750s, Indian trade essentially funded the expansion of the British Empire. Minorities, Hindu bankers and regional princes allied with Britons to secure a share of power. One minority group in particular, Sikhs, worked closely with the British in the Punjab. Indeed, the last Sikh guru, Gobind Singh, helped bring down the Mughal Empire as the British reached into India. Professing loyalty towards neither Mughal Muslims nor Hindu royals, Sikhs pursued their own business interests. Their leaders preached a religious doctrine which promised enlightenment to those who worked and bustled in a busy city, an approach close enough to that of Protestant Britons. Similarly, Sikhs focused on business efficiency, honesty and pride in wealth. After 1757, when British soldiers routed Mughal rulers (and their French allies) at Plassey, British imperialists would control India, remaining dominant in the region until 1947.

Like the Ottoman and Safavid empires, the Mughal Empire did not secure the loyalty of most people, and all three functioned without economic unity. Rather than reward traders for the wealth they generated, Mughals felt threatened by merchants and their ideas. Steep inequality meant peasants had no reason to commit to elite-run economies whose focus was glorious monumental architecture instead of productive commerce. Mughal elites, like those in the Ottoman and Safavid empires, resisted new financial ideas, new technologies, and inhibited the productive potential of the people they ruled. After 1700, while commercial and print culture spread along with rising literacy and numeracy in Europe, Muslim rulers hindered trade by refusing to allow printing in Arabic. Traditional word-of-mouth deals and hands in pockets stood in for international trade and global investment.

Of course, elites everywhere reaped profits while the masses struggled. The Taj Mahal, like Versailles in France, was built at great cost in both money and labour – the people gained next to nothing. The difference, however, was the degree to which Western Europeans were extending global trading networks and setting the terms of trade. By 1750, while standards of living slowly rose in Europe, they stagnated or declined in the three Muslim empires.

Indian Ocean trade – Asian commerce

Far from the comforts of palatial power, Muslim merchants traded in the Indian Ocean, as they had for centuries. After Ming China turned inwards in the 1430s (see discussion herein), Gujaratis and Egyptians directed much of the ocean trade in the region. Thus, even as Muslim rulers restrained commercial growth at home, Islam spread to Indonesia through merchant wanderers, freed from aristocratic constraints.

After the Portuguese navigator Vasco da Gama rounded the southern tip of Africa in 1497 to reach East Africa and the Indian Ocean, Europeans stumbled into an ancient and thriving trade system. The system connected Africa to Arabia, India and all of East Asia – the fabled land of commercial riches. Africa's interior linked to this oceanic trade through numerous coastal cities, where a mixed Bantu–Arabic hybrid language known as Swahili could be heard on docks and ports. Humming Swahili ports such as Mombasa and Malindi sat at the intersection of long-distance trade routes, where luxury goods entered Africa's interior while gold and ivory were exported to the world.

As it happened, the arrival of the Portuguese coincided with a crisis in gold production in many parts of Africa's interior. Fragmented rule among independent, freewheeling traders in Swahili towns meant easy pickings for Portuguese gunboats. Since these towns harboured great wealth, the Portuguese quickly set about pirating them. At the beginning of the sixteenth century, Portuguese sailors sacked the Kilwa Sultanate and other Swahili cities. By 1700, they had seized Swahili ports, controlling the rich trade passing through them.

The Swahili city-states sat at the westernmost point of a vast Indian Ocean trading circuit that connected Arabic traders to Hindu family networks across South and Southeast Asia. This was an open trading world, free of Europeans, capitalism or Christianity. Buddhist kingdoms in Vietnam, Cambodia and Thailand, and innumerable Southeast Asian islands, sent product into China in a relationship where China predominated. However, across the seas the exchange network premised upon relative equality among the many states, if not absolute harmony. European traders thus entered a functioning world with only small-scale rivalries. These mixed societies were well used to trading with diverse groups. None expected to dominate the whole system. Yet, in the early modern era, European merchants would exploit these lightly organized, small states and the small-scale factionalism that did exist, to dominate it wholesale.

This was no utopian trading paradise. Royal monopolies existed as elsewhere, and tribute systems of forced payment went from weaker kings to strong. Thousands of small kingdoms, islands and minor states populated a vast water world linking Africa, India, Arabia and China. Competitive chaos was the flavour, in a complex economic environment that no one empire, sultan or king regulated. This was a winner-takes-all world of outright rivalry, but usually free of large-scale violence and without powerful guns on boats.

In East Asia, as elsewhere, slave labour sustained commerce, with Malays often providing the forced labour for independent Chinese traders. The Manila Galleons, loaded with silver bullion from the Americas, enslaved Asian workers whose lives mirrored those from Africa in their hopelessness. Merchants swapped, stole and prospered through piracy, a practice common to the area. Europeans adeptly joined in these practices.

> The Portuguese, Spanish, Dutch, French and English introduced superior gun power into existing trade networks, however, which weighed negotiations in their favour, and they entered a turbulent world of Asian commerce. Piratic sea nomads roamed from island to island around the southern Philippines stealing and looting at will. Here, a sixteenth-century Portuguese sailor (with a biased world view) describes a maritime society in the straits of Malacca:
>
> > These men in these islands are greater thieves than any in the world, and they are powerful and have many *paraos* (boats) They sail about plundering, from their country up to the Moluccas and Banda, and among all the islands around Java; and they take women to sea. They have fairs where they dispose of the merchandise they steal and sell the slaves they capture. They run all round the island of Sumatra. They are mainly corsairs. . . . They take their spoils to Jumaia, which is near Pahang, where they have a fair continually. Those who do not carry on this kind of robbery come in their large well-built *pungajavas* with merchandise.[2]

In the 1600s, Europeans thus joined a loosely defined, extensive trading area along the Asian coasts of the Indian and Pacific Oceans, free of strong, centralized states such as the Muslim empires or China. Ethnic and cultural connections facilitated trade and fostered trust within merchant networks. From the Middle East to Asia, merchant families and groups hustled and bustled for profit: Jains, Hindus, Armenians, Jews, Parsees, Malays and Chinese all traded from enclaves in hundreds of cities and ports. Hindu advisers known as *dubash* in particular specialized in simplifying trader interactions, providing agency services for merchants to exchange goods and monies free of confusion. Malayan, Javan and Indonesian kingdoms bustled with ports full of Japanese, Chinese and others who competed with arriving Europeans.

Pushy Portuguese

When Portuguese merchants arrived in Melaka in 1509, locals met them warmly as fellow traders. These strangely confident Christians searching for allies against Muslim merchants found partners in Asia and access to the riches of the spice trade. Asian merchants and rulers later had reasons for regret. Portuguese soon sought control of the spice trade in India and Ceylon rather than a share of it. The Portuguese took the key city of Malacca in 1511, capitalizing on earlier alliances, and by 1557 they controlled trading posts in Hong Kong and Macau, even threatening China.

The arrival of Europeans increased regional conflict. The Portuguese saw no importance in offering gifts to trade partners. This was common practice in the region, and, when Muslim sultans complained, Europeans responded with violence or looting. Dutch merchants too had no compunction about using violence in Indonesian ports, killing a Javanese prince who obstructed profits in 1596. The founding of Spanish Manila in 1571 would connect global trade networks more tightly, and here, Spaniards customarily abused Filipino merchants and chiefs. The goal was to ship tin, spices and rice from the region into markets dominated by Europeans, for European profit, not to collaborate.

By the seventeenth century mercantilist European nations – purposely bent on accruing wealth in bullion – entrenched jealous competition and conflict in the region. They fought anybody, including each other, to secure gains. In the century after 1600 the Dutch East India Company pushed out Portuguese merchants. By 1641 they took Malacca and other Portuguese enclaves from their Christian rivals, dominating Ceylon, Macau and numerous Indian port cities. The Dutch then pushed out the Portuguese and created a trade monopoly between the Netherlands and East Indies that made them the seventeenth-century power in the region.

Princely gains

As in Africa, Asian trade was not a simple one-way relationship, dominated by Europeans. Trade supported affluent royal dynasties in Asia, who worked with the Portuguese or Dutch to forge monopolies on commerce. Local princes and merchants gained from trading deals and, as elsewhere, broader populations remained poor. Royals such as the Nguyen princes in Vietnam worked their peasantry to the bone, importing military goods for the king's defence and personal gain. As in Africa and the Arab world, local conflict and rivalries facilitated European incursions. A half-century of warfare between the Le dynasty and Trinh lords in the North and the Nguyen lords in the south from 1627 to 1673 destroyed social stability in Vietnam. As in the Muslim empires, strong investment-based economies did not develop in the Indian Ocean. Instead, a small number of connected merchants and elites enjoyed most of the wealth produced from trading with Europeans (Figure 4.4).

Indian Ocean trade boomed in the seventeenth century and continued to grow into the eighteenth. But by 1750 Europeans only possessed minor footholds in ports rather than real power over Southeast Asian states, where merchants, kings and sultans traded on their own terms. Western traders met robust Asian dynasties or chiefs. Only after 1750 did they begin to dominate the region through superior military power and more industrial forms of production and warfare. Europeans began colonizing cities, hinterlands and ultimately setting up territorial empires in the 1800s.

In the eighteenth century, however, as Europeans encroached, different regions in Asia increasingly exported one major cash crop – spices and peppers from Indonesia or cinnamon from Sri Lanka. More and more, gains went not to local traders or princes but to European merchants and monarchs and eventually the broader

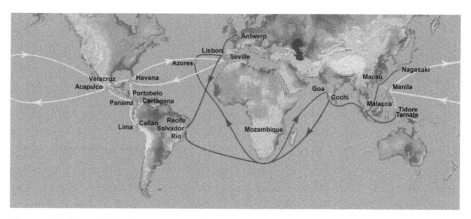

Figure 4.4 Dutch Empire *c.* 1800 (Wikimedia Commons).

European economies. The products themselves ended up in the dishes or homes of westerners, as the Dutch, British and French initiated a process of domination of the Indian Ocean that continued into the mid-twentieth century.

Ultimately in this era, Europeans, like others, aspired to trade with China, the enduring giant of global commerce. To the degree Europeans began extracting wealth from weaker states in the eighteenth century, this was nothing new in history. Europeans were, unbeknownst to them, emulating a pattern of economic influence across East and Southeast Asia that the state of China had for centuries considered their right. In Southeast Asia, Chinese migrant traders had partnered with kings as a minority merchant class for centuries, and were interested only in profits, not in developing local economies. Trade, before and after Europeans arrived, was no morality tale.

China – Majestic confidence

Like Portuguese or Dutch shippers, pirates or Muslim rulers, Chinese emperors and merchants cared first and foremost for their own financial and political interests. This had long been Chinese tradition. Over 2,000 years ago the influential Qin era Legalist Shang Yang (d. 338 BCE) influenced many, championing a strong army and rich country as the basis of a successful state. For centuries, Chinese rulers had looked to enrich themselves by dominating neighbouring Asian economies. Early European intrusions possibly even helped the Chinese court. Portuguese traders were preferred to Japanese pirates, who had long terrorized Chinese ships. Indeed, conflict with Japanese buccaneers partly influenced the Yongle Emperors fateful decision to stop Chinese merchants exploring the seas in 1433 – just as Europeans were initiating their efforts at ocean explorations! (Figure 4.5)

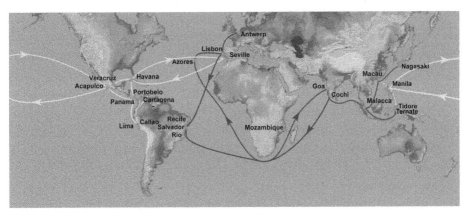

Figure 4.5 Manila Galleons trade routes (Wikimedia Commons).

Foreign policy

China had been the most sophisticated and largest economy on earth for centuries, producing tea, silks, porcelains, paper and cotton in vast quantities. Its economy was fabled, envied across the known world in Eurasia. Most Chinese people engaged in trade of some kind, either directly or by connecting their agricultural production to urban merchants. However, the Chinese state did little to improve its revenue system in these centuries, relying on foreign tribute and agricultural taxes. Entrenched interests continued to control economies, with the sole goal of maintaining inherited prestige or position. Even more than in other kingdoms, Chinese rulers kept tight controls on the circulation of wealth. The imperial court manipulated economic life from the capital without consideration of broader societal needs.

Because of rising inflation, the court had ceased printing of paper money in the fifteenth century. Much sought-after silver specie now replaced paper currency, and the imperial court's growing dependence on American silver brought China deeper into the global economy. Accruing silver became the heart of Chinese policy into the eighteenth century. Bullion dug up under the rule of Spanish overlords in the Americas ended up in Chinese courts, enriching neither Spanish nor Chinese peasants. Similar to Spanish court policy, Ming economic planning suffered under bureaucratic ineptness and royal self-interest. The whim of a given emperor often dictated policy. Consistency and predictability – the goal of most merchants then as now – were rare. The consequences of bad decision-making were never scrutinized, in stark contrast to Dutch or English markets, where merchants not only advised rulers but sometimes even dominated cities and economies. While bullion flowed to China, the British and other European powers benefitted most from the silver trade.

Since Confucian thinking held little respect for merchant life, the Ming elite did not support international trade. Though emperors and their staff allowed merchants to trade freely, they did not encourage it or participate in it. More often, Chinese migrants departed the mainland to make money, dominating the Indian and Pacific Ocean networks until Europeans arrived. Overseas Chinese traders did collaborate with Spanish and Portuguese merchants in the 1600s. While the Ming court generally disdained Europeans, well-organized Chinese merchants traded throughout the Indian Ocean region to ensure that silver and other goods flowed to China.

Peasant pains

Ming emperors and the Chinese people eventually paid a price for fiscal incompetence, losing their kingdom in 1644. The dynasty finally fell due to mismanagement of the economy, which provided an opportunity for the invading Manchu Qing dynasty, foreigners from the north who remained in power until 1911. Through these centuries the Chinese people would suffer at the expense of imperial life. In the years after 1650, from conflict following the fall of the Ming, hundreds of thousands of workers moved from home to form diaspora communities in settlements everywhere from Asia to the Americas. Chinese peasants moved to work on sugar plantations and farms in Indonesia and other parts of Asia.

Traditional Chinese thought placed peasants among the first ranks of working people. But in practice Ming elites showed little respect for them, forcing some farmers through decree to plant mulberry bushes the court could swap for foreign silver. The incoming foreign-elite Qing had even less respect, implementing the *baojia* system, where official surveillance persecuted and pursued the peasantry to maintain obedience. Women had even fewer rights under the Qing than under the Ming, as greater submission was expected. Qing culture subjected more women of high class to the agony of foot binding, which signalled women's elite status while pleasing the eyes of powerful men.

If Chinese peasants suffered, others in inland regions did too. In the 1700s, Central Asian steppe nomads and pastoralists found themselves threatened from three sides by the Ottoman, Chinese and Russian military machines. After 1697, the Qing expanded territorially, taking Mongolia and surrounding steppe lands, giving China economic control of Xinjiang and Tibet in the 1720s and 1730s. Here, China reached its current geographic extent, meeting Indian and Russian borders.

For steppe people, Qing supremacy signalled the end of lifeways common to the Silk Roads for two millennia. Trade declined because Atlantic Ocean seafarers moved goods quicker and cheaper around the world's oceans. Of central importance to world trade since the time of the Han and Rome 2,000 years earlier, the steppe world diminished in global importance, as the loosely organized region fell easily to Chinese power. Steppe nomads and pastoralist populations gradually retreated into isolation, becoming poverty-stricken areas disconnected from ocean routes and commercial networks, kowtowing to Chinese officials out of fear. Nomadic tribal societies like the Uzbek, Kazak and Turkmen minorities struggled to maintain independence, while subject to tribute payments and humiliating deference to the larger military states surrounding them. The Chinese state itself gained from new connections to the New World. Some of the new foods arrived from the Americas – like corn, which grew in these barren regions and at higher altitudes – became staples of Chinese life, helping to grow Asian populations in this era.

Paying the price

While Chinese leaders enjoyed imported silver and maize, they refused to trade openly with foreigners, fearing if the economy opened up, their power base would collapse. Henceforth, China tightly regulated trade with Europeans. In 1699 the Qing established the Canton System, which controlled the number of foreign traders in ports. This roused resentment among European traders and weakened China's internal economy because merchants looked elsewhere. By 1750, China had entered a period of decline. Corruption and inefficiency remained endemic in government administration. Ethnic disunity spurred disdain for Qing rule, similar to discord in Muslim empires. In the 1700s, millions of peasants died from starvation. Beijing remained reliant on silver imports to fuel the economy, exposing the government and Chinese peasants to economic disruptions from changes in global supplies of the precious metal. Elite gain led to China's national decline in this era.

Japan – Closed for business

Japanese elites insulated commerce from foreign influence even more than China did. The country's traditional glorification of a martial life, and elites' firm desire for domestic stability, made the uncertainties of open trade far too risky. Following almost a century of civil war in the 1500s, the powerful daimyo Toyotomi Hideyoshi took control in 1585 and began to pacific Japan. Overseas, however, he invaded China and Korea in the 1590s, inviting a military fiasco that wasted massive lives and resources. Still, the nation unified thereafter and in 1603, the shogun Tokugawa Iesayu and his family began an uninterrupted reign that lasted until 1868, when European incursions disrupted Japanese life forever.

For most of this period, Japan remained economically stable and relatively prosperous. Trade increased in the seventeenth century as Jesuits, Dutch and Portuguese connected Japan to distant trade circuits for the first time. Population growth was gradual as economic productivity increased, so wealth was generated and shared to the point that by 1750 Japan was as prosperous as England and Holland. Like both these small nations, Japan had a small population and a high standard of living. The difference though was that Japanese elites expelled Dutch traders in 1641.

Though limited trade was permitted for a while after, the 'closed country' policy sharply limited Japan's exposure to the global economy developing around it.

The domestic economy thus remained small. Inequality went unchallenged, as elsewhere. Shoguns controlled vassal lords called *daimyo*, about 200 of whom served their emperor around the country. Daimyo managed large landholdings, which the Tokugawa shogunate required them to maintain. Their duties included making lengthy and expensive annual trips to the capital, where some family members remained as hostages, in a show of loyalty to the shogun. Japanese men of affluence were expected to keep luxurious gardens, wear expensive silk clothing and maintain frequent visits to theatres and castles, usually remaining indebted to a web of overlords loyal to the shogun. Daimyo controlled what limited global commerce Japanese engaged in, reaping rewards by supplying the Shogunate with lead, gunpowder and guns.

Elites and rulers could force anybody suspected of disloyalty to commit suicide – so risks were high for those who developed new ideas or threatening ambitions. Beneath the warrior daimyo class, merchants and artisans were forbidden to wear swords, enjoying no political and limited economic power, and the peasantry suffered from severe restrictions on movement and ideas, with few rights compared to those in Western Europe. Samurai could literally slice their social inferiors in half if they felt disrespected. As in China, Japanese villages had to pay taxes and provide labour to imperial nobles. After 1600, the lowest *buraku* caste was deemed outside society, comparable to untouchables in India, with no rights as humans whatsoever. Tokugawa culture stifled both economic innovation and challenges to the social order in these centuries.

Conclusion – The price of isolation

In Japan, then, a closed militarized society built on agricultural production prevailed into the nineteenth century. Only the arrival of American sailors in 1854 would force Japan to open its trade doors, leading to a remarkable movement to modernize and industrialize the country from 1868. Japan would modernize quickly, emerging as a great power in the early twentieth century. But until the mid-nineteenth century, both Japanese and Chinese leaders felt confident that they had no need to accommodate to growing European power. Both societies would be weakened and suffer great consequences in the 1800s as a result.

Keywords

Atlantic economy
Big men
chattel slavery
economic growth

Further reading

Findley, Carter V. *The Turks in World History*. New York: Oxford University Press Inc, 2007. A broad overview of the role of Turkish people from the ancient world through early modern history to the present, explaining, among other themes, economic life and interaction in the regions dominated by Turkish peoples.

Keay, John. *India: A History*. London: Harper Press, 2010. All-encompassing, wide-ranging history of the continent from ancient times to present, with five thoroughly researched chapters on the early modern era.

Lockard, Craig A. *Southeast Asia in World History*. Vancouver, BC: Langara College, 2011. A concise history of the economic crossroads of Asia, exploring the regions connections to both China and India, and centrality for maritime trading networks to the Middle East and Europe.

Ringrose, David. *Expansion and Global Interaction, 1200–1700*, 2nd ed. New Jersey: Pearson, 2012. This excellent brief global history of the late medieval and early modern world clearly explains many of the political as well as economic trends that were shaping human societies in this period.

Streusand, Douglas E. *Islamic Gunpowder Empires: Ottomans, Safavids, and Mughals*. Boulder, CO: Westview Press, 2010. This is a study of the three Muslim empires and their connection to an integrated trade system extending across Eurasia.

5

Dollars and violence

Chapter Outline

Situating the chapter

In the mid-seventeenth century British elites began aggressively challenging Dutch economic pre-eminence, to the point that Britain would dominate trade in the eighteenth century, ousting their Northwest European rivals. After 1752 the Dutch suffered a series of defeats to their rivals, the British, in the Anglo-Dutch Wars. The British would soon become more powerful and economically influential worldwide than the Dutch.

Yet it was the Dutch who first theorized – or legally justified – the idea of free trade. The inspiration came from world historical rivalries in the South China Sea. The Dutch intellectual Hugo Grotius had proclaimed, in 1609's *Mare Liberum*, the importance of freedom of the oceans, promoting open trade as a basic good for all humanity. In reality it was good for Holland, in their successful attempt to oust the Portuguese from the spice trade in Asia and in access to China. But the English were listening. Both nations would find ways to benefit from 'free' trade they were not direct participants in: the silver trade would enrich North-western Europe, even though the mines and labour were in the hands of other powers and local elites.

Tellingly, the father of capitalism, Adam Smith, would later note that Grotius was the first important thinker to attempt to lay a global legal-economic framework over the world's oceans, applicable to all nations. By 1750, global economic competition with Britain hastened Dutch decline, just as they had previously brought Portuguese and Spanish decline. The British would then proclaim the ideology of free trade, when it suited them (Figure 5.1).

In our era, Europeans went searching for profits in distant, vast Asian markets. But what they found in the Americas was ultimately far easier to exploit. Though long-distance indigenous American trading networks had existed for centuries, they were not dense, and were simpler compared to those in Asia. Exploitation of these simpler economies was made easier by superior European military prowess and the diseases they hosted on their bodies.

Figure 5.1 Portrait of Hugo Grotius by Michiel Jansz. van Mierevelt, 1631 (Wikimedia Commons).

Vast American resources would help make Europe a rich continent by the late eighteenth century, far richer than China. By 1750 Europeans dominated American markets, enjoying sugar from the Caribbean, tobacco from North America, and beaver pelts from Canada. By 1776 a new power would slowly arise in the north with all the benefits of new lands and resources, run by white Christians of European descent in a burgeoning young state, the United States of America. The ideas of Grotius, Smith and the aspiration for control of the seas would bring about the rise of the new American power. Economics and violence were central to the founding of the new nation too, as we shall see.

Narrative

The Spanish dollar

South and Central America

Of course, for much of our era, the United States did not exist. But the foundations of its later power were being laid nonetheless by European nations. In the century between 1500 and 1600, Native Americans died wretchedly from diseases introduced by Europeans, against which they had no immunity. Estimates vary, but something like 15–20 million people likely died following the arrival of Europeans. Though zealous Europeans purposely persecuted Indians in these centuries, epidemics killed most people. Indeed, from a physiological and epidemiological standpoint, this was just another version of the Black Death which, carried unknowingly by Mongols, had decimated Europe in the fourteenth century. Pandemics throughout history have wiped out vast numbers of human beings.

As in Africa, Europeans encountered a complex trade system, where dominant groups coerced weaker regional ones. Chief among these dominant entities were the Azteca and Inca, who developed sophisticated irrigation and terraced systems to successfully produce food and goods for their wealthy societies. As in Africa these were typically complex chiefdoms rather than states. A lack of iron-ore metallurgy severely limited their ability to defend militarily against Europeans or to harness the power of nature as was common in Eurasian states. Lacking beasts of burden also limited the ability of American populations to move goods fast and far or develop wealthy economies.

The Aztec Empire, like so many others worldwide, was a tribute state that extracted wealth from subject peoples. Godlike emperors and their aristocracy enjoyed furs, jewellery, rubber or precious stones from weaker groups, under threat of retribution. Aztec imperialism relied upon economies of pilgrimage to shrines. Here, important rituals and symbolic ceremonies were controlled by nobles who, alone, were allowed to possess sacred items as potsherds, incense burners or feathered shields. As in the religious crusades in medieval Europe or the annual Muslim haj, belief and ceremony were part of commercial exchange, with large movements of people for religious purposes periodically stimulating markets. In an economy centred on cacao, corn and obsidian production, a highly stratified nobility of religious and military rulers lived in comfort, while slaves or workers survived however they could (Figure 5.2).

Further South, the Incan state organized goods exchange similarly. They built fortresses to protect trade routes over a road system and along coastal mountains that spanned 800 miles. The Inca state was even more authoritarian than the Aztec, however. The dynasty controlled the centralized economy with an iron hand, ensuring supplies of potatoes, maize and peanuts flowed to elites. No money-based market developed in the South.

Ruling a region far greater than modern Peru, the Inca ran the largest land-based empire on earth in 1500. After overthrowing the Chimu people in the 1400s, the empire grew into the largest state in the Americas, with a complex economy based on deference from conquered peoples. The economy was based on the *mita*, a combination of forced labour from subject populations and communal labour. This system constructed the famous Andean roads that crossed the Andes. Economic life comprised crafting of baskets of reed, shaping leather for clothing or transportation. Complex impressive pottery was produced as it had for centuries.

Figure 5.2 Native American medicine, 1565. The various methods employed by the Seminole Indians to treat their sick (© Getty Images).

To maintain order, the Inca developed a complex system of organized food distribution. Produce was conveyed from large centralized warehouses which connected small towns and villages. The powerful used water to control agriculture and economic life, and though the lowest ranks of Inca society suffered harsh conditions, this system functioned well prior to the Spaniards' arrival. Incan emperors owned all wealth; they *were* the state in effect. After death their possessions even remained with them. Hence wealth could not be passed on, reinvested or reused as elsewhere. Wealth in this economy remained with the dead.

Native negotiations

Like elites in other societies, Indian rulers usually acted in their own interests. They did not simply lay down and accept European intrusions. To survive in a post-contact world, some individuals and leaders negotiated, allying or partnering with foreigners. Some Indians became powerful elites in Spanish America, acquiring grand homes and riches. Indian merchants moved into the upper classes to mix with Spanish families. Some Native Americans even worked as slave catchers, allying with Europeans to find escaped African slaves. Europeans tended to dominate throughout the Americas, but indigenous elites found ways to thrive in the circumstances.

Just as there was never one unified European plan to conquer the Americas, nor was there one common indigenous response to foreign incursion. Some allied with Europeans, some fought and many fought or traded with each other as elsewhere. Consequently, the Spanish found willing allies in their aim to dominate the Aztec and Inca. Along with vast wealth, Cortes found Aztec societies riven with conflict and internal resentments. Since tribute was the basis of the Aztec economy, weaker populations contributed to Azteca wealth accumulation. Indeed, this had long been the pattern. After the Maya declined in the ninth century, the Toltec and Mixtec ruled much of modern Mexico for centuries. They were in turn subjugated by the Aztecs in the fifteenth century. Harsh Azteca dominion over other indigenous peoples would haunt them once the Spanish arrived in their capital Tenochtitlan.

From bad to worse

Still, when Pizarro and his Spanish conquistadors conquered the Inca in 1532, they set off a transformation of the native economy that worsened life for most Indians. Earlier rule by indigenous elites was presumably preferable to a shocking New World of Spanish diseases with new economic practices. Pizarro had defeated the Inca by tricking the emperor Atahualpa, asking him to meet unarmed, European soldiers, who were in fact armed and ready, executing him (although he had himself earlier executed his older brother to take the throne). The Spaniards looted a large room full of gold and silver, setting about the gradual decline and subjugation of the Inca. They duly demolished palaces, temples and storehouses that were the basis of the Incan economy. By 1550, the Spanish had defeated both the Aztec and Inca. Mexico City and Lima thus developed into the two major urban centres of the Spanish-dominated **Atlantic economy**. These two cities became the capitals of New Spain, serving as legal and administrative centres of the new economy.

The most obvious economic impact on Central and South America was the transformation from self-sustaining agricultural economies into centres of global silver bullion production after 1540. In particular, silver from the Potosi mine in modern Bolivia lubricated the New World economy, from America to China, providing much of the bullion Europeans exchanged for Chinese silks and porcelains. Labour conditions were horrendous. The Spanish forced workers to carry ore on their backs from hundreds of feet inside the mountain. Workers suffered terrible mercury poisoning as they separated the silver. Potosi was a wild boom town where corruption and violence ruled. Free of control from any one ethnic group, opportunist minority merchants – often forced to emigrate because they were unwelcomed in burgeoning European states – managed most commerce. Commercially minded Basques, a minority in Spain, mingled with Chinese traders and Sephardic Jews, all of whom traded with Iberians and Africans.

South America would subsequently provide bullion for the booming Atlantic and Pacific trade routes for centuries. Brazil alone in the 1700s was the source of 80 per cent of the world's gold, around 2 million pounds, and a diamond boom in the eighteenth century sent vast amounts to the necklaces and ringed fingers of the wealthy in the 1700s. European credit markets could emerge due to the widespread dispersal of silver bullion around the world, with the new connected markets pushing profits towards Europe, while the actual metals went to China.

Since Europeans lacked numbers in New Spain, they could not extract America's wealth without new sources of labour. The mountain of silver required so much forced labour that when Indians started dying in the 1560s, Spaniards started to import African slaves to supplement natives. Vast lands offered the potential for great riches to opportunistic Spaniards and Portuguese, but labour was short on the ground. The plantation system that they would develop, to produce and move goods across the Atlantic, in fact *revived* global slavery, and made West Africa the centre of a terrible new transatlantic slave trade.

The plantation complex system, long present in the medieval Mediterranean, was now transplanted to the Americas. Columbus brought existing knowledge of sugarcane with him – his family was in the business. Slaves and Indians worked with sugar predominantly but were also exploited in all manner of occupation. They processed indigo for the beautiful blue clothes of distant nobles, working with toxic paste in damp ditches. Sugar processing was particularly miserable though. Its production demanded of workers an incessant fast pace and long hours to produce product and profit. Deadlines, fast-paced market competition and new expectations of revenue worked people to death in the new global sugar business. More labourers could always be found from Africa to replace those who died, like a macabre, steady supply of replacement machine parts. European-style capitalism was slowly transforming indigenous economies.

Iberian empires

Up until around 1650, most trade between American and European markets went through Portugal and Spain. Both monarchies had long struggled to access trade in Eurasia and searched for ways to evade Muslim and Italian middlemen. Their brief role as dominant traders would end though in the seventeenth century. By 1750, their monopoly on Atlantic trade would be challenged by the arrival of Dutch, English and French traders and settlers, which weakened both Iberian powers (Figure 5.3).

Portugal

The Portuguese were the first to integrate the global economy. Due to Spain's domination of the Iberian Peninsula, Portuguese merchants were forced to look outwards to sea, to explore Africa and the Americas. Struggling to access Ottoman and Asian markets, Portuguese merchants exported basic primary products as fish, oils, salt, animal hides and wine. A small country with less than a million people, the Portuguese nonetheless initiated commercial links that enabled the emergence of modern European empires. They branched out from basic primary products to instigate the enslavement of Africans, first shipping slaves to Brazil around 1538. By 1570 over 50 Brazilian mills produced sugar on slave plantations, with around 100 slaves labouring miserably on each one.

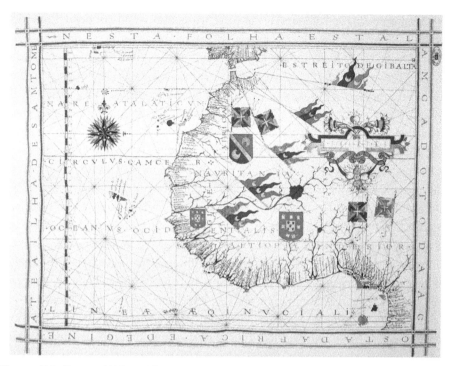

Figure 5.3 Portugal/West Africa: Nautical (Portolan) chart of West Africa. Fernão Vaz Dourado (1520–*c.* 1580), 1571. Portuguese explorer Prince Henry, known as the Navigator, was the first European to methodically explore Africa (© Bridgeman Images).

Expeditions down the western coast of the African continent began in the 1400s. Portuguese merchants first gained control of the North African port of Ceuta in modern Morocco by 1415. Portuguese sailors developed a navigational technique, called the ***volta do mar***, that allowed mariners to swing out into the Atlantic, sail south toward the Cape of Good Hope, then use Atlantic wind patterns to return safely. By 1450, Portuguese merchants were in the African Gold Coast, gaining experience which later helped them to find their way to the Americas, and which initiated the slave trade.

At first the Portuguese emulated the medieval approach of Venetian merchants, with only limited contact or influence in small coastal trading-posts. Gradually, though, superior gunpowder technology provided them a new element of coercion and changed the terms of negotiations in their favour. Quick profits came from gun sales or even from providing protection services for African elites. As they would in the Americas, Basque, Armenian and Portuguese-Jewish trading networks provided investment or insurance services that facilitated Portuguese exploration. There were always many parties to transactions in the burgeoning global trade centred on the Americas. Europeans may have developed what became merchant and then industrial capitalism, but they did it alongside traders from across Eurasia, and the world at large.

The impact on natives in Brazil was immense. Portuguese importers initially sought brazil wood for its highly prized red dye (hence the name of the country). Soon though plantation owners worked slaves to death producing sugar, rum or tobacco. Sugar plantations were carved out of the land, with huge donations doled out by the Portuguese crown to adventurers.

Until sugar prices crashed in the 1670s, Portugal's colonial empire accounted for much of the sugar produced worldwide. Thereafter, however, the Portuguese state rapidly declined in wealth and power. The Caribbean would become the key sugar-exporting region, controlled and colonized by the English. Most of the wealth accrued by rich Portuguese would in time be used to pay debts to English financiers, as that nation expanded internationally to replace both Portugal and Spain as the principal colonizer and enslaver in the Americas.

Spain

As many students know, Spanish adventurers led by Columbus arrived in the Americas in 1492, and, thus, a small kingdom ruled by aristocratic Catholic families stumbled upon new continents. The Habsburgs had already ousted Muslims and Jews from Iberia in 1492. By 1521, the family governed economic life in the kingdom and were deeply committed to spreading Christianity worldwide while looting for riches. The dynasty and the well-connected attained exorbitant wealth from Atlantic trade; gold and silver from the Americas were melted into bars, shipped across the oceans into state coffers that Spanish rulers could use as personal treasure chests (Figure 5.4).

Long-standing Eurasian trade connections inspired the first Spanish voyages. The impetus to explore came from Spain's centuries-old connection to the Muslim world in the Mediterranean. Iberian explorers learned about sailing away from shore from Muslim traders and merchants in North Africa. They had earlier been exposed to Indian and Chinese scientific techniques and mathematics, figuring out how to use a compass to sail out of sight of land. Broader Eurasian ideas and technologies, then, aided European explorers.

Long-standing economic competition also contributed to new discoveries in the Americas. Just as Spanish traders had blocked Portuguese access to wider markets, the Spanish in turn had been frustrated by Ottoman Muslim traders. The Ottoman Turks had controlled routes from the Mediterranean over steppes and sea into Asia for centuries before 1500. Once they ventured across the Atlantic and Pacific, however, Spanish explorers sailed some of the longest voyages ever attempted. Polynesians had sailed across the Pacific Ocean, but the Spanish exploration prompted massive trade connections and cultural exchange, so the effects would dwarf earlier Polynesian voyages. They would be duly rewarded (Figure 5.5).

Spanish traders shipped the first African slaves across the Atlantic in 1510. In 1521 the Catholic pope and the fanatically devout Emperor Charles V sanctioned the **asiento system**, which both sanctioned and stimulated the shipment of more

Figure 5.4 Charles V. Portrait of Charles V as a child (Ghent, 1500–Cuacos de Yuste, 1588), Emperor of the Holy Roman Empire (© Getty Images).

slaves, by granting royal licence. From 1550 sugar production boomed on the island of Cuba, and by 1530 gold from the Americas began flowing back to Spain. The Habsburgs sent royal administrators to organize labour and to collect bulk shipments of silver bullion from mines. Even with this windfall, however, Spanish rulers exacted high taxes from their subjects, who remained among the most heavily taxed in Europe. Those in power failed to develop an economic infrastructure or sophisticated economy to effectively absorb the great inflows of precious metals in these centuries. Spain's wealth would not last as a result. Inflation would persist in weakening a small economy.

Spanish conquistadors, adventurers and priests moved into Asia in the 1520s, taking control of the fragmented Philippines to dominate the main islands. No centralized state existed to contest Magellan or other Spanish adventurers. Instead, thousands of minor chiefs competed for power in the islands. Once the Spanish arrived, the native population was forced to leave traditional lands, over time providing labour for priests and nobles in farm communities, bringing a heavily Catholic influence on life in the Philippines. Manila would develop into an important trading post and way station in Spain's growing trans-Pacific commerce in the sixteenth century.

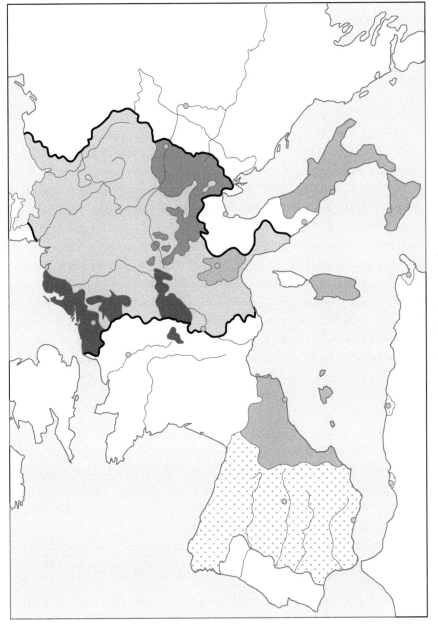

Figure 5.5 Charles V inheritance by 1519 (Wikimedia Commons).

Wasted earnings

Showing little inclination towards financial innovation, a wealthy class of Spanish churchmen and military families allied tightly with the monarchy, meaning Spain made little practical use of the riches the Americas provided. The Spanish Crown favoured the upper classes at the expense of the peasantry; politically connected merchants received land grants to become rich in the Americas. Nobles earned revenue from trade licenses, taxation or cheap peasant labour. Spanish merino wool was exported for profit, so the best arable land was taken from peasants and used to raise sheep.

The Spanish economy suffered greatly from inflation, a consequence of the flow of silver from Potosi and Mexico into small Spanish markets. Indeed, the supply of bullion tripled in Europe in the 1600s, prompting a huge rise in prices of basic staples, while real wages lagged behind across Europe. Peasants in Spain suffered most, having to pay higher rents or produce more food for lords. As in most countries, Spain's leaders showed little sense of responsibility towards the working poor or impoverished. Rather, they assumed hunger and suffering to be natural, sent from the heavens, even as volumes of gold and silver flowed from American mines.

For all the riches accrued in the Americas, the cost of living doubled in Spain after 1550, as inflation hit those with fixed incomes hardest. The poor – peasants, people without property and regular wage earners – all found their money purchased far less, decade after decade, as wages stagnated due to a global market shift known as the **Price Revolution**. While some gained, notably landowners, wealthy merchants and securely tenured renters, starvation occurred in Spain, uprisings increased and discontent continued for almost a century. The clearest sign that life for the majority in Spain declined with the influx of bullion was the country's *decrease* in population across the seventeenth century.

Indeed, peasants throughout Europe suffered because of the inflationary effects of Spanish bullion. Though all the accumulated wealth helped seed industrial capitalism over centuries, everyday labourers did not gain. Spanish rulers squandered gold and silver on extravagant structures and palatial residences rather than infrastructure or economic development. As a result, and despite the American windfall, Spain's influence over international trade declined after 1600.

The decline of Spain is all the more remarkable because the Spanish peso was the dollar of the early modern world, the world's first commonly used global currency. Spain was the most powerful European state in 1500. The monarchy and the landed gentry possessed vast plots of Spanish land named *latifundia*, resisting market valuation which provided new capital for English and Dutch nobility who made money from land. In old as in New Spain, conquistadors and crown cronies enjoyed land grants from the monarchy. Since the Spanish did not produce manufactured products for markets, the English and Dutch instead sold wares to the Spanish elite.

Indeed, the Spanish state declared bankruptcy eight times between 1530 and 1700, as royals and their cronies wasted gold on aggressive wars to dominate Europe or to re-Catholicize newly Protestant states. The Spanish royal family spent massive sums invading England in 1588, inviting a national disaster and defeat, which wiped out its military. This inaugurated the state's slow decline, coincident with England's rise.

The Spanish Empire remained strong through the seventeenth century at least, financed by 16,000 tonnes of silver extracted from the Americas. Roughly 180 tonnes of gold entered Europe through Spain in this era, but by 1750 that wealth would aid neither Spain nor Portugal, which were both weakening powers.

Anti-market fundamentalism

In addition to elite extravagance, Spanish intolerance towards non-Christians also slowed economic development. Spain might have gained from the rich agricultural heritage left by Muslims in the Iberian Peninsula, but by expelling Muslims in 1492, they lost advanced horticultural and irrigation knowledge. Religious intolerance towards Muslims, Jews and Protestants forced talented traders and thinkers to move to rival nations. Catholic zealotry forced the most skilled populations in agriculture or trade to depart. After 1700, while England and Holland slowly adopted more modern, industrial-capitalist, practices and strengthened global trade connections, the Spanish state remained committed to mercantilist thinking, storing gold in treasure chests or spending it on architectural splendour and warfare.

In its colonizing mission, Spain thus prioritized proselytization over profits. The Dutch, English (and to some extent the Catholic French) were far more interested in profits and business. Though they too professed similar views of the supposed immorality of indigenous traditions, they prioritized profits over piety (Figure 5.6).

Indeed, the seventeenth-century rise of the Netherlands as a global commercial power owed much to its hard-won independence from Habsburg Spain. In 1568 the Dutch revolted against Spanish rule in an effort to gain economic and political independence. Conflict persisted for decades, while trade gradually shifted north to the Dutch city of Amsterdam, which, after 1600, became the main European commercial entrepôt. By 1598, Spain's national debt was fifteen times higher than its income. By 1648, when the Spanish lost the war to the Dutch, the crown was out of money, with ruined finances and unable to get credit – from mostly Dutch and English bankers. The Spanish economy essentially collapsed by 1750, by which time the peso was worth a third of its 1650 value.

Western Europe was growing richer in this era in general. Between 1500 and 1700 Spain's economy grew roughly about 20 per cent, similar to France's and Portugal's. Italy's stagnated fatally as trade moved away from the Mediterranean. During these years, however, Britain and Holland saw their economies grow 200–300 per cent, from a similar starting point. Dutch provinces sent more wealth into Spain from international trade than even the bullion from the Americas had! Entrenched

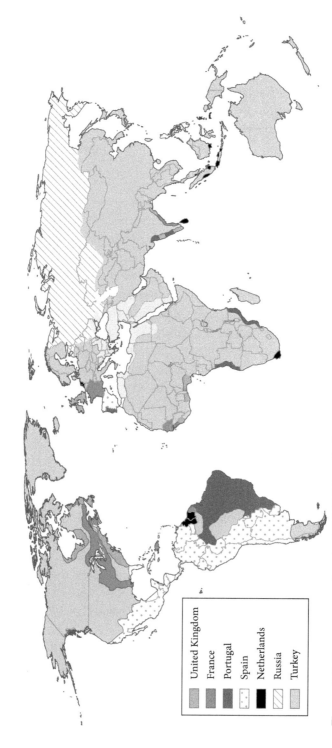

Figure 5.6 European empires in 1754 (Wikimedia Commons).

United Kingdom
France
Portugal
Spain
Netherlands
Russia
Turkey

Spanish economic interests kept the spoils of commerce for themselves, like most elites in Asia and worldwide. But meanwhile, the British were coming.

North America – Slave trading

In North America, settlers from England and France arrived in increasing numbers after 1600. Like the Iberian powers in Africa, they met powerful indigenous societies with complex economic systems. Native American economies were typically hierarchical, where local chiefs redistributed goods and services to wider populations. Indigenous societies relied on complex kinship networks that worked according to reciprocal obligations and responsibilities. They were usually honour based, as opposed to government by imperial command, written contract or law.

Everyday people in the Americas were probably better off than the masses in Eurasia. Though many endured lean seasons in certain years, they were far less likely to suffer chronic hunger than people in strong centralized states from Europe to China. Natives prided themselves on cleanliness, unlike people in cities across Eurasia who rarely washed. The first English settlers constantly referred to hard-working, healthy natives who enjoyed nutritious diets. They were mostly untouched by disease, in stark contrast to common European peasants and labourers with disfigured skin and a basic diet, who toiled in harsh conditions for increasingly profit-minded agricultural and manufacturing enterprises, working hard and long for monetary gain.

The seventeenth-century Jesuit missionary Pierre Biard foresaw the possibility that Europeans might be addicted to profit and productivity, criticizing European tendencies towards hustle-bustle, while citing approvingly that North Americans Indians lived easier lives.

He wrote: 'their days are all nothing but pastime. They are never in a hurry. Quite different from us, who can never do anything without hurry and worry; worry, I say, because our desire tyrannizes over us and banishes peace from our actions.'[1]

In the south of what is today the United States, the tribal system consisted of diverse populations competing in a mixed economy of agriculture and foraging. American foods such as squash, beans, pumpkins and corns that would soon feed millions around the world provided sustenance. Most economic activity focused on food production; those too intent on competition and personal enrichment could find themselves shunned within or banished from kinship systems.

Though Indians tended to live healthier lives than their Old World counterparts, socio-economic inequality was common in North American tribal life also. Dominant groups, and elites within those groups, possessed more than others. Pocahontas's father Powhatan, for instance, controlled around thirty client tribes, and used his position as a major chief to maintain economic dominance. Native elites in fact both gained and lost by negotiating trade relationships with Europeans and playing the powers off one another. Elites enjoyed manufactured goods otherwise unavailable to them, like metal bowls, hatchets, knives and guns. Yet, over time, they became more and more dependent on Europeans to provide them with these goods, and so suffered worsening terms of trade as power disparities increased. Dependency was the ultimate outcome, for all natives.

Collaboration and alliances in North America

As elsewhere, Europeans did not just turn up and take what they wished. Like Africa rulers, Native American elites negotiated the earliest transactions with white merchants from a position of parity or power. France's development of a fur-trading empire in North America after 1608, to create New France, formed on roughly equal terms with natives. English relationships with Indians often proved more fraught due to English arrogance, but they too sought to establish trading relationships with Indian communities, from New England to the Carolinas.

Natives participated in global trade with their own desire for exotic items. From the Cherokee in the south to the Huron in the north, Indians desired items of European origin as important status symbols. Many Indian communities valued practical European manufactured goods that they could not produce themselves, such as metal bowls, knives, hatchets and guns. Over time, however, natives became dependent on such European goods and they suffered worsening terms of trade as a result.

Throughout the seventeenth and eighteenth centuries ever more Native Americans saw their ways of life shattered under the pressure of growing European populations. Europeans brought attitudes and assumptions about wealth, land, labour and legal rights that ran contrary to native interests. Most Indians had long possessed a more communal attitude to land, called **usufruct** rights. This was premised upon sharing the fruits of the land. Deaf to indigenous attitudes to land and property, people from England, Holland or France found it perfectly natural to delineate land: hedges and fences were a sign of order, of efficiency and legal proof of ownership. Europeans fervently fenced off property to exclude and dominate North American tribes; the assumption being that since Indians didn't want to demarcate the land, they were not using it, so it was freely available (Figure 5.7).

The Thirteen Colonies on the east coast of North America were first settled by the French and English. In the North, French settlers founded Port Royal in 1604 and Quebec in 1608. The English then founded Jamestown in 1607. Dutch settlers inhabited New Amsterdam in 1633, which would become New York. Though most early settlements ended in desolation and hunger, many more Europeans came over time.

Slavery constituted a large part of economic life from the earliest days in North America. European colonizers imported the majority of African slaves into Central and South America, but large numbers went to North America too. The first Africans

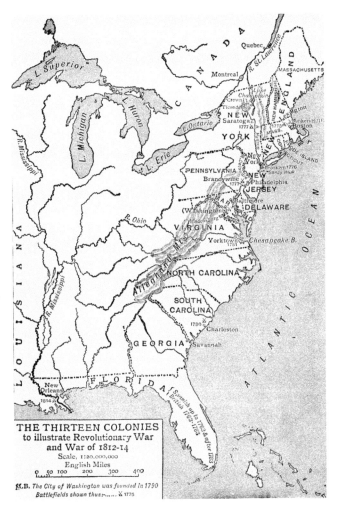

Figure 5.7 Map showing the Thirteen Colonies, to illustrate the Revolutionary War and War of 1812–14. The Thirteen Colonies were British colonies established on the Atlantic coast of North America between 1607 and 1733 (© Bridgeman Images).

arrived in Virginia in 1619. By the end of the seventeenth century the Chesapeake colonies relied more and more on slaves to cultivate tobacco. English colonists exploited not only African labour but also African knowledge. West Africans understood rice cultivation, which was sorely needed in the Carolinas to feed growing populations in the 1600s.

Colonies varied in type and formation. In 1733, social reformers founded Georgia as an anti-slavery colony, where the poor of England could go to learn farming and develop themselves into hard-working, successful subjects of the English king. In time, however, royalist colonial leaders rebelled against the plans of social reformers. They looked north with envy to the Carolinas, where they saw wealthy white slaveowners. In 1751, proprietors fed up with rebellious Georgians surrendered the colony to the Crown and Georgia developed as a slave colony like the Carolinas and Virginia to the north. English elites who enjoyed land grants from the British crown ran the North American colonies in plantation style, shipping white servants or indentured labourers over to work the land. Reform lost out to repression.

In the southern colonies, the craze for tobacco smoking prompted intense land cultivation and great fortunes for white southerners. Tobacco, first imported from the Caribbean, changed the land and economy in North America forever. By 1750, it was the dominant crop in the economy, encouraging further slave imports through the 1800s and, of course, the addictive habit of smoking.

Northern cities such as Boston, Philadelphia and New York were, from the beginning, more concentrated on global trade and free labour rather than slave economies as in the south. Though slavery existed throughout the region, most northern colonies such as Massachusetts in New England were not plantation based and did not depend on slavery. Instead, they built family economies, with homesteads and farms feeding minor industry or factories, emulating the model of industrializing England. Fishing and logging remained the mainstay of economic life into the late eighteenth century and American independence in 1783. Wealth inequality was hence far less prominent in the north than the south. Working conditions were accordingly superior, including access to literacy, nutrition and rights, ideas that stemmed from increasingly liberal nations like England, France and Holland and were more accepted in the north than the south.

European economies – Profiting from violence

The Spanish and Portuguese did not invent plantations or slavery. These were systems of commerce and oppression long in place in the Old World. North-western Europeans – in particular the Dutch and English – did, however, introduce a new type of commerce in the centuries after 1600. This was an economic system hell-bent on the pursuit of profit and riches, and it would develop into modern capitalism.

As in recent centuries, the flow of money and bullion around the world, although passing through the hands of many traders and rulers in many societies, would enrich a small number of people and entities the most. From 1849 on gold rushes from California to South Africa would vastly increase the world's money supply, make fortunes for the few, but also create new markets and trade networks; in our case a few small nations in Northwest Europe controlled the new credit markets developing slowly around the world as a result from the increase in silver flows, primarily England and Holland. From 1500 to 1800, around a third of the world's silver supply ended up in China, and just as importantly became the currency of trade globally. Then as now, those who controlled the money made the money.

But even with the vast growth in trade across the Americas and Asia, Europe remained a minor player in the minds of most rulers, well into the 1700s. Leaders of

Ming China, Mughal India and Ottoman Turkey had no reason to fear Western merchants or to imagine Europeans would challenge their authority after 1800. It would have seemed unlikely that men in small northern European states would be able to dictate terms to long-standing, powerful empires. Indeed, most European states, in the west of Ireland, Scotland, much of Scandinavia and most of Central and South Europe, persevered with traditional subsistence agriculture economies, raising stock, or crops such as rye, barley and wheat. Very little changed in most agricultural economies between 1500 and 1750.

Yet, for better or worse, North-western Europeans initiated a new form of commerce, and thus economic life, in these centuries. First, Western European monarchs acquiesced to demands for trading rights from middling merchants and entrepreneurs. Second, Europe's traders proved greedier and more aggressive than others, and third, European financiers were more innovative in developing instruments for making money out of money. Ultimately, the layering of credit-based markets around the globe provided hegemonic control for a small number of Europeans with money and power, without the cost of military domination, land grabs or direct domination. As with multinational corporations today, everything was done on the cheap, increasing profits while limiting on-the-ground interaction. This was the origin of modern capitalism as we know it.

Some Turkish thinkers, presumably with their own prejudices, considered Europeans as particularly calculating and covetous in their dealings with other peoples. In one seventeenth-century Turkish novel, the adventurer Evliya Celebi is appalled at the great harm done to Native Americans by Europeans. Columbus, named here as Kolon, is seen by Indians in the story as thus:

They cursed those priests and Kolon, saying, 'Our world used to be peaceful, but it has been filled with a greedy people, men of this world who make war every year and shorten our lives.'[2]

Monarchs and merchants

Even before Europeans began settling the Americas, markets in Europe were undergoing a substantial transition. After 1500, regional commercial centres like Venice, Genoa, Lisbon, Lyons, Bruges and Seville were challenged by Antwerp in Belgium, which emerged as an international centre for trading in luxury items. Italian trade, like that across the steppes and Middle East, was eventually supplanted by commerce in the North of Europe. Italian traders in Cairo, Istanbul and Alexandria had long searched for spices and luxury goods prior to 1500. Venetian and Genoan merchant families fought for access to wider markets for centuries, but these small independent city-states had limited military means. By 1500 they were declining in influence, losing control of trade routes to English, French or Dutch merchants. Competition was creating winners and losers in commerce.

Like royals worldwide, European monarchs tried to tax populations to maintain power and glory, or to outdo rival families. As elsewhere, European merchants aimed to enrich themselves via commercial gain at the expense of their royal overlords. But profit-seeking merchants of North and West of Europe proved especially vigorous. Crucially, uniquely in this era, rulers in Holland and England acquiesced to traders' demands for autonomy, which would turn out to be a win-win approach.

In the seventeenth century, some European thinkers slowly began to argue that royal-imposed regulations, requirements and restrictions stifled profits and commerce rather than encouraging them. By the 1600s, European investors, royal or otherwise, readily funded exploration, using private wealth to support overseas colonization and otherwise expand global trade. They and their merchants got rich together.

European trade was already growing by 1500. Its share of global wealth doubled prior to the continent's global expansion. By the sixteenth century Europeans were trading far more with each other too. Baltic traders shipped caviar, whale oil, potash, grains and leathers from Russian ports. Scandinavians sent timber, wool, irons, tar, pitch, flax and hemp through European seas and rivers. Continental European trade grew even as the continent's economic powers competed with each other for global markets.

Greed is good?

After 1600 a new mentality regarding business developed in the northwest of Europe: the notion that all people, not just rulers, might aspire to acquisition and affluence. What's more, rulers, wealthy traders and aspiring middling types were able to pursue and display wealth free of shame. Workers in western parts of Europe readily got in on the act, pushing for higher wages in the 1600s with which to purchase exotic trinkets or luxuries from afar. Because of this social pressure from below, wages rose in North-western Europe, creating relatively egalitarian societies (mainly among men) in Holland and England. Indeed, wages were already higher in Western Europe compared to elsewhere, so this constituted a great increase in spending power for common people.

Steadily, a new business culture emerged that measured time by money, where items such as clocks marked hours of labour, and where managers used metrics to pressure workers to make more. In stark contrast, and more indicative of the world at large, Chinese elites in this era considered clocks mere trivialities, mere toys with no connection to production, to be owned and enjoyed only by elites. Few societies employed the notion of rushing, to make money or to meet a mechanical deadline. Whether this new form of measurement was a positive or negative for humanity remains an open question.

Financial instruments

In addition, from roughly 1650 North-western Europeans developed – or newly imagined – financial services that facilitated trade worldwide. Marine insurance, bartered in European coffee shops, persuaded those with money to invest and speculate overseas. Central banks provided monetary security to motivate wealthy investors. Funding and construction of physical infrastructure – docks, canals, roads and harbours – aided shipping, loading and offloading of goods quickly and cheaply. A budding newspaper trade provided crucial information for traders, sharing details in print that investors could utilize to predict and increase confidence.

An aggressive tendency to plunder ancient trade routes accompanied these European commercial innovations. Increasingly, by 1750 Europeans began to impose new ways of doing business wherever they sailed. This combination of overseas venturing and economic innovation subsequently enabled the first intercontinental empires to develop in the eighteenth century. Thereafter, the European model – imperial, nation-state economic system – intruded upon diverse societies into the twentieth century, either through outright colonization or through economic pressure.

In contrast, traditional trade patterns everywhere else worldwide functioned without systematic financial institutions to stoke the interest of the rich. Asian, Arab and African empires continued to place economic authority in the hands of political or religious elites, who in essence *were* the state. In Europe, merchants wrenched the reins of economic power away from monarchs, boosting domestic economies and national power through overseas expansion, while still deferring to the symbolic power of royal families.

Holland perhaps best symbolized this new way of doing business, where merchants dominated or shaped the state. This small nation moved away from restricted medieval, regional economies to a penchant for international trade, profiteering through finance, competition and consumption. By comparison, the French state regulated and dictated commercial activity, akin to rulers elsewhere in Eurasia. While in England, a mixture of private profit and state control developed.

Holland

The Dutch were the masters of trade in this era. Already in 1550 Dutch traders organized close to half of European commerce, each transaction enriching the Dutch economy accordingly. The Dutch state built up a vast merchant navy that secured shipping lanes, providing low freight costs to increase volumes and sales. Dutch merchants profited from international trade by specializing in moving other people's products. In the century before 1700, Dutch ships carried the majority of global shipping, and wealth and products from Russia, Southeast Asia, Turkey and the Americas enriched the Dutch economy. By organizing logistics, they could profit equally from Portuguese imports or Chinese exports.

After the Dutch captured the Southeast Asian Spice Islands in 1605, the republic's wealth increased considerably. Merchant elites, unrestrained by monarchs as was often the case, built Dutch companies, which worked as autonomous entities overseas, free from royal encroachment. Tellingly, the Dutch were so prosperous at home that few felt the need to emigrate. As an interesting side effect, their efforts to build settler societies like New Netherlands in North America foundered as the English settled in the region. New Amsterdam thus became New York.

Once Dutch soldiers fended off Spanish dominance in 1648, Holland no longer had to pay to maintain a high-cost foreign army. As the Dutch expanded to dominate trade globally, Spanish rulers were now forced to ask for loans from Dutch burghers! Whereas Spanish merchants were exploited and treated like open banks by the Habsburgs, those in Holland were a central component of the power elite. Madrid, Venice and Lisbon had long been centres of commerce, but the heart of the financial world now moved to Holland. A small state that uniquely favoured merchants and traders, Holland developed a privileged political and economic class, instead of rule by monarch or emperor. Elected officeholders, not absolute monarchs, cultivated a system of commerce that could openly exploit international markets without filling the pockets of need of indolent royals.

Faith in productivity

The Dutch made particularly efficient use of limited land, draining large lowland tracts that were often underwater. Using peat for energy, farmers rotated crops frequently, increasing food production significantly. Better methods of husbandry increased animal stocks, turnips fed animals in winter, while clover replenished nitrogen levels in soil. This same shortage of land also sent Dutch adventurers overseas to find new ways to turn a profit.

Dutch financiers created innovative financial mechanisms – for monetary exchange, insurance, credit. They invented a new institution, the stock exchange. The world's first central bank, the Bank of Amsterdam, offered access to capital at low rates. Established in 1609, the bank enticed investors in joining foreign ventures. New business practices like bookkeeping, currency exchange and the first securities markets meant money could create more money. Firms organized to pool skills and increase supplies of cash at hand, and social networks gave business ventures wide scope to make connections freely. Around the world in other places, small family enterprises, limited in their capacity to expand, remained the norm. But in Holland, private partnerships and limited liability companies proved better at adjusting to the needs of traders, complementing family businesses at home, but offering greater economies of scale for global trade.

Dutch tolerance also facilitated a cosmopolitan business culture. In 1492, Jews forced to leave Spain had found refuge in Holland, where they helped develop financial markets connecting Europe to Asia. After the Dutch Revolt against Spain in 1648, refugees such as Flemings, Jews, Walloons and merchants of any stripe who wished to trade were welcomed in Dutch towns. With a reputation for fair play among traders, Holland become the centre of a new global system of finance after 1700.

Dutch traders used this accumulating wealth to exploit overseas societies. Soldier-merchants set up a string of trading forts around the world: along the West African coast to Angola, down into South Africa, across Arabia, along the Malabar Coast west of India and east into Ceylon. By 1600 they had taken Portuguese colonies, competing with and beating the Portuguese in Brazil, Africa and Spanish America. In India, relatively isolated port cities detached from central Indian rule could not fend off foreign intrusions. So, when Dutch traders demanded concessions, they were usually conceded to with minimal resistance.

Between 1600 and 1750 the Dutch East India Company (VOC) controlled the export of millions of products, Dutch-made and otherwise. This inaugurated centuries of colonial involvement in Southeast Asia, as the company built connections with East Asia via ports in Canton, Taiwan and Nagasaki. The VOC built harbours, factories and trading hubs, to become in essence the first major global corporation. Connecting markets in Holland to the world's trade, the VOC offered stock options, reinvested profits from the spice trade, distributed profits to shareholders and accrued great wealth.

The tiny country of Holland thus introduced a new, unique attitude to domestic and international trade – the seeds of capitalism. The Dutch built seafaring towns, fishing ports and docks, connecting inland manufacturing centres and productive agriculture to global financial markets, using a large reserve of capital to profit from others' trade. It was in effect the first capitalist nation.

European trading nations did not only compete globally, they openly questioned each other's approaches to making money. What seems distinct is that Western Europeans began philosophizing about trade, forming philosophies and ideologies that justified ocean domination, positing a love of wealth and an appreciation of consumption. In 1664, as most Eurasian societies were frustrating traders or closing borders, the English mercantile economist intellectual Thomas Mun expressed envy at Dutch economic tactics. Here he cites Dutch hypocrisy at a supposed 'live and let live' attitude that was in reality one of harsh competition and suspicion:

> Behold then the true form and worth of forraign trade, which is The great Revenue of the King, The honour of the Kingdom, The Noble profession of the Merchant, The School of our Arts, The supply of our wants, The employment of our poor, The improvement of our Lands, The Nurcery of our Mariners, The walls of the Kingdoms, The means of our Treasure, The Sinnews of our wars, The terror of our Enemies. For all which great and weighty reasons, do so many well-governed States highly countenance the profession, and carefully cherish the action, not only with Policy to encrease it, but also with power to protect it from

all forraign injuries; because they know it is a Principal in Reason of State to maintain and defend that which doth Support them and their estates.[3]

The English aristocrat George Downing apparently agreed. When open trade suited the Dutch, open seas and free trade should prevail, but when it was in regions they controlled it was closed trade.

As he put it, somewhat sarcastically: 'It is *mare liberum* in the British Seas but *mare clausum* on ye Coast of Africa and in ye East Indies.'[4]

England

A commitment to competitive, worldwide expansion soon became the emblem of England, another marginal early modern state. Only about 2.5 million people populated the British Isles in 1500, having actually declined from 5 million owing to the Black Death. The only commercial participation this small island enjoyed at this time was in producing raw materials such as cotton for overseas markets. Even as late as 1600, over 66 per cent of exports were still basic woollen goods. From 1600, though, the English forced the Dutch to contest trade everywhere. The Dutch lost to the English repeatedly, as the Spanish and Portuguese had previously to them. Like the Catholic states before them, the Protestant Dutch would be ousted by a rising nation who made better use of its land, human resources and military, and was, at root, greedier.

Religious differences stemming from the Protestant Reformation in 1517 had amplified Dutch animosity towards Catholic Spain. Likewise, religious conflict motivated new economic attitudes in England. With Henry VIII's rejection of the Catholic Church in 1533 the English crown took a quarter of the nation's best land in a sudden windfall, dispossessing the church of its lucrative properties. When the pope excommunicated Henry for divorcing the Spanish Catherine of Aragon, Henry immediately married Anne Boleyn of France, to widen what became a permanent Catholic–Protestant division in Western Christendom. Vast tracts of highly valuable church lands were made available to noble cronies of the Tudors, who used new wealth to make England richer through trade.

Just as the Portuguese and Spanish had laid the path for Holland, Dutch adventurers thus laid the foundation for British imperialism, providing expertise and shipping advice that the British built on after 1650. The first English settlements in the 1620s were in the Caribbean, where Dutch traders provided credit, technology and skills, to facilitate planting of tobacco and sugar. English merchants followed Dutch forays into India also: English traders arrived first in Madras in 1639, then in Bombay in 1661, working to buy coffee, cloths and tea to connect to markets in China. The British soon chose to sell and ship slaves to the Caribbean. In cities like New Amsterdam, named after the Dutch city, English traders developed new centres of commerce in the

Americas, ousting the Dutch by 1665, and renaming it New York. This provided a base for further English expansion in the East Coast. In Australia and South Africa too, the British replaced Dutch settlers and populated those regions with English-speakers.

Women and peasants – Domestic resources

Worldwide, elites exploited the labour of common people in their own societies, both male and female. As in Holland, British women worked in the family and contributed considerably to the national economy. In both places, women played a dynamic role in economic life, planning and managing household consumption of goods and foods to keep families fed. Women in these more liberal states suffered fewer of the cultural restrictions found elsewhere regarding commerce and social life. North-western European cultures did not generally question whether women could manage finances or work in public. In addition, the bulk of the population, peasants, male or female, had greater freedom to move, especially in England. There were no official controls on movement, and since serfdom had long been abolished, people moved freely to find work, something unimaginable in most foreign lands.

We know that Europeans became voracious for global products in the 1600s. We know too that more people across all social strata participated in commerce by 1700. But huge sections of society were excluded from consumption in most parts of the world, including low-caste people, women, peasants or the enslaved. In North-western Europe, women participated and contributed to commerce, free of stigma. In moneymaking England, rural peddlers travelled the country offering wares to homemakers to the apparent pleasure of some homemakers. One gentleman noted the following in 1609 of women in England: 'A gentlewoman that lov'd to bable away her mony in Bone-laces, pinnies, and such toyes, often usd this short Ejaculation: God love me, but as I love a Pedlar!'[5]

By maximizing the labour of women and workers more widely, nations like England and Holland became richer overall. It is no surprise Napoleon is said to have derisively called England a 'nation of shopkeepers'.

Colonial resources

The first English plantations were not in the Americas, but nearby in the Ulster region of Northern Ireland. New beliefs about trade and land usage informed English expansion into its smaller neighbouring island of Ireland in the 1560s, which created the settlement of Protestant Britons on Catholic Irish soils. Elite English economic plantations took land from Irish peasants after 1550, initiating a process of colonization that would bring the British a global empire. Irish meat and dairy products comprised a key source of nutrition and profit for the English beginning with the reign of Queen Elizabeth (d. 1603).

Elizabethan explorers soon began searching the Americas for further riches. In 1602 English traders arrived in the Caribbean, and by 1607 had settled Jamestown on the eastern seaboard of North America. In the 1620s, English merchants focused on India. Soon Indian calico covered the bodies of English aristocrats, as imported wares began to change dress styles and inspire new consumer aspirations. As in Ireland, Indians did not welcome such incursions. Conflict was constant. William Hawkins, one of the earliest adventurers to Surat in India, was insulted and robbed by Mughal officials in 1608. Yet the British began to establish factories regardless, as their greater military technologies overpowered Indians.

British elites intentionally created laws to justify their economic gains. In 1700 and 1720, supported by the pointed guns of a strong navy, English officials imposed the Calico Acts, which prevented cheap Indian cotton from entering England, bolstering English production and bringing profits to England. Commercial laws were forced upon weaker foreign states anywhere the British sailed. Hostility with the Dutch was relentless. For 200 years after 1652, the Navigation Acts legally justified exclusion of other nations from using English ships to trade, ensuring more wealth flowed to Britain.

By developing the world's first robust navy, British ships easily intercepted hundreds of other nation's vessels each year, harassing commercial opponents through a ferocious process of what was in essence state-sanctioned piracy. As a result of maritime acts, British naval aggression turned a small state into an unrivalled sea power after 1700. With increased prosperity derived from global and domestic trading, the population at home grew from 4 million to 8 million between 1600 and 1800, even as many looked abroad to emigrate.

The British reached imperial power status by the late eighteenth century, and the protection of British merchants became a key aim of the state. The famed British navy became both a military and merchant organization, benefitting from strong official support. Royal monopolies granted to favoured allies made the monarch's friends rich in Ireland, India or the Americas. The monarchy rarely oversaw trade ventures directly. Instead, it granted private traders or companies licenses or charters, so long as they shared profits with the sovereign.

By the time of the American Revolution in 1776, over 2 million people lived in North America, mostly speaking English, not Dutch or French as might have been. They formed a nation with an Anglo elite, that traded with England primarily even after revolutionary strife. By the late eighteenth century, the British also had a foothold in India, and would dominate that huge subcontinent until 1947, enabling Britain to avoid serious losses from American independence.

British slaving

By the 1700s, British merchants supplied more slaves to North America than any other nation. The British were late to the slave trade, but made up for lost time in response to a surge in sugar demand after 1650. Though slavery in the Americas preceded the arrival of English traders, it is no small irony that the state developing the greatest domestic social freedoms was at the same time arranging, shipping and profiting from millions of enslaved humans. The first ventures began under the Royal African Company, chartered in 1660. Initially focused on acquiring West African gold, the company soon added slaves to its list of profitable commodities. Though it rarely actually made profits in its first decade, company activities helped normalize slave trading as a component of England's growing global trade.

The British would dominate the slave trade through the 1700s, shipping millions of people to the Caribbean and North America. Almost all slaving took place under the auspice of private companies run by merchants. Prior to the rise of abolitionist sentiment, slavery seemed perfectly normal. Tens of thousands of English sailors had in fact been enslaved in the fifteenth and sixteenth centuries by North African Muslim slavers, the Barbary Pirates. So English traders' entry into human trading networks elicited few moral qualms back home, until the late 1700s when moralists, both religious and secular, began to denounce it and advocate for abolition. British slavers were the major players until more enlightened Britons fought for abolition in 1807.

Despite the enormous human suffering of the slave trade, the wealth that flowed into Britain from slavery was a minor portion of national wealth. British slavery produced sugar above all else, which comprised about 2.5 per cent of overall GDP. Slave shipments comprised less than 3 per cent of English shipping tonnage in this era overall. Britain's busiest year shipping slaves was 1792, when 204 ships left England. Yet that year over 14,000 vessels were registered to trade, meaning that less than 2 per cent of British ships were directly involved in slavery.

Most global trade in fact occurred across Asia or within Europe. Intra-European trade developed in commercial networks based in Antwerp, Amsterdam and London. Domestic industries such as textiles, finance and insurance created more wealth to reinvest globally. Income from the slave trade, of course, injected wealth into the economy, but it was not the sole or primary stimulus for the eventual industrialization that would make Britain the most powerful nation on earth by the nineteenth century.

Self-interest as a belief system

By 1750, England was a nation with a large fund of wealth stored in a central bank, a financial institution which backed debt and prevented bankruptcies. The Bank of England oversaw a complex economic system where loans and money flowed freely. Such innovations funded overseas expansion by creating banknotes backed by gold and silver. The investor class trusted in the system, and because they felt secure in their property rights in liberal England, they could rest assured they would keep profits gained in their ventures.

In North America, merchant-run ventures such as the Plymouth Company, Bristol Company and Virginia Company of London illustrated to investors that traders knew best. Informed private investors made decisions instead of monarchs and

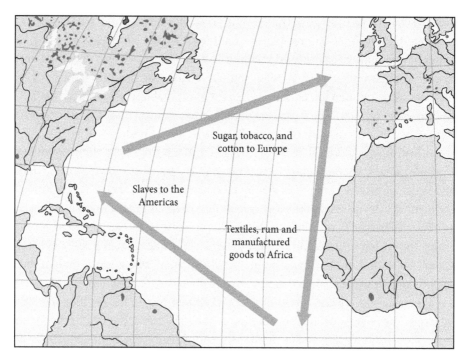

Sugar, tobacco, and
cotton to Europe

Slaves to the
Americas

Textiles, rum and
manufactured
goods to Africa

Figure 5.8 Triangular trade/slave trade (Wikimedia Commons).

aristocrats, proving a more efficient use of human and material resources and a better way to make money. The idea of joint-stock companies helped organize businesses and profits. Though countless people lost money (or died doing the work), a culture of commerce provided for constant opportunity to inspire people to keep trying.

Participation in the triangular trade enriched Britain as it did other European nations. The Americas also provided important nutrients from fish, energy from sugar, not to mention new desires to consume and smoke tobacco. Though imports from the brutal American economy contributed, Britain's economic growth in the eighteenth century was mostly due to home manufacture and global export. The highest estimates calculate that wealth derived from colonies for the British in these centuries was about 15 per cent of total (Figure 5.8).

English society became remarkably and uniquely commercialized between 1500 and 1750. In this period, a constitutional monarchy emerged that encouraged trade more than absolute rulers in Europe or elsewhere. Philosophers espoused the virtue of wealth and accumulation. Economic and agricultural productivity increased substantially, while the rumblings of capitalism and consumerism emerged in the eighteenth century.

By 1750, as Spain and Portugal faded into commercial irrelevance, England's military and merchant adventurers ousted the Dutch from markets worldwide. They also began to overpower their ancient rivals, the French, shaping an empire from

India to the Caribbean and North America, that would dominate global trade into the twentieth century. While Spanish monarchs and merchants extracted metals from the Americas to get rich, the Dutch and English invented new wealth in European markets by trading globally.

England and Holland employed efficient, modern approaches to economic innovation. Both had strong central states, but left economic growth to a wide array of actors, near and far. The French combined both approaches; a strong belief in landed wealth along with a commitment to overseas commerce. France remained comparatively centralized financially, but just as in most empires and kingdoms worldwide, royals and their cronies made decisions regarding trade in France, not better equipped merchants. This hindered French growth over time.

France

The histories of England and France intertwined for centuries before 1500. Royals and nobles in both countries developed strong, central monarchical states, with powerful military and economic capabilities. French expansion into North America began in 1605 just before the English settled in Jamestown. By 1624, French trading forts were established on the west coast of Africa, prior to English expansion into India and Africa, and the two rivals would try to undo each other wherever they could through the 1700s. However, domestic struggles and overseas military losses to British navy vessels weakened French power by the late eighteenth century, culminating in the devastating French Revolution in 1789. British commerce continued to grow throughout the eighteenth century, while French commerce took a markedly different turn after 1750, when imperial defeats, bad rule and economic crisis brought revolutionary turmoil and misery for millions of people.

Intransigent elites

Where in England an experimental curiosity regarding the potential profits of trade prompted emergent capitalism, French practices changed little from medieval finances. Intellectual theories idealized small-scale agriculture and local protectionism rather than open trade. The French economy was inhibited by the paranoia of absolutist rulers, endemic corruption and vast inequality that culminated in colossal upheaval in revolution and war.

As in Spain, French religious intolerance and political disunity stifled commercial growth in our period. Sixteenth-century religious strife discouraged those inclined to trade, exemplified best by the St. Bartholomew's Day massacre in 1572, when enraged Catholics slaughtered tens of thousands of Protestants, forcing many to flee abroad. After Louis XIV revoked the religiously tolerant Edict of Nantes in 1685, factional strife forced industrious French Protestants (Huguenots) to move to England or Holland. The nation's economy suffered consequently, as productive Huguenots – like Jews had been for centuries – were dispersed to Europeans trade centres such as London and Amsterdam, understandably disinclined to work for the French crown's economy.

Through the seventeenth century, France was the most powerful state in Europe, yet wealth was centred upon the king and his cronies. Income derived from victories in European wars, overseas trade and peasant labour flowed mainly to royal coffers, managed by a controller of finance loyal to the monarch. As in Spain, most of the wealth rested in the palaces of monarchs and their cronies rather than flowing to other classes or the economy.

Whereas English nobles paid taxes to the crown, French aristocrats were committed to avoid them. By the late seventeenth century, the English parliament held a body of representatives who maintained the right to approve new taxes to fund economic growth, whereas in France, Central and Eastern Europe, royals imposed taxes by diktat without asking for authorization. The French crown often dismissed debts or missed payments on interest, so international lenders – usually the Dutch or English – charged them higher interest rates. Forced loans became the only way for French royals to generate money and sustain a princely extravagance that thwarted national prosperity.

Running up debts

From the era of Henry IV (d. 1610) until the revolution of 1789, French kings swam in debt, and habitually taxed peasants and farmers to fund their wars and high living. The Valois dynasty clashed with their Habsburg rivals through the sixteenth century. Unlike English and Dutch leaders, French kings habitually interfered in financial decisions, shaping a localized court economy based on patronage, where merchants kowtowed to find favour with court. Instead of consultation, condescension informed questions around money.

French trade theories remained mired in conventional thinking. Jean-Baptiste Colbert (d. 1683) took absolute control of French finances under Louis XIV and persisted down a mercantilist path, even as the English and Dutch transitioned to a more fluid early **capitalism**. Colbert increased revenues by reducing corruption, but France's economy failed to modernize. Into the eighteenth century, French theorists called physiocrats remained committed to the belief that land, not trade, was the fundamental source of wealth. Like most worldwide, they could not imagine financial innovations that might use money to create money.

Ultimately, the famous Bourbon king Louis XIV (d. 1715), with Colbert's help, ruined the nation's fragmented economy through relentless military aggression. Like the Spanish Bourbons before him, upon his death he left an indebted state with enemies throughout Europe. Patronage fuelled Louis's court-based economy. Sycophants who produced nothing gained lands and favour if they attended court. French rulers simply could not extract enough from the peasantry to fund warfare or Louis's flamboyant court life, centred on his palace at Versailles. Between his death and the revolution in 1789, disorder and conflict characterized French economic life.

Autocracy as a rule

With minor variations, through the 1700s, Dutch, English and French societies became more centralized, modern nation-states. In varying degrees, merchants took power from absolute rulers to create national wealth in all three states and to unify economic ties across the country. In France, regional economies were not connected to the court particularly. In England and Holland, though, networks slowly connected the whole nation to one economy. France was more typical of the world at large, however. Elsewhere in Europe, economic fragmentation, traditional medieval economies, or a mixture of both, remained the model, as rural life and noble extravagance persisted through this era.

Located next to France, the bewilderingly complex Holy Roman Empire consisted of hundreds of tiny German-speaking principalities. Vast plots of unproductive land were owned by the church, obstinate landlords dominated peasants on feudal domains and gigantic Habsburg family-owned territories served as play gardens for the connected. In this fragmented Central European polity, tiny localities functioned relatively free from a strong state. Limited commerce enriched regional overlords, who provided protection for serfs or labourers as long as they worked hard. Since no large tax base existed to draw upon, nobles abused peasants to extract the maximum they could. Throughout Central and Eastern Europe, large landowners controlled grain production, literally holding peasants' lives in their hands, increasing the likelihood of poverty or hunger, while resisting market mechanisms or connections to international trade.

The European continent east of France was also mired in frequent conflict and insecurity. The horrors of the religiously divided Thirty Years War (1618–48) meant that for decades, roaming warriors were paid or paid off to fight for one side or another. As in the Crusades, war *was* the economy. Mobility was impossible and trade duly declined. While the greedy Bourbons fought the aggressive Habsburgs in endless royal rivalries, a third of the population of Central Europe suffered death.

Into the 1700s, the emerging state of Prussia in Germany would spend the great majority of its assets on militarization instead of commercialization. War, or preparation for it, was the main expenditure in a society where an ethos of frugality was sacred, and trade or profits were considered inconsequential. When the German Hohenzollern dynasty grabbed lands in war after 1701, they were handed to loyal military elites. The economy remained regimentally planned and controlled, rigidly constrained from growth or productivity.

Serfdom in the east

To the east, peasant lives actually worsened in this era! Farmworkers across Central and Eastern Europe subsisted just above starvation levels, dependent upon elites and possessing no sense of rights. Excessive taxation east of Germany extracted revenue

Figure 5.9 Peter the Great, Peter I or Pyotr Alexeyevich Romanov (1672–1725) ruled the Tsardom of Russia and later the Russian empire (© Bridgeman Images).

from a desperate peasantry through the era, generating negligible income for those in power while punishing the poor. In Russia, Poland and much of the region into the Balkans, labourers had to give five or six days a week service to lords, functioning effectively in complete servitude. By dominating peasants through the sixteenth and seventeenth centuries, Polish elites converted huge landholdings into self-serving, grain exporting plantations (Figure 5.9).

Russian life was illustrative of great inequality and exceptional in its harshness. In the 1500s a strong Russian state emerged among the knights of Eastern Europe, who fought off raiding Mongol groups from the steppes. Though the port of Archangel became a major depot for shipping to and from Europe, the burgeoning Russian state had limited access to the sea and weak links to long-distance trade networks. Lords and rulers exacted everything they could from labourers in what was in essence a state kleptocracy. *Boyars*, wealthy nobles who had been granted fiefs by the tsars, were similar to Ottoman *timars*, owning both the peasants and their labour.

After visiting Holland and England, Peter the Great (d. 1725) was deeply impressed and tried to develop a vigorous, modern economy akin to those emerging in Western Europe. He was inspired by his travels to open Russia to Western European values, and attempted to Westernize Russia. Yet while elites learned French and adopted Western attitudes, little changed for the masses, as most wealth eventually amassed in the hands of his family and friends. As in Prussia, Peter's was a war economy rather than a market for exchange. A giant at 6' 7" in a time when most men didn't reach 5' 7", Peter was so impressed by Western Europe he gifted Russian lands to Western elites to forge strong connections. His successors proved weaker rulers than Peter and lacked the same commitment to develop Russia economically.

Peter enriched the court and region around St. Petersburg, but reversed the few freedoms Russian serfs possessed. In 1649, peasants were legally classified as serfs, owned by their lords. Peter enriched favoured nobles while suppressing others, as he built a stronger personal, autocratic Russian state. As an indication of general disrespect for the Russian poor, his rule included fantasy military exercises in which he and his friends shot and killed actual men, who served as toy soldiers for his pleasure. Russian life was brutal at all levels: husbands habitually whipped wives and children, who worked on farms and tilled the land under strict supervision.

Russian wealth did increase during Peter's reign. Victory in the Great Northern War of 1700–21 won lands and resources from a declining Swedish monarchy. But conflict with the neighbouring Ottoman Empire, always costly, frustrated Russia's expansion to the south. Russian expansion extended to Asia in this era, as the state competed for resources with Chinese and Mongol tribes. In 1689, the Treaty of Nerchinsk settled disagreements between China and Russia, as both gained enormously at the expense of steppe societies. Russian and Chinese armies subjugated steppe tribes, initiating large-scale logging and mining for the benefit of state coffers. Over time, the Russian state steadily pressured Siberian populations, who had lived off reindeer and fur-trading, to submit to Russian control and surrender lands for agricultural purposes. Resisting Cossack populations were starved into submission, dying in huge numbers during the eighteenth century.

Russia, like China, became a huge multi-ethnic imperial entity through early modern expansion. It developed a top-down imperial approach to politics: democracy and commerce were never on the agenda. Outside of the growing cities of St Petersburg, Moscow and Kiev, diverse pastoralists and herders lived off the land as they always had. Some Russian merchants did look overseas, expanding into Alaska to compete with the English in Canada and trading down the St Lawrence and Mississippi Rivers. Though Russian traders sold pelts from fur-bearing animals to Europeans and Asian markets, no international Russian empire developed.

In sum, east of the Elbe River in Germany, personal bondage was customary through our period, lasting in some places well into the twentieth century. Dominant lords owned land, labour and wealth, openly exploiting peasants for personal benefit.

Trade remained medieval in manner and scale, and few indications of economic growth were apparent. Little would change in the ensuing centuries, until the Russian Revolution of 1917 – motivated by a supposed desire for equality – reshaped the region, and eventually the world.

Conclusion – The price of progress

In 1917, Russian rebels proposed a radical revolutionary political and economic system, Communism, which would purportedly, once and for all, bring justice to the world's workers and smash capitalism and its insecurity and inequality. In 1776, just at the end of our era, Adam Smith scoured the world's early modern economic trade systems and published a bible of sorts for capitalism, the hugely influential *Wealth of Nations*. This founding text of modern economics spread a new set of capitalist beliefs to inspire those interested in commerce: self-interest is virtuous, the pursuit of profit helps enrich people, encouraging others to work harder; all of society gains. This was the newly minted notion of **progress**, and this orientation and attitude still hold sway in most economic systems around the world. Commitments to one or the other of these systems would constitute the central ideological divide in twentieth-century conflict: communism versus capitalism shaped the century. As most students know, Communism did not fare particularly well in the long run.

As influential as Smith would become, no one thinker, state or social group planned the early modern economy or 'invented capitalism', however. Rather, millions of individual traders, enterprises, state representatives and indigenous people forged a new Atlantic trading system. This early modern global economic system developed from their many interactions. It was not modern capitalism, but it was the foundation upon which the current system emerged. It was founded, as we have seen, on exploitation and violence.

Whether worker conditions improved in the centuries between 1500 and 1750 is an open question. The pace of work certainly increased for most labourers, whose productivity was regularly measured by managers. Slaving from 1500 to 1650 was milder in quantity than in later centuries. It grew in number and intensity in the 1700s because of the rising demands of industrial competition, in an increasingly capitalized, connected world. How most people felt about their material life or economic status in the early modern era is hard to know. Did poor people care about inequality? Did rich people rack themselves with guilt over their comforts? We don't really know, but we do know they were humans like us, many of whom suffered greatly and lived in poverty.

Disparities abound in the historical sources. Archives are full of the records of Dutch and English companies, but contain little that reveal the experiences of subjugated populations. The voices of Eastern European peasants are even more silent than those of Indians or African slaves who were at least partially recorded by their colonizers. Most Chinese, Arab or Indian merchants did not find it necessary to record transactions regarding trade. The voices of the masses remain hard to discern. They did not appear to expect economic mobility, but surely they resented their status and plight to some degree.

Thus, enduringly difficult questions abound in world history regarding how Europeans became so globally dominant after 1750. To what degree was European wealth premised upon accumulation of capital derived from slavery? Did they innovate, with a more precise scientific world view that measured the world more accurately? Did higher wages prompt desire to tinker, and create efficient labour-saving devices? Were Europeans just lucky? Were they exceptionally wicked?

As the past two chapters demonstrate, the vast majority of humans suffered great cruelty in this period, to the economic benefit of a small number of elites. Peasants, slaves and workers laboured to kick-start what would become a growing world economy in the late eighteenth century. More tolerant societies helped ideas germinate, were more stable and more productive. Europeans had a greater penchant for trade than others, and literacy and education became more freely available to more Europeans around 1750. Though we may not know precisely how most people felt in this era, we have a good sense of what they believed. And to this we will turn in the next chapter.

Keywords

Asiento system
Capitalism
Volta do mar
Progress
Price Revolution
Usufruct

Further reading

Curtin, Philip D. *Cross-Cultural Trade in World History*. Cambridge: Cambridge University Press, 1984. Curtin presents interesting case studies from this period that shed light on the collaboration of local elites with powerful states and demonstrates the wild variety of interactions between colonizers and colonized.

Gunn, Geoffrey C. *First Globalization: The Eurasian Exchange, 1500–1800*. Lanham, MD: Rowman & Littlefield, 2003. Gunn argues very little happened in this era that owed much to European talents. Instead, all aspects of growth and development had precursors in Islam, Asia and the Americas.

Israel, J. *Dutch Primacy in World Trade, 1585–1740*. New York: Oxford University Press. 1990. A thorough and detailed study of the Dutch Republic, a tiny nation that dominated world trade, shipping and finance in the early modern era, tracing the Dutch trading collapse in the mid-1700s.

Klein, Herbert S. *African Slavery in Latin America and the Caribbean*. Oxford: Oxford University Press, 2007. A deeply researched socio-economic history of slavery, focusing on the Afro-American experience in Latin America and the Caribbean, covering the Portuguese-, Spanish- and French-speaking regions of the Americas and the Caribbean.

Neal, Larry and Rondo E. Cameron. *A Concise Economic History of the World: From Paleolithic Times to the Present*. New York: Oxford University Press, 2016. A classic text in its fourth edition, covering all periods of history and all regions of the world, comparing approaches to wealth creation and economic patterns and systems.

Interlude 3 – Economic obstinance

Disdain for commerce

As might be expected, the Spanish Empire reaped immense rewards from its takeover in the Americas in this era. Spain remained strong until 1650, financed by 16,000 tonnes of silver in the centuries after 1500. Roughly 180 tonnes of gold entered Europe via Spain in this era, but by 1750 that wealth would not reside in Spain or Portugal. Both had become weakened, increasingly unimportant powers in Europe by then. This was primarily a result of resistance among Iberian elites to economic innovation and inflexibility towards new market forces, which were increasingly controlled from Protestant states like Holland and England.

Intolerance towards non-Christians in Spain also handicapped the Spanish monarchy and economy. Spain might have gained from a rich agricultural heritage left by Muslims, who had resided in the Iberian Peninsula for centuries. Yet advanced horticulture and irrigation methods Muslims provided were lost when they were expelled in 1492. Religious intolerance towards Muslims, Jews and Christian Protestants forced talented traders to move to other nations. Spanish Catholic zealotry thus compelled the most skilled populations in agriculture or trade to depart. By 1700, while England and Holland moved towards modern industrial-capitalist practices and learned to benefit from global trade connections, the Spanish state remained committed to mercantilist thinking, storing gold in treasure chests instead of investing, insuring or innovating with regard to monies (Figure I.3.1).

Catholic states focused more on evangelizing their form of Christianity than developing trade relations. The Dutch, English (and to some extent the Catholic French) were far more interested in profits and business. Though they all professed similar views of the inherent inferiority of indigenous traditions they encountered, they were less bothered by diverse spiritual notions, persistently more focused on profits than piety.

Figure I.3.1 Pirate treasure – Spanish doubloons (© Getty Images).

Irritation towards uncompromising Spanish elites spread in Holland around 1600. Holland was a country with a very different set of class and commercial relations. In 1568 the Dutch, tired of being taxed to fund Spanish wars, revolted against Spanish rule in a bid for political independence. By 1598, Spain's national debt was fifteen times higher than its income. As the conflict dragged on for decades, trade gradually shifted north to the Dutch city of Amsterdam, which after 1600 became Europe's central commercial entrepôt. By 1648, when the Dutch finally beat them, the Spanish crown was out of money. The dynasty's ruined finances meant Spain was unable to secure credit, now loaned by mostly Dutch and English bankers. The Spanish economy essentially collapsed by 1750, by which time the peso was worth a third of its 1650 value.

Between 1500 and 1700 Spain's economy grew roughly about 20 per cent, similar to that of France's and Portugal's. Italian trade stagnated as trade moved away from the Mediterranean. During these years, though, Britain and Holland saw their economies grow 200–300 per cent, from a comparable starting point. The tiny Dutch provinces in fact pushed more wealth into Spain from international trade than American bullion had! As in Asia and most of the world, entrenched economic interests kept the spoils of commerce in Spain, thus preventing the spread of complex economies or early industrial production. Spain would be a poor, weak country in Europe thereafter, well into the twentieth century.

6

Criticism and conformity –
Early modern minds

Situating the chapter

Between 1500 and 1750, Islam continued to expand, spreading from the Middle East into Southeast Asia. Meanwhile ancient Eurasian traditions such as Confucianism, Buddhism and Hinduism also gained adherents in South and East Asian societies. As we have seen, Europeans crossed the world in search of wealth and power, Christianizing millions in the process (Figure 6.1).

As in past centuries, religious and philosophical concepts were never permanent or straightforward – rather, they were transferred, reinterpreted and reshaped to suit specific circumstances. Though new ideas about existence and meaning developed in our era, tradition remained the norm – few could dare question conventional worldviews. Then as now, most believers did not know of the origin of their belief systems or traditions, and imbibed them from childhood, through social and familial conventions.

In Europe towards 1750, however, some started questioning the privileging of sacred thought. North-western Europeans, in particular, advocated secular and scientific ideas, based on practical, rather than supernatural, understandings of nature. This was a significant intellectual change, as European thinkers compiled new empirical learning in dictionaries of learning like the *Encyclopedie*, published in France in 1751. This bible of knowledge aimed to record all the world's learning thus far, a veritable early modern Wikipedia.

In a period of bloody conflict over religious convictions, tolerant new philosophies championed broad principles of tolerance that developed into the individual rights regime of the modern democratic world. Those societies that fostered lenience concerning faith or cultural difference would, perhaps not coincidentally, prosper the most, by drawing on the ideas of many minds rather than just a few. Those societies where a tiny minority of male political and religious elites enforced ancient, assumed truths, declined in power and wealth. Then as now, knowledge was power.

By the end of this chapter, readers should be able to:

- Synthesize different cultural perspectives from around the world.
- Understand how religious and philosophical views changed or persisted.
- Evaluate patterns of transmission between complex and smaller societies.
- Explain how conventional views were transformed because of new geographic findings.
- Appraise the ways in which religious and political leaders in different regions approached scientific thought.
- Analyse the consequences of new ideas for different regions of the world.
- Hypothesize to what extent tolerance aided overall social development in certain regions.

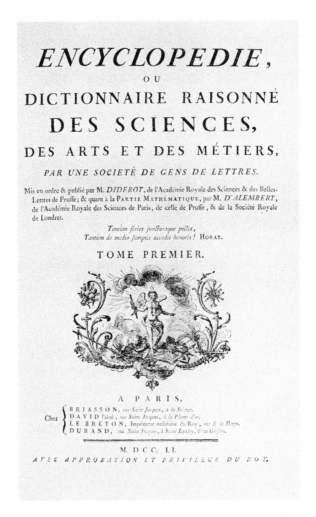

Figure 6.1 Title page of Denis Diderot's *Encyclopedie*, 1751 (© Getty Images).

Narrative

Atlantic crosscurrents – Challenging convention

Early modern sources for the most part don't tell us exactly what protagonists really thought in private, but we do know that the intellectual world changed more between 1500 and 1750 than in the previous 1000 years. A more rational method arose for examining the human condition, which the ancient Greeks had eulogized but which had been lost to history for centuries: **Reason**. Intellectual debate and the idea of reason as a guide to life entered history more systematically than ever before. Religious doubt, even direct criticism towards received wisdom, spread widely towards the eighteenth century in Europe. Though all traditions had their sceptics, scepticism grew most among thought leaders especially there, if predominantly in the west.

Scientifically inclined minds began interrogating the content of the heavens, the soils, substances like water and air, even the long-misunderstood mystery of the human body itself. All societies had done this to some degree, but in Europe by 1750, new thinking emerged from multiplying sources. More than ever, secular thinkers subjected priests, politicians, princes or other patriarchal figures to suspicion.

Everything changed with regard to human explanations for life on earth in this era. Long-standing **ontological** arguments – about the nature of existence – that relied on no basic premise other than 'God must exist', or long-practised tradition, were confronted with explanations drawing on reason, empirical proof and practical evidence. This meant the idea of being a human being on earth would alter immeasurably all over the world in the eighteenth and nineteenth centuries. Innumerable texts would appear, in ink, to question ancient traditions.

The printed word

Crucially in the early modern era, print literacy grew far more in Western Europe than elsewhere worldwide. Printed pages spread new scientific, military and technological concepts, drawn from many minds, to a wider population. Aside from enabling Europeans to dominate indigenous and ancient societies, the printing press opened minds to the possibility that a wide array of world views existed, based on different conceptions of reality, space and time. Publications in seventeenth- and eighteenth-century Europe abounded like never before anywhere. Travellers' accounts, novels and memoirs helped people imagine a new, more wide-ranging array of cultures worldwide.

Between 1500 and 1750, guided by print material, a new consciousness arose on the critical subject of truth itself. The emergence of a **public sphere**, particularly in North-western Europe, freed even ordinary people to question accepted dogma through open debate, newspapers, political protests and pamphlets. Such argumentation humbled dogmatic leaders, some of whom even began to empathize towards lesser types in their own societies or those in other cultures. The seeds of free speech, individual rights, the right to public assembly, to protest – later so common in democracies – emerged in these centuries, out of print culture. An information revolution of sorts occurred by the eighteenth century, which empowered the literate few.

Nevertheless, amidst these first hints of tolerance and critical thinking, two centuries of conflict and cruel domination of foreign peoples ensued. Print also contributed to the growth of propaganda. It could provide an apparent imprimatur of truth to bad ideas too. Reading words in print that justified racism, sexism, nationalism or prejudice could convince, or educate, otherwise reasonable people to act out of hate too.

Europeans excelled not only in intellectual dissent but also in exerting military dominance over around the globe. Europeans explained away wholesale violence against indigenous peoples by calling on their belief in the superiority of Christian theology. Europeans fought each other incessantly over religious differences, whereas elites in China, the Ottoman Empire, India and elsewhere strove to preserve social order by suppressing such dangerous questions. Governing monarchs and administrative mandarins across Africa and Asia insulated their societies from the encroachment of new ideas, in the process closing talented minds to new possibilities.

Testing tradition

For most of the early modern era, people maintained the same orthodox world views as they had for a thousand years. Yet in all complex societies, gifted minds used systematic thought to question convention. In China, philosophers like Wang Yangming broached new understandings of science and mathematics, building on earlier Chinese science. Indian and Arab astronomers continued to explore nature through mathematical approaches, as they had for centuries. The Indian saint Chaitanya even propagated a new form of secular thinking based on the material world, to supplement Hindu ethics. Yet in these sophisticated states allied political and religious authorities inhibited unorthodox explorations, shackling the minds of great thinkers and suppressing burgeoning scientific thought.

The discovery of New Worlds in the Americas after 1492 changed everything, opening up new intellectual possibilities for humankind. Atlantic crossings prompted new understandings of geography to inspire the imaginations of European thinkers. When westerners sailed to distant parts of the earth in the decades after 1500, they returned with more than gold or corroboration of new human societies; they brought back a new unbridled vision of a world with limitless possibilities, inviting new perspectives on the diversity and complexity of societies on earth, of nature and of intellectual possibility. These expanded geographic horizons, owing to overseas adventures, had a profound impact on intellectual and religious thought in Europe, emboldening attempts to harness nature and creating a new scientific paradigm for understanding the world (Figure 6.2).

Within Europe at this time, Martin Luther tore apart the predominant Western religious world view, Catholicism, beginning centuries of intellectual competition in the Christian world. Politically, after 1513, theorists such as Machiavelli posited secular, realist philosophies of power, bereft of regard for tradition or the spiritual world, based on power in the here and now. These were conflict-inducing ideas, put in print, that would kill many, but would over time bring forth a culture of debate.

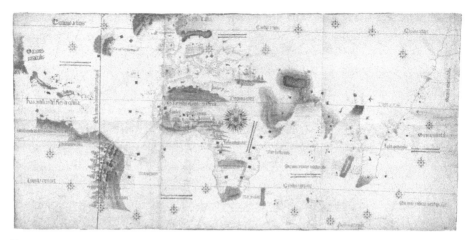

Figure 6.2 Cantino Planisphere – earliest Portuguese map, 1502 (© Getty Images).

Mixing minds

Not so long ago, Western historians claimed this new rational, methodical approach to the world found in Europe was **endogenous** – internally developed by particularly inquisitive and innovative European minds. But external, **exogenous**, global influences certainly influenced new ways of thinking. Peoples from the Americas and from societies across Eurasia had long asked similarly exploratory questions. Multiple factors, then, enabled a small number of Europeans to imagine new forms of intellectual, philosophical, mathematical and religious worlds – it was a world historical process, not solely a European one. That said, it was Europeans who set out to conquer new lands and to develop new scientific theories.

Encounters among deeply dissimilar societies increased in this era. Many traditions were challenged, forced to readjust or simply lost followers. World religions and philosophies had long been a muddled bundle of ideas, composed of untidy notions and unfathomable beliefs, fluidly imagined and construed differently by different people at different times. So new attitudes towards geography, the skies, the earth and the people on it were bound to cause turmoil, and they did.

Far from the Atlantic Ocean, across Eurasia, contrasting world views competed as they always had. The Caucasus region bordering Europe and Asia had always mixed religious philosophies from Catholic Europe and Christian Orthodox Russia with Islamic Sunni, Shia and Sufi concepts. Believers in Armenia for instance – the site of the first conversion to Christianity in the fourth century CE – combined elements of Zoroastrian sun-circles with a Christian cross, buttressed by persistent pagan practices.

But this era brought even more world views into competition. By 1750 people on all continents would have to reconsider their heritage and certain conventions regarding the past, the present and the future. The incorporation of the Americas into the world often diminished the authority of Old World traditions, stimulating efforts to imagine New World views to explain the world of the early modern era.

Fundamentalists find the Americas

Spanish conquistadors were not interested in learning about the beliefs of indigenous Indians. Catholic voyagers, more even than other Eurasian societies, were firmly committed to evangelizing newly encountered peoples. It is ironic, therefore, that new global encounters would strike at the unity of Catholic Christianity. The existence of strange new people, unmentioned in the Old and New Testaments, undermined the truth claims of Christian clerics and the papacy that for over a thousand years had upheld the faith. Despairing attempts by priests and preachers to explain the existence of newfound Indians prompted only further questioning and greater fracturing in the centuries to come.

In 1509 Pope Julius II, unfamiliar with native views or traditions, authorized Catholic monarchs, missionaries and explorers to convert the Americas en masse. Though Spanish and Portuguese missionaries often claimed success in mass conversions, they faced frequent disappointment. Indians, like Africans and Asians, were often satisfied with their own long-held traditions. Some, however, found it fruitful to form alliances with Europeans and were very interested in certain aspects of the new religion. Local chiefs discovered the selective incorporation of Christian teachings often augmented their own standing, and so took what components of Christianity suited them. Hence a merging of traditional world views took place over time in many places.

Although Spanish Christians conquered the Americas, they usually met resistance. Catholicism, as it emerged in Mexico, remained infused with earlier elements of native traditions, to the point that was in some cases little more than a superficial overlaying of Christianity on indigenous understandings. Moreover, religious orthodoxy proved difficult to enforce. Local populations fused Christian notions with their own philosophies in syncretic, practical ways, just as pagans in Europe had done upon the spread of the Christian faith in Europe, a thousand years prior.

Catholic certainty

While voyagers spread Christianity afar, the Catholic Church in Europe was itself the unwilling recipient of new ideas. The Protestant Reformation split Christendom in 1517 irrevocably between Catholics and Protestants. It was provoked by the church's unwillingness to reform in the face of criticism. Nonetheless, while adherents were lost in Europe, because of Spanish and Portuguese colonization efforts, by the 1600s, Catholicism became the dominant world view in the south and central regions of America. In the North, splintered versions of Protestantism prevailed in eastern North American colonies, as a result of Dutch, English and Northern European emigration.

Catholic and Protestant Europeans thus competed to colonize the Americas with New World views that altered natives' worlds immeasurably. In North America, church elders imbued Protestant societies with an Anglo-Dutch credo of self-governance, combined with a disdain for the hierarchy of the papacy in Rome. Protestants tended to question all elites just as they had protested Catholic rule, which eventually broadened social and political representation in the North. Indeed, the Puritans, radical Protestants who openly strived for a new society, eliminated the Catholic hierarchical 'chain of command', preferring instead a 'priesthood of all believers', in which individuals should decide what was right or wrong based upon their own conscience, premised upon one's own reading of the bible. This was not Catholic Europe, nor was it the world view that would spread in Catholic South and Central America.

Spanish incursions into Native American lands began in earnest in 1493, after Pope Alexander IV issued a bull proclaiming that Spain should possess all lands west of the Cape Verde islands off Africa. Spain's great rival, Portugal, protested, so the two countries signed a border agreement in 1494, the Treaty of Tordesillas, dividing any new lands discovered between them. At root, it meant that Europeans would now consider the Americas Catholic lands, regardless of the beliefs of millions of natives. Spanish clerics had long **proselytized** – attempted to convert – throughout Iberia itself. They forced resistant Jews to leave Spain in 1492, while making some Muslims convert to Catholicism (Moriscos). In the 1494 treaty the pope coincidentally sanctioned slaving posts on the African continent, asserting Catholic claims for the enormous expanses of new lands, and the inner souls of their inhabitants. Newfound trade routes also conveniently helped challenge the ancient Muslim enemy.

Columbus, like most early adventurers, was a fervent Catholic. The Spanish named most of the Spanish ships in the first transatlantic voyages after Catholic saints. They considered the conversions of lost souls among native peoples a principal goal of colonization. While Spanish soldiers slaughtered resisting Indians, priests welcomed the chance to save native souls. The adventurers' deep faith inspired them to spread their convictions to natives, even while their bodies carried diseases that killed millions.

The new landed nobility who migrated from Old to New Spain took control of vast American lands. A huge cleric population migrated alongside these middling aristocrats to rule native populations and shape a European-descent Catholic cultural elite. Settlers enriched the church through tithes, the main tax on land and wealth in New Spain. They also took control of the people they met.

Gods' wrath

Beaten by both European guns and germs, the Aztec and Inca logically presumed their gods were angry with them. Since they had seemingly been abandoned, they had no choice but to convert to the conqueror's faith, which was apparently truer.

The supernatural underpinnings of indigenous world views did not help fend off the arriving Spaniards. A certain fatalism almost predicted the end of their civilization.

Aztec cosmology was based on the god Ometeotl, who had spawned four lesser deities, and Quetzalcoatl, the god of light, mercy and wind in the east, who recreated the people after destroying earlier populations to form the Azteca. The Azteca, it was said, chose Tenochtitlan as their capital because they saw there an eagle atop a prickly pear cactus eating a snake, a sign that their gods had told them to look for. The Azteca believed this world would end with massive earthquakes. To support the gods, Azteca had to capture thousands of victims for sacrifice, and in gory rituals slice human supplicants with knives of obsidian. Alas, we cannot know Aztec attitudes to such practices, since Spanish priests and soldiers destroyed most Azteca codices – just as the Azteca had earlier destroyed Toltec cultural artefacts when they came to power.

Spaniards overcame Indians through a mixture of technology and awe-inspiring rituals. Spanish guns, horses and ceremonies overawed preliterate Indians, and though natives suffered so much in the face of Spanish conquest, many accepted the sacred assertions of Spanish crown and church authority. Spanish ships, for instance, baffled the Aztec aristocracy, who apparently believed ships were floating sea mountains. Along with remarkable ships and a new faith, the Spanish brought disease and violence, which demoralized their victims.

Many missionaries, in fact, respected native rites. Just as Africans and Indians responded differently to foreign incursions, the Spanish did not approach natives in a uniform way – church people, soldiers, fortune hunters and administrators differed in their evaluation of native beliefs. Some Spanish priests preserved native manuscripts, and upright men like Bartolomo de las Casas expressed bitter shame at the brutality of soldiers and other evangelists. De las Casas even positioned himself as the indigenous peoples' protector after 1516, defending their rights in front of the Spanish crown, against other officials who insisted Catholic theology justified enslaving Indians. Indeed, the Spanish king responded by outlawing Indian slavery. But, in a bitter irony, this spurred development of the Atlantic slave trade as the Spanish sought more African slaves to replace natives. Elsewhere, open-minded thinkers set up universities in Mexico City and Lima in 1551 to inculcate learning in new lands.

The battle between clashing cosmologies was in any case decided by physiological factors that nobody understood. Disease from Eurasia curtailed indigenous resistance, spiritual or physical. Native Americans simply had no immunity to the pathogens of Eurasia arriving with Spanish bodies. Even minor viruses like pneumonia or measles sapped body and spirit, and since it was palpably clear white people were not dying, Indians assumed they must either be gods or possess better gods. The misery of seeing dying family and friends thus facilitated conversions to Christianity. In 1521 one conquistador converted 30,000 Indians as he enslaved countless more.

Though the Spanish struggled to win souls voluntarily from natives, they succeeded in extracting labour. New Spain shipped tonnes of bullion, dug out by coerced natives to Europe to fight religious wars between the two main factions of Christians. The Spanish emperor Charles V was already busy battling Muslims and

Jews in the 1520s when he chose to counter Protestantism with military action. He and his royal rival, the Catholic Francis I of France, also competed to win papal favour, resisting the growing challenge of Protestantism in the Netherlands, England and Germany.

Like Spain, Portugal was in essence a theocracy, a Christian society founded with the express goal of ejecting Islam from Iberia since the twelfth century. In this era, both nations viewed global exploration as a religious endeavour, intended to counter Islam while gaining riches for Christianity. The Portuguese sailor-monarch Prince Henry (d. 1460) was a devoted Catholic whose aim was to outmanoeuvre Muslims who had controlled trade routes for centuries. Like the Spaniards, Portuguese understanding of Indians in Brazil was shaped by religious preconceptions. Conversion of Indians was central to European plans for subjugation. Firm-handed Jesuits forced thousands of labourers into settlements to work on ranches and vineyards. Indeed, it was largely through the Jesuits and other learned orders, that those driven by the desire to counter Protestantism made Catholic Christianity a major global religion outside of Europe,

In these centuries, Spanish or Portuguese Catholics could not or would not conceive that other peoples had alternate world views, often longer-standing traditions, with equally sophisticated ritual behaviours and explanations for human existence. Even in India, when Da Gama reached Calicut in 1498, he assumed that Hindu temples – most centuries older than the earliest European churches – were Christian. So hard did Christians try to manipulate Indian culture into existing world views that one seventeenth-century writer claimed Indians were probably the Ten Lost Tribes of Israel.

Theories of how to wage just wars, derived from the fourteenth-century religious scholar Thomas Aquinas, helped Catholic states rationalize the cruel consequences of their expansion. For many Catholics the domination of weaker societies in the Americas was proof of the Lord's plan for Christianity to spread globally. In Africa, Christian priests and princes stretched devout notions of fair warfare to the extreme, claiming that war was no sin if the victims deserved it! African slaves had clearly erred in rejecting Christianity they asserted; their fate was just in the eyes of God. Such thinking helped justify slave trading and forced labour – both of which enriched Christian European cultures in this era.

Africa – Indigenous beliefs, Christianity and Islam

Sub-Saharan beliefs – South of the Sahara

Like most regions worldwide in this era, sub-Saharan African societies did not consider spirituality or religious practice a separate realm from everyday life. There was no distinct religious or secular sphere as for many in today's world. Instead, beliefs were deeply interwoven with daily life, shaping social systems in every conceivable way, arguably even more than in Christian or Muslim states. In regions not controlled by centralized political states, spiritual affiliations served as the main networks to tie people together. In the eighteenth century West African Igbo society adherence to the Aro Chukwu oracle tied together a large number of different communities. African shamans would control shrines, using their power to punish wrongdoers, serving to bind together societies that lacked political elites or written legal systems. In more complex states with aristocracies and kings such as the Kongo, religious leaders played essential roles in limiting the power of elites, preserving spiritual ethics that decried excessive greed and overweening power.

The more isolated sub-Saharan African societies were not exposed to Islam or Christianity, though they possessed their own complex cosmologies and belief structures. The tribes of the Gold Coast region of West Africa combined veneration of ancestors, who lived in a spirit world, with regional and collective gods, all of whom derived from a single ultimate being, *Nyame*. The Akan people believed in condemning personal greed, to encourage a communitarian ethic. This began to change after 1700, though, as the growing Atlantic slave system introduced and spread a money-centred commerce that put a new premium on individual wealth.

Honour was often an important concept underlying spiritual practices in sub-Saharan Africa. In Eastern and Central Africa, tribes deeply venerated religious diviners or spiritual doctors. Often, it was difficult to enter the ranks of these social groups, who were not considered wealthy but were instead highly respected for their knowledge. The process by which one became such a figure was demanding. This challenge in itself brought honour both to the person and to the society that possessed such a diviner.

Islam and Christianity in North Africa

After 1500, Christianity and Islam spread through Africa. Islamic beliefs had long justified the enslavement of Africans. Similarly, Atlantic slavery, driven by Europeans, was buttressed by a monotheistic world view Europeans felt sure Africans would welcome. The spread of Catholic, and later Protestant, Christianity, into sub-Saharan Africa accompanied the development of the Atlantic slave trade, usually via the establishment of small European settlements.

Many African kings and individuals found the message of Christianity alluring. Portuguese priests won many converts in the Kongo state after the king accepted the new religion. In Kongo, most people integrated Catholicism into established practices rather than supplanting old ways. Leaders in Benin converted to Christianity partly out of practicality, to facilitate trade relations with the Portuguese, and Kongolese aristocrats employed European monks and priests as scribes and advisers. The masses saw Christian preachers as a new kind of priest, but whose god was just one more spiritual manifestation among many of their own. In general, cultural mingling took place in the spiritual realm.

> Though few questioned the ethics of European incursions, some intellectuals sensed or knew colonization invited morally dubious behaviors. As early as the sixteenth century, the noted French juror Jean Bodin (d. 1596) formed legal and moral arguments against the practice of enslavement, noting it was depraved, let alone unprofitable. But the words of ethical jurists could not counter stronger forces of economic and religious interests. Colonization and the Atlantic slave trade grew through these centuries, driven by faith and greed. Christian kings such as Alfonso of Portugal wanted African converts as much as African gold. So, monarchs made deals with local royals, offering guns in exchange for African conversions, such as this one in 1514:
>
> > With a very good will we send you the clergy that you have asked for . . . when we see that you have embraced the teachings of Christianity like a good and faithful Christian, there will be nothing in our realms which we shall not be glad to favour you, whether it be arms for cannon and all other weapons of war . . . we earnestly recommend that you order your markets to be opened and trade to be carried on freely.[1]

Ironically, early modern Europeans were simply the most recent Christians on the African continent, where the religion had initially formed in the Roman era. One of the oldest Christian cultures on earth was in Africa: Ethiopian kings claimed descent from the biblical King Solomon and the Queen of Sheba. One of the most important Church Fathers, St. Augustine, was from North Africa. But as Christianity entered African kingdoms, Islam expanded in several regions of sub-Saharan Africa too, similarly blending with local practices as it spread.

In our era, Solomonic kings of the Ethiopian region of East Africa also confronted growing Islamic emirates, which expanded through Somali populations. These Muslim emirates derived their power and wealth from connections to Indian Ocean trade and the Sunni-led Ottoman Empire. This conflict led to the partial breakdown of the thousand-year-old Christian Ethiopian state and its partial replacement by a patchwork of Islamic societies in the east.

Africans usually adopted Islam in coastal East Africa and the interior of West Africa via Sufi Muslim brotherhoods. Brotherhoods such as the Qadiriyya spread Sufi ideas wide. These often fit well with pre-existing ethical traditions that similarly stressed the subordination of individual greed to the collective good. African beliefs thus coexisted with traditional communalistic forms of Islam that all denounced individualism. Diverse African systems of belief absorbed different flavours of Muslim or Christian doctrine, integrating the two major religions into established regional practices.

The Islamic world

While Christians and Muslims mingled with or overcame indigenous African belief systems, they also interacted with each other in the Mediterranean and Africa. This was a continuation of rivalry that stemmed from the eleventh-century Crusades. Outside of the Americas, this was an era of Islamic expansion. The loss of Constantinople in 1453 had been an enormous shock to European Christians; 'Fear of the Turk' (or Muslim) haunted Christendom into the eighteenth century. However, while Christianity continued to spread widely in the Americas and Africa during and after our era, Islam's expansion was mostly over by 1750. Muslim philosophers and scientists inquired into the nature of the universe in this era, as they had for centuries, but, as we will see, conservative Muslim rulers prevented the transmission of scientific ideas at the very point Europeans embraced them, with great consequences for the future.

Ottoman Empire: Tolerance and traditionalism

Ottoman rule ultimately constrained Islamic thought in these centuries. Building on centuries of Sunni expansion, between 1500 and 1600, the Turkish Ottomans grew in power and influence in the Muslim world, with a firm commitment to maintaining Sunnism as it had been interpreted for centuries. They conquered Mecca, the spiritual centre of Islam, in 1517, and would soon dominate most of the Middle East and Central Asia, including the Balkans region of Eastern Europe. By the 1520s, Ottoman Turks seriously threatened Christendom. From the Balkans region, Turks captured an annual quota of enslaved Christian boys. Sent to the sultan as *devshirme* and forcibly converted to Islam, these slave boys gained exalted civil or military positions in Janissary units. This practice, along with the Ottoman sultan's well-known desire for Christian concubines, helped make Christian Europe acutely aware of encroaching Turkic Muslim power. This partly explains why Europeans in the Americas were so intolerant of indigenous faiths: they felt compelled to conquer other parts of the world for Christendom in order to counter the spread of Islam.

Sunni Ottomans offered considerable toleration towards non-Muslims in the empire. Though this was not tolerance as we might understand it today, nothing like the pervasive Christian anti-Semitism prevailed in the Ottoman world. Rulers did divide subject populations by religion, but minorities could practice their beliefs freely. As long as religious minorities in the Balkans, for instance, sent regular taxes to the sultan, they could maintain their own beliefs with some autonomy. Typically, however, from the Balkans to Africa, the upper classes readily converted to Islam for either economic or political gain, or out of conviction. Peasants often usually converted without consultation and acculturated into the religion over time, generation by generation. As in Africa or the Americas, most people continued practising a mixture of traditional and new practices that suited their needs.

Multi-ethnic and multilingual, the Ottoman Empire was more diverse than Christian or Asian states. The Ottoman branded Syrian, Greek or Armenian Christians and Jewish minorities conspicuously, as *dhimmis*, but they allowed them to live in peace. A relative lenience towards tax-paying provinces meant that regions like Albania and Montenegro freely mixed Jewish, Christian and Muslim motifs and symbols in clothing and culture. While Christians in Europe persecuted Jews, and as Japanese or Chinese leaders expelled Christians from their lands, Ottomans allowed loyal minorities to practice their faiths openly.

New strains of the Hebrew tradition even emerged within the Ottoman Empire in this era. Isaac Luria (d. 1572) founded a new, transformed Judaism known as Kabbalah in the sixteenth century. This renewed cosmopolitan Judaism (akin to Sufism in its mysticism) incorporated mathematics and literary analysis, exploring numerology and the hidden meanings in sacred texts. Followers believed they could save all of humanity by praying and practising correct action through a divine spark of insight. Such ideas crisscrossed the empire free of the anti-heretical persecution found in Europe for so long. In 1666 the self-proclaimed Jewish messiah Sabbatia Zevi (d. 1676) went as far as to announce he would take the sultan's crown; he was ridiculed and exiled by the sultan's supporters, but Jews in the empire suffered no collective punishment, as might have been expected elsewhere. Both Luria and Zevi generated renewed fervour among European Jews and shaped a resurgence in the Jewish faith inside the Muslim empire.

Limiting debate

Muslim political and religious elites mixed a commitment to tradition with tolerance in this era. Neither as violent as Christian Europe nor as dogmatic as Asian empires, Ottoman rulers accepted the existence of different faiths, without resorting to burning or torturing as their European counterparts did. This does not mean, however, that Ottoman sultans or imams accepted open criticism of Islam, or indeed new sciences that they feared might challenge religious orthodoxy.

Rulers and elites governed the Ottoman Empire with a firm hand, countenancing neither dissent nor innovation. The Ottomans placed Islam at centre of all life, combining both secular and religious power in the position of the sultan. The empire vested great authority in the clergy, which restricted unorthodox thinking. This discouraged intellectual exploration, while encouraging corruption, compliance and conformity. In the 1600s, therefore, a stultified intellectual orthodoxy became endemic. All activity, commercial, religious or cerebral, was expected to express the sultan's power, to the point the state controlled intellectual life. As in China, the Ottomans prioritized social stability over new ideas or social progress.

Some Europeans such as Francis Bacon conceded there were many possible sources of faiths. In 1620 he wrote:

Neither is it to be forgotten that in every age natural philosophy has had a troublesome and hard to deal with adversary – namely, superstition, and the blind and immoderate zeal of religion. For we see among the Greeks that those who first proposed to men's then uninitiated ears the natural causes for thunder and for storms were thereupon found guilty of impiety. Nor was much more forbearance shown by some of the ancient fathers of the Christian church to those who on most convincing grounds (such as no one in his senses would now think of contradicting) maintained that the earth was round, and of consequence asserted the existence of the antipodes.[2]

Because intellectual debate on the cosmos, nature or society brought uncertainty, Ottoman elites suppressed it. They feared print technology since it promoted debate. The first book was published in the Ottoman Empire in 1493, and printing might have developed as it did in Europe. But religious leaders resisted technologies that spread words and ideas, or invited subversive thinking. The irony is that fifteenth-century Europeans first learned of paper production from the Islamic world through Spanish Muslims. But, after a prayer book was printed in 1610, a century passed before a Greek Orthodox printer in Syria printed the second, in 1706. By contrast, the fledgling English colonies in North America had a working press by 1640, and a woman in colonial Maryland, Dinah Nuthead, operated one by 1695. China, Japan and Korea all printed many books by 1595, and India printed large numbers of books in the seventeenth century.

Some Muslim scholars such as Ibrahim Muteferrika (d. 1745) advocated for the printing press. Indeed by 1726, works on geography and the natural sciences were published. Around 1,000 titles circulated, including secular texts. But Ottoman rulers shut down the presses in 1742, convinced that the printed word was irreligious. This decision brought a century-long decline in the empire's fortunes. Weak and dogmatic, the Ottoman Empire by the mid-eighteenth century became known as the 'sick man of Europe'.

There is an historical irony here, since Arabs had studied astronomy and mathematics for centuries, and Turkic thinkers had long studied the heavens in Central Asia. Turkic scholars such as Ulugh Beg (d. 1449) studied astronomy through observations and instrumentation in Samarkand well before the Scientific Revolution.

Muslim scholars gathered data tables, copied and translated texts, and some likely found their way to Europe. But the Muslim world failed to sustain these scientific explorations.

Just at the point Europeans began exploring the heavens and earth by theorizing and experimenting, the Sunni world welcomed an even more doctrinaire strain of Islam, Wahhabism. An exceptionally fundamentalist world view arose in the eighteenth century, espoused by Muhammad Ibn Saud, a Saudi leader who accepted the ultra-conservative ideas of Muhammad ibn Abd al-Wahhab (d. 1792). Spreading outward from the new Saudi kingdom, centred on the holy city of Mecca, Wahhabism discouraged Muslims further from the study of science, innovation or curiosity towards other world views. Madrasas taught the Quran, exploring religious legal traditions exclusively, but not science or technology.

Sunni intellectual orthodoxy hardened among Muslim elites in the eighteenth and nineteenth centuries. By interpreting Islam through an orthodox lens, those in power aspired to purified understandings of Islam, relying on tradition. They suppressed mathematical, philosophical and scientific ideas that had percolated through the Muslim world as long ago as the thirteenth century. They would fall behind in the coming centuries.

Safavid security – Sunni versus Shia

Sunni elites in the Ottoman Empire rejected more than science or secularism. They resisted alternative views of Islam too. They considered Sufism as a mystical threat to continuity, so it remained confined to less powerful merchants, travellers and mystics. The other major strand of Islamic belief, Shiism, remained a major threat, since it was the centrepiece of Persian philosophy.

Sunni Ottomans competed with their key rivals, the Persian Safavids, who were Shiite. Unlike the Protestant–Catholic divide that erupted in 1517, the schism between Sunnis and Shias originated with Islam's seventh-century origins. It hardened in this era, when militant Persian Safavids came to power in 1501, committed to another version of Islam. Though originally founded by Sufi orders, the Persian dynasty practised Shiism, and stridently resisted Sunnism.

The Safavid dynasty originated in 1501 with growing mystical devotion towards a new charismatic leader, a fourteen-year-old boy named Ismail who religious leaders declared the messiah. Known as the *shah* – ruler of all – he brought about the conversion of all Persians to Shiism. Claiming to be the twelfth imam, Shiites considered him the saviour they had long expected to return to earth. He also claimed to be the reincarnation of all the great prophets of the past: Moses, Jesus, Muhammad, Abraham, Noah, Adam (even Alexander the Great!) 'Twelver' Shiism hence became the official religion of Persia and most followers remain known as twelvers (differentiated today from seveners and other sects who regard different imams as the true successor to Muhammad).

Intellectually, the Safavids allowed their scholars greater latitude in pursuing inquisitive studies than their Ottoman counterparts. The renowned school of Isfahan brought a seventeenth-century cultural renaissance – men like Mir Damad (d. 1632) studied the nature of the cosmos, stressing the connection of all humans through space and time. The mystic philosopher Mir Fendereski (d. 1640) and his follower Mulla Sadra, (d. 1640) formed an influential school of transcendence that delved into the origin of all humanity on earth. The ideas of Mulla Sadra, regarded as the second most important Muslim thinker after the medieval philosopher Avicenna, foreshadowed modern religious ecumenical studies.

Indeed, Persian scholars questioned existence in a manner similar to that of twentieth-century European existentialist thinkers. Persian thought to some degree mirrored innovative European ideas in this era, but Persian culture, like Ottoman society, did not allow for scientific investigation beyond mystical philosophy. Rather than applying science for practical uses, Persians, like Indians, studied pure science in theory only.

Some, like the important Iranian poet and student of ethics Mohsen Fayz Kashani (d. 1680), spoke of aspiring towards self-perfection through intuition. Still, he nonetheless directed Islamic thought back towards traditional theology. Intellectual deviants, mystics, and other theologians, he argued, had gone astray from the **hadiths** and Koran. Through such powerful traditional thinking Persian thinkers stifled innovative thought. By 1722 the Safavids, like the Ottomans, succumbed to military and political decline. Persian thought did not flourish after this point, and constant conflict with their Ottoman rival undermined Safavid stability.

Insecurity increased in the region also through conflict with Sunni Pashtun minorities (in modern Afghanistan). Afghan culture was shaped profoundly by the poetry of Khushal Khan Khattak (d. 1689) a famous fighter whose voluminous writings and ideas inspired Afghans to resist Persian Safavid and Indian Mughal incursions. A notable female poet-warrior, Nazo Tokhi (d. 1717), likewise inspired Sunnis across Afghanistan. This female fighter led armies, motivating the formation of a separate Afghan identity, distinct from Ottoman Sunni or Iranian Safavid culture. A complex culture thus emerged in the Afghan region, with an identity forged through its geographical location between the Ottomans and Safavids to the west, and the Mughal Empire in modern-day India to the southeast (Figure 6.3).

Mughals – Muslim rule in Hindu India

Like Pashtuns and other Afghans, the majority Hindu population of India resisted the encroachment of neighbouring Islamic empires. Though culturally Hindu and Buddhist for over a thousand years, most of India in this era was actually ruled by a dynasty of Sunni Turkic Muslims. From 1526 until the mid-eighteenth century, the Mughal Empire dominated modern-day India and Pakistan, after which the British would invade.

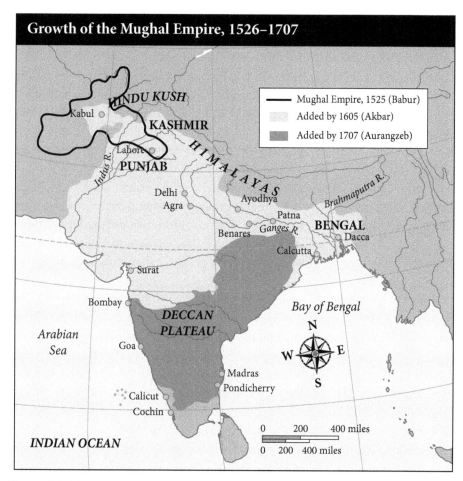

Figure 6.3 Mughal Empire growth, 1525–1707 (Wikimedia Commons).

Though more accepting of religious minorities than the Safavids, Mughal leaders were similarly cautious about permitting freethinking scholars to influence society. The Mughals initially inclined towards an open pursuit of ideas. Emperor Akbar (d. 1605) supported literature and poetry, studying the Persian language and recognizing the great diversity of philosophies in central Eurasia and beyond. Akbar freely entertained representatives of different schools of Islam, Christianity, Buddhism, Jainism, Hinduism and Judaism, enjoying spiritual lectures in his court. He even devised a new religion combining these world views – with him as its prophet! However, when Akbar attempted to contain religious conflict in Mughal society, orthodox Sunni religious leaders condemned him for his lenience.

As elsewhere, Indian thinkers pondered how to improve society for the good of all. Chaitanya Mahaprabhu (d. 1534) looked to reform civilization through the Hindu concepts of yoga and pure love. He led the Hindu Bhakti reform movement and taught that by enthusiastic singing, dancing and chanting the many god's names, perfect poetry could be produced, and all people could improve themselves and the world. Known later as Hare Krishna, this inspiring thinker broadened Hinduism's appeal, and has since spread worldwide through missionary activity and joyful action.

Non-applied science

Like Persians and Arabs, Indians had developed home-grown methods of studying nature and the universe well before Europeans. The sixteenth-century Kerala School calculated elliptical orbits for planets, continuing a long Indian tradition of cosmology. Indians had invented the mathematical notion of zero in the seventh century. Hindu advances continued in this era, as scholars strove to pinpoint *pi* to a specific number of digits, a crucial component for understanding mathematics.

Intellectuals such as Achyuta Pisharati (d. 1621) explored nature empirically, measuring tides, moons and planetary motion. Traditional mysticism informed Pisharati's understanding of nature and approach to medicinal healing of the body; Brahmanic prayers were central to his work and the stream of followers who developed his ideas. His students studied Sanskrit poetry and hymns to understand mathematics, the body and the universe. Others such as Mulla Mahmud Jaunpuri (d. 1651) developed theories of logic and astronomy, while Kamalakara (d. 1700) produced volumes on astronomical and mathematical calculations to understand trigonometry. His advanced formulae helped advance science using Arabic numerals, which the West made use of later. Jagannatha Samrat (d. 1744), like Kamalakara, developed Muslim science, working on instrumentation, astronomy and mathematics to grasp the nature of the cosmos.

But Mughal India put much of this sophisticated knowledge to ceremonial or philosophical use rather than practical application. Like in Persia and Asia, pure science did not develop into applied technology in India. As often occurred across Eurasia, stubborn rulers obstructed the dissemination of new thought. When Jaunpuri tried to persuade Emperor Shah Jahan to build an observatory, religious leaders fearful of losing control intervened. As elsewhere, in India, Sunni orthodox elites resisted freethinking and preferred to contain secular inquiry. Like Fashani in Persia, Ahmad Sirhindi (d. 1624) redirected Islamic thinking back towards orthodoxy, countering both foreign ideas and unorthodox local cultural forms such as Sufism. An important follower of Sirhindi, Shah Waliullah (d. 1762) moved the Mughals further towards hard-line thinking in the eighteenth century, promoting the enforcement of Islamic sharia law via the all-powerful caliph. Waliullah rejected not only Sufi mysticism but also scientific innovation.

Though gifted with remarkable thinkers, India was fragmented politically and religiously. High-caste Hindus considered their Muslim overlords ritually unclean and thus disdained the Islamic elite. Muslim Moghul tolerance of the Hindu majority waned after 1700. Emperor Aurangzeb (d. 1707) subjected Hindu populations to religious oppression and repressive taxation, antagonizing vast numbers of Indians. Previous Mughal emperors had refrained from forcing wholesale conversions on the Hindu population. Some upper-class Hindus converted to Islam out of economic practicality, while continuing Hindu practices. But this elite collaboration only served to diminish loyalty from the lower classes and regional Hindu social groups. Such tensions between Hindu and Muslim world views therefore weakened an already loosely unified empire and prevented a common Hindu approach to understanding nature.

Further intellectual fragmentation developed with the rise of Sikh kingdoms in the Punjab region of India. Beginning in the sixteenth century, a new major religion developed, essentially mixing Hindu and Muslim creeds, under the leader and founder of Sikhism, Guru Nanak (d. 1539). Sikhs aspired to a life of accomplishment, with regard to both family and business, openly criticizing corruption in elite Muslim and Hindu circles. Emperor Aurangzeb's intolerant attitude towards Hinduism provoked not only Indian irritation but also a major Sikh revolt in the 1700s. Decades of dissent through the later seventeenth and early eighteenth centuries served to fracture the weakening Mughals, with Muslims, Hindus and Sikhs at odds in the region.

The arrival at Indian ports of Europeans with gunboats would further fragment India. Indian intellectuals, rulers and peasants would have to confront Dutch, English and French adventurers who, along with the Portuguese, brought a wholly different world view by the 1600s. The Portuguese had been on the Indian coast since the early 1500s, and by 1612, the British East India Company began building forts and trading posts around Bombay, using its harbour as a base from which to expand its control over India. When Muslim kingdoms fought Hindus in the southern Vijayanagar kingdom, Europeans used the opportunity to establish and solidify bases at Goa, Cochin and Colombo. Fragmentation served Europeans nicely (Figure 6.4).

Like Indians in the Americas, Indians in Asia were regionally diverse, and likewise this division provided opportunity for foreigners to dominate the subcontinent. Regional rivals such as the southern warrior queen Keladi Chennamma (d. 1689) fought Mughal armies in the south of the continent, willingly making pacts with European traders with no loyalty to the Mughal Empire.

Though female fighters such as Keladi led soldiers into battle, chauvinism towards women persisted throughout the Muslim world. In Mughal society, as in the Ottoman and Safavid empires, women played little or no part in intellectual life. Ottoman sultans employed up to 5,000 women as sexual slaves in harems, to demonstrate status and sexual potency, while husbands and sons expected deference from wives and mothers. By 1750, at least some European women could openly criticize patriarchal society, but women in Muslim societies could not engage publicly with ideas. In the Muslim world, as in the Confucian, Hindu and Buddhist traditions that shaped much of Asia, it was generally accepted that women served an important role in society. But in Islam, as in Asia, that role was mostly confined to family and home.

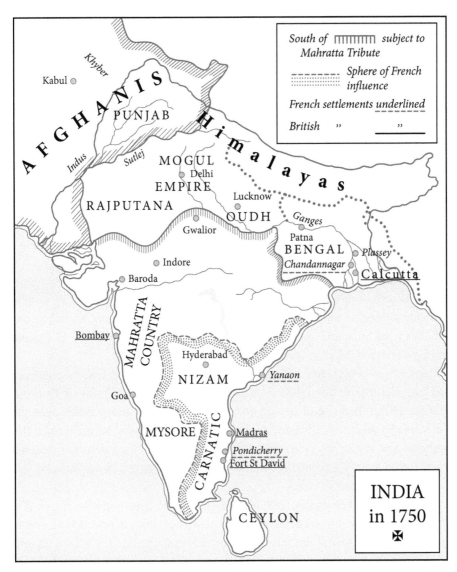

Figure 6.4 Map of Fragmented India in 1750. http://etc.usf.edu/maps/pages/3600/3671/3671.htm. Accessed 22 March 2021.

As in Islam, Asian traditions had long ago settled on women's subservience to men. Hence, women could not rise to counter traditional world views in either the Arab world or Asia.

Arab, Indian or Asian perspectives generally explored the realm of natural philosophy, studying nature for its own sake, rather than seeking to manipulate it scientifically to benefit humanity. This limited useful application of intellectual exploration.

Asian ideas – Mixing mindsets

Monotheistic ideas would also spread into Asia to challenge traditional world views in this era. Along with the onslaught of European science, advocates of Islam and Christianity made great inroads into Asian societies between 1500 and 1750.

Absorbing monotheism

Most prominently, traders introduced Islamic ideas into Southeast Asia (where more Muslims live today than in the Middle East). The sultan of Aceh converted his people to Sunni Islam in 1600 and the Javanese followed in 1625. Commerce served as the vehicle for conversion, which was both spiritual and practical. Both kingdoms received key protection from Ottoman Turks in return for spices. Converting to Islam served the practical needs of elites in both societies.

While Muslims won converts in Southeast Asian islands, Spanish and Portuguese Christians arrived in the islands of the Philippines, a region populated by animist-practising natives in which Asian and Muslim merchants had long traded. Spanish Catholics used force and coercion to control and convert most of the Philippines, creating a unique Christian society in Asia.

Spaniards, of course, faced fierce resistance from natives. The fearless indigenous chief Lapu-lapu famously killed Ferdinand Magellan in 1521, refusing to declare loyalty to Philip II's Spain or convert to Catholicism. While native rebels attempted to repel the Spanish, the Spaniards worked to expel Chinese and Japanese rivals from Southeast Asia throughout the seventeenth century. Following extensive missionary efforts, Catholic priests began the process of Christianizing the Philippines, bringing over 300 years of Spanish rule.

Often, when Catholicism spread into indigenous societies, native women lost the social standing they enjoyed before the Spanish arrival. Indeed, priests took over the rituals and ceremonies that native women had long managed. As more Spanish arrived through the 1600s, *indios*, or Filipino natives, found themselves relegated to the bottom of the social order. Native Malays, some of whom sided with the Spanish, were ultimately enslaved, forced to build the galleons that moved silver from Mexico to Spain and China via Manila.

Catholic certainty of one true God contrasted with the more fluid, fragmented religious world views of Asians. In most of Southeast Asia, for centuries, a loose mingling of world views prevailed in everyday practice, not one faith. Hindu or Muslim rulers generally conquered societies who remained animist or practised forms of Buddhism. The spread of Chinese ideas faced similar limits in South-east Asia. In Vietnam, for instance, though Confucian thinking prevailed to some degree, Vietnamese people still practised a diverse mixture of traditional beliefs. Everywhere in Asia, mixed mindsets prevailed over doctrinaire monotheism.

Japan

Confucianism, or more accurately Neo-Confucianism, began to shape Japanese thought in this era, known in Japanese history as the Edo Period (1603–1868). Influential Confucian scholars such as Fujiwara Seika (d. 1619) and Hayashi Razan (d. 1657) dissented from the long-established Japanese Shinto and Zen Buddhist world views. Confucian thought would continue to influence elite thought in Tokugawa society until Americans arrived in the 1850s. This was for good reason: stability remained the overall objective and Confucianism extolled stability. A century of military conflict had culminated in the Battle of Sekigahara in 1600, bringing victory for the warlord Tokugawa Ieyasu and unification of the country. The Japanese emperor, revered as a god, served as the spiritual figurehead for those in power through these centuries.

Like others in Asia, Japanese people employed a mixed approach to devotion, practising Shinto, Confucianism and Buddhism in various measures from day to day. Buddhism continued to prevail in Japan as it also served the Japanese state. Wealthy temples registered families to secure taxation and stability for government. Although populations throughout Asia continued to practice Buddhism in this era, the ancient tradition spread only to Tibet, where Mongol khans announced the first Dalai Lama in 1578, bringing Tibetan Buddhism to the region. It was constrained in growth by both Confucianism and Islam.

Under the Tokugawa dynasty, Japan became increasingly suspicious of foreign influences and ideas. To ensure cultural isolation and aid consolidation of his new dynasty, Tokugawa Ieyasu had banned Christianity and foreigners in 1612. Portuguese missionaries' hopes for mass conversion thus perished. There were consequences for this isolation. In the 1770s, for instance, Japanese physicians were dumbfounded to find Dutch anatomy books illustrating dissection and other modern physiological practices. Some Japanese thinkers avidly pursued what became known as Dutch Learning in the late eighteenth century, but concerned warlords allowed only limited contact with Europeans. Japan would thus be shaped by varying cultural traditions but not welcome science or modernity.

The Chinese way

In the sixteenth century, as Confucian ideas spread in Asia, China's technical expertise in the intellectual realm also increased with print culture and resultant rising literacy. One indicator of growing literacy is that more of the population felt confident enough to attempt the notoriously difficult civil service examinations, with even lower-class applicants aspiring to reach the highest levels of learning.

Continuing a long Chinese tradition of studying astronomy and cosmology, the renowned Neo-Confucian scholar Wang Yangming (d. 1529) pursued the study of empirical, provable science. He scrutinized ancient texts with a critical eye, and advocated for new scholarship and investigation. A campaigner for education, learning and active inquiry, Wang brazenly declared that Confucius was merely a historical figure, to be critiqued, and that new visionaries should aspire to change Chinese culture. Working to influence urban elites, he offered a new optimistic view of human nature. Yet, by 1700 his ideas fell out of favour, as the more ethereal ideas of the philosopher Liu Zongzhou (d. 1645) influenced court and state. Liu updated and criticized Wang's ideas, inclining all-powerful emperors to oppose the practical, objective study of nature and focus on further updating ancient Confucian thought for its own sake.

Just as Neo-Confucian thought was cemented in Chinese intellectual life in the sixteenth century, Europeans began arriving with strategies for converting huge numbers of Chinese to Christianity. After Portuguese Jesuits arrived in China in 1583, Catholic Christianity spread throughout Asia and entered the centre of the formidable kingdom. Just as Native Americans had to reckon with alien Christian ideas, Confucian emperors now had to contend with foreign ideas for which they were ill-prepared. Portuguese kings sent missions to aggressively convert Chinese people to Christianity, spreading the gospels to leaders, with an eye to converting masses. The Jesuit Order, founded by Ignatius of Loyola in the 1530s, aimed at the direct education and conversion of elites, so that masses conversions might soon follow. The Italian Jesuit scholar Matteo Ricci (d. 1610) moved to China and even attempted to synthesize Confucianism with Christianity, impressing the emperor with his knowledge of astronomy and mathematics.

As in the Muslim world, however, emperors subdued Chinese intellectuals. They discouraged innovative thinkers from studying anything but the classics, which meant that only poetry and prose from the 2,000-year-old Han world could be published. Hence a world view expressed in literature revolved around a sphere where demons, ghosts, folk tales and ethereal happenings prevailed. Published around 1750, one of the major works of Chinese literature was replete with supernatural content. Its author Pu Songling mixed reality with fantasy, and through enchanted exposition, her narrator tried to improve moral standards and expose corruption:

LI. – DEATH BY LAUGHING.

A Mr. Sun Ching-hsia, a marshal of undergraduates, told me that in his village there was a certain man who had been killed by the rebels when they passed through the place. The man's head was left hanging down on his chest; and as soon as the rebels had gone, his servants secured the body and were about to bury it. Hearing, however, a sound of breathing, they looked more closely, and found that the windpipe was not wholly severed; and, setting his head in its proper place, they carried him back home. In twenty-four hours he began to moan; and by dint of carefully feeding him with a spoon, within six months he had quite recovered.[3]

Japanese and Chinese cultures, more so than Islamic and Christian traditions, tended to take a syncretic approach to ideas, so both societies showed considerable interest in the new religion from Europe at various times. Christianity seemed just another flavour of thought to Asians, with some principles such as self-denial and patriarchy not dissimilar to the basic tenets of Confucianism. Christianity also helped rulers counter the intellectual fluidity and more tolerant aspects of Buddhist thinking that they feared. But when it became apparent after a few years that Jesuits intended Christianity to be the one and only true religion, and that European science was also more developed that Chinese, emperors and elites reacted against European thought. Emperors probed European astronomy and science for their own purposes, but the Chinese never succumbed to European attempts at mass conversion of the Chinese to Western religion.

The Ming dynasty collapsed in 1644 after a 300-year reign. Widespread corruption among the scholarly elite and court pandering made it risky to refute Confucian dogma. The last emperor had no idea there was even a problem until invading Qing soldiers entered the gates of the Forbidden City capital. The Chinese scholarly elite studied history and classical texts in addition to mathematics, but were expected to contribute to social order, not focus on theories of trade, science or social reform. The need for patronage encouraged sycophantism, which limited the ability of Chinese intellectuals to ponder new ideas. Intellectuals provided practical counsel against greed, and spread an ethos of egalitarianism, but rather than engage in cosmic explorations, technological innovation or social and political critiques, they focused mostly on the rote memorization of Neo-Confucian texts for official advancement through bureaucratic examinations. After 1644 the new Qing rulers were even more hard line. They sponsored art and scholarship, but mainly in order to prevent thinkers from contemplating new ideas. The Qing dynasty tortured or murdered those who offered dissented; nobody could criticize elites or tradition. Passing exams remained a central component of Chinese philosophy, inhibiting innovative or original thought into the twentieth century.

Self-serving views were the norm worldwide of course. Like Europeans and others, Chinese emperors felt sure they were a 'chosen people'. Japanese emperors and religious elites would surely have agreed there were inferior races subject to their own divine preeminence. *Kirishitan Monogatari*, anti-Christian propaganda from 1639, aimed to expel foreigners from Japan in tones strikingly similar to anti-Semitic Europeans. The following excerpt describes one Japanese writer's perception of arriving European priests:

A Southern Barbarian trading vessel came to our shores. From this ship for the first time emerged an unnamable creature, somewhat similar in shape to a human being, but looking more like a long-nosed goblin . . . the length of his nose was the first thing that attracted attention: it was like conch shell. . . . His head was small. . . . On his hands and feet he had long claws . . . his voice was like the screech of an owl.[4]

As in all societies, there were exceptional thinkers in Asia at this time. The Kangxi emperor, who ruled for sixty years until 1722, studied Jesuit scholarship and encouraged learning. He also maintained the cultural superiority of Chinese civilization, and claimed Europeans derived basic mathematical principles from the 2,500-year-old Chinese *Book of Changes*. He permitted 'evidentiary research', or **kaozheng**, an empiricist approach to geology, medicine, mathematics and earth sciences. He also allowed the tradition of ministers challenging autocratic and ill-informed emperors. But this was a very modest version of dissent, compared to the often-combative councils forming in Europe against arbitrary rule. While dabbling in science, Kangxi nonetheless directed Chinese thought towards a reliance on calendars and a commitment to ritual behaviour. Mathematics and numbers served to order the world, maintain harmony and ultimately support imperial rule, not to shape science and technology.

Conclusion

In China, as in much of Eurasia, some people pursued innovative inquiry into reality and life on earth, free of metaphysical mysticism. Many elites appreciated Western science, and some emperors found it a worthy pursuit. But by the time of the Qing dynasty, decades of disruption left a subjugated, mostly passive, intellectual community, who, like the Mughals and most of the Muslim world, did not consider scientific exploration worthwhile. In the coming centuries, China too would pay a steep price for a conservative approach to innovative thinking.

> At this time Europeans began to explore and describe the world and all that was in it, in works such as the *Encyclopedie*. Some even criticized ethnic prejudice, including condescension towards Muslims, Africans and Asians. Voltaire famously replied to his countryman Bossuet's *Universal History of 1681*:
>
> > This great writer takes but a slight notice of the Arabians who founded so potent an empire and so flourishing a religion; he makes mention of them as a swarm of barbarians. He expatiates on the Egyptians; but he is silent on the Indians and the Chinese, nations as ancient at least, and as considerable as the people of Egypt.[5]

Indeed, when Jesuit priests began translating Confucian texts into French in 1687, an important world historical moment had passed. Just at the point many Eurasian empires rejected intellectual innovation, ideas from those cultures began to permeate European thought. This privileged Europeans with a more sophisticated, more global understanding of the world, of nature, and of other cultures, arming Christian states with knowledge they could use to expand globally in the 1700s and 1800s. At the historical juncture of the eighteenth century, most societies on earth would remain committed to ideas that had worked for centuries, for good reason. However, the previously marginal Christian societies of Western Europe would move towards a very different approach, as we shall see in the next chapter.

Keywords

Reason
Ontological
Public Sphere
Endogenous
Exogenous
Proselytize
Hadiths
Kaozheng

Further reading

Austen, Ralph A. *Trans-Saharan Africa in World History*. Oxford: Oxford University Press, 2010. Tracks the influence of Islam in all aspects of life in this vast region of Africa, shaping law, trade, ideas, literacy and urban life.

Canny, Nicholas P. and Philip D. Morgan. *The Oxford Handbook of the Atlantic World, c.1450-c.1850*. Oxford : Oxford University Press, 2011. Thirty-seven essays providing a comprehensive overview of Atlantic history from 1450 to 1850, many of which focus on ideas stemming from religion, faith and intellectual cross-pollination.

Hastings, Adrian. *The Church in Africa: 1450–1950*. Oxford: Clarendon Press, 1994. This is a comprehensive, exhaustive exploration of the role of Christianity in one part of the world, with views from both native leaders and incoming Europeans.

Northrup, David. *Africa's Discovery of Europe: 1450–1850*, 2nd ed. New York: Oxford University Press, 2009. Northrup analyses the views of elites in Africa, offering a consideration of African understandings of Europeans using available sources with African perspectives.

Thornton, Russell. *American Indian Holocaust and Survival: A Population History since 1492*. Norman: University of Oklahoma Press, 1987. Russell presents a fascinating analysis of the eradication of millions of people from the earth after Europeans arrived in the Americas, showing how little memory of these events still resonate today.

7

European ideas – Early modern minds

Situating the chapter

In 1500, there was little difference between European societies and others worldwide with regard to approaches to intellectual and philosophical life. The centrality of religion, low general literacy and broad respect for received wisdom shaped cultures and intellectual life, from the elite to the commoner. Most Europeans accepted the

Figure 7.1 Alexis, friend of Martin Luther, after he is struck by lightning during their travels, 1505 (© Bridgeman Images).

words of clerics, ministers and ancient authorities without question. Few dared challenge conventional axioms. Most knew only of parish beliefs and heard only what clerics told them. Kings or royals were invested with sacral power almost everywhere; the touch of some European monarchs purportedly healed sickness. Like elsewhere, European values were encircled within a world view of pious acceptance. Accepted notions were usually those of the aristocracy – valour, loyalty and a code of honour. Adherence to traditional views tended to safeguard social norms, while the supernatural occupied daily life for most all over the world, Europe included.

Yet by 1750 a transformation was underway. Western Europeans, particularly in North-western Europe, publicly debated new ideas in areas of individual rights, social criticism and scientific understanding. More people from lower sections of society began volunteering ideas regarding life, society and nature. Compared to tribal, peasant or imperial populations worldwide, European culture developed into a hodgepodge of competing possibilities, which opened doors to a modern world (Figure 7.1).

Europe – Violence and tolerance

But in the early 1500s, almost all Europeans accepted the religious world view of the pope and the political power of local princes. Charles V ruled the Holy Roman Empire from 1519, the private inheritor of vast areas of Europe. From this base, he oversaw a wide Catholic expansion across Europe, Eurasia and into newfound lands in Asia and the Western Hemisphere. Catholics believed that the ordained clergy succeeded directly from Christ's apostles and worshipped Mary, the mother of Jesus. The bread and wine of the mass were (and are) for Catholics the actual body and blood of Jesus, interpreted literally. The Christian notion of a Great Chain of Being informed attitudes towards existence, premised upon a static, set hierarchy. Questioning religious understandings of the heavens, the earth and nature was neither expected nor allowed. Catholics expected to convert the entire world in the 1500s, and it must have seemed quite plausible.

However, in 1517, Martin Luther's fervent commitment to his personal view of Christianity forever undermined the legitimacy of a universal Catholic Christendom. Europe, and the world, changed forever. A century of turmoil resulted from the Protestant Reformation, which brought forth not only plenty of spilled blood but also a flood of critiques against Catholic dogma. This assault on Catholic thought opened up floodgates for criticism of all manner of social norms. Quite ironically, Luther's challenge of the Catholic Church, an institution with over a thousand years of authority, stemmed from a natural, electrical, process scientists would later explain, but which in the 1500s seemed proof of supernatural power residing in the heavens. Caught in a lightning storm one night and fearing a horrible death, a terrified Luther cried out loud that he would become a monk and serve the Lord's purpose if only he could live. He lived, and he changed forever religious life in the West.

For a decade prior to 1517, the corruption and avarice on display in the upper echelons of the church had repulsed Luther. He wondered what kind of church would sell **indulgences** – a way to absolve the sins of those with the means to contribute money. Luther inadvertently encouraged literacy, arguing that individuals could find meaning in the New Testament by reading for themselves. They could grasp the drama of Jesus's life and the stories contained within, free of the need of intermediaries such as priests, popes or for that matter any authority figure. Hence, although he did not intend this, the modern, intellectual notion of individual thinking and the principle of autonomy took root.

A cleavage in Christendom had already existed since 1054, between the Catholic world and Orthodox Christianity which prevailed in Russia, Greece and the Balkans. Though the two churches had excommunicated each other, they ruled broadly different regions, and conflict was rare. But Protestantism was a different challenge. Protestant belief rested on the basic – and much more offensive for Catholics – premise that the pope had no authority, and that individuals should read scripture themselves, in stark contrast to the almost universally illiterate cultures of Eastern Orthodox Christianity. After the sixteenth century, from the Reformation's origins in Germany, dissent prevailed in the west of Europe, while suppression shaped Eastern European thought.

Luther found fertile ground for dissent. Freed of an intervening Catholic clergy, Protestant princes after 1517 reformed their regional churches in their own moulds. Once Luther's ideas spread, accompanied by printed translations of the Bible in local languages, wider European publics considered the Bible and all of history in a new light. Indeed, after the Protestant Reformation, intellectual minorities in Europeans cities could rarely be fully suppressed, or ignored. Even non-religious, hereditary nobles could no longer assume that their populations abided by traditional understandings of social order. New understandings of social and religious order brought great change to Europe, and great violence.

Violence as a way of life

The Protestant Reformation ended a thousand years of dominant Catholic Christian rule in Western Europe, and prompted the creation of new nations with splintered religious allegiances. There had always been factions, 'heretic' groups that challenged the Catholic hierarchy, and intellectual opponents of Catholic dogma. But this new questioning of traditional religious authority opened the possibility of challenging other kinds of thought, including political and scientific ideas. Still, though over time the Reformation inspired a European culture of open inquiry, in its immediate aftermath violence and suspicion prevailed. Indeed, the freedom to opine on matters of faith produced more than a century of great acrimony and bloodshed in Europe.

For two centuries, peace and security, the ostensible goal of political and religious elites everywhere, disappeared in Europe. As always, the poorest suffered most. Divisions over Luther's radical, deeply religious, ideas brought civil war, with over 100,000 deaths in Germany alone during the Peasants War (1524–5). Common people, emboldened by Luther's challenge to the supreme authority of Rome, aired social and economic grievances through armed protest. They suffered vicious retaliation at the hands of ruling elites, and found little support from Luther himself.

Unlike Roman Catholics, Protestants splintered quickly, lacking a single religious orthodoxy, and this had important consequences. Though Protestantism split into two main groups, the Lutheran and Reformed churches, countless dissenting subgroups eventually emerged. In 1540s Geneva, John Calvin moved Protestantism even further away from Rome, arguing that those who govern society should be selected from among the elders of the community. Cities, he argued, should be run by a council of ministers, laypeople who could manage their own problems without resort to the power of bishops. Calvinism was a severe system of thought, rejecting the aesthetic aspects of Catholicism, demanding an exacting morality, while encouraging people to read the Bible for themselves. The key Calvinist belief was **predestination** – God decides who will go to heaven before they are even born. Though, according to Calvinists, there was nothing a person could do to earn salvation, many reasoned that leading a moral and prosperous life on earth was surely a sign that God had predestined them for heaven.

By the late seventeenth century, Protestant sects mushroomed in Europe, with most people remaining loyal to their local parish rather than any broad, national, let alone global, entity. From 1525, Reformed Calvinists persecuted other Protestant sects, like the Anabaptists and Baptists who refused to baptize children. Still, over time, Puritans, Baptists, Huguenots, Quakers, Moravians and many smaller sects within the Protestant tradition settled into relative peace, sharing a common opposition to the ancient Catholicism they had broken with.

The Catholic Church responded forcefully to the Protestant breakaway. Violence erupted across Europe, splitting nations, cities and even families between the two new forms of Christianity. The Council of Trent, meeting from 1545 to 1563, attempted to reform the Catholic Church, to educate clerics and to reaffirm the churches commitment to good deeds and the masses. Nothing much changed intellectually or institutionally though. The Catholic priesthood remained in place, and the Church still considered ancient doctrines sacred. It did send out new monastic orders, such as the Jesuits, to reconvert Protestants and convert Indians and Asians, but this was doubling down on the past, not considering the present.

The Peace of Augsburg of 1555 briefly brought order back to European life. The terms of the peace included the innovative legal concept of *eius regio, cuius religio* ('whose realm, his religion'), which proclaimed that princes and kings would decide the faith of the regions they ruled. Nonetheless, Catholic and Protestant rulers, supported by armies of fanatics or mercenaries, re-engaged in vicious religious wars soon after, lasting until the end of the Thirty Years War in 1648.

For most of the sixteenth century religious conflict fractured France. The French Wars of Religion from 1562 to 1598 destroyed social stability, as royal houses competed for power, while the masses fought for whoever would best protect them. French Protestants (Calvinists and Huguenots) resisted the dominant Catholic population. Both sides attacked each other mercilessly, even inside churches. The St. Bartholomew's Day massacre in 1572, in which Catholic mobs in Paris killed every Protestant they could find – perhaps as many as 70,000 – encapsulated a century of religious intolerance and loathing. Many Protestants soon fled France to escape persecution, ensuring a Catholic majority in France. Well over a million people died in this French civil war.

Ireland also traces its modern disunity to this period. Protestant English nobles staked out new lands in Catholic Ireland in the 1550s, displacing Catholics, prompting centuries of violence and eventual British domination of the Irish. Religious conflict continued to afflict England, Scotland and Ireland through the seventeenth century. The complex English Civil War (1642–51), which also embroiled the Irish, Scottish and Welsh, was in part a conflict between Catholics and Protestants, but also between differing branches of Protestantism. Hundreds of thousands died and millions suffered as England and Scotland, like Northern Ireland today, became resolutely Protestant and the south of Ireland remained Catholic.

When the fervent Protestant and short-term dictator of England Oliver Cromwell invaded Ireland to create a new Protestant English utopia, he praised the murder of thousands of Catholic children and women, few of whom were combatants. Though it is unclear whether 800 or several thousand of those murdered were civilians, no sympathy extended to Irish Catholics who were, like Africans or Indians, considered subhuman. From Dublin Cromwell wrote in 1649:

Sir, It hath pleased God to bless our endeavors at Drogheda. After battery, we stormed it. The Enemy were about 3000 strong in the Town. They made a stout resistance; and near 1,000 of our men being entered, the Enemy forced them out again. . . . I believe we put to the sword the whole number of the defendants.[1]

While some Europeans considered the exploitation of weaker people and robbery of their lands might please God, others felt divinely sanctioned by a god who apparently wanted to clear land for them in the Americas. William Bradford, the governor of Massachusetts, claimed in the 1650s: 'The good hand of God favored our beginnings, sweeping away great multitudes of the natives . . . that he might make room for us.'[2]

Spain continued to deploy religious devotion as an instrument of state policy. The general stalemate between emerging Protestant states and the Catholic Church monopolized the energies of Spanish monarchs for centuries. The **Spanish Inquisition** was a particularly brutal affront to humanity, a programme of religious persecution that maimed or murdered tens of thousands of accused heretics, church critics and Jews in Spain, France, Italy and central Europe. Phillip II of Spain introduced the *auto-da-fe*, horrific show trials which publicly tortured apostates, Jews and Muslims in a bid to enforce Catholic orthodoxy in Spain. Though numbers are disputed, scholars estimate that tens of thousands of people endured agonizing pain for being Protestant or otherwise challenging Catholic dogma.

The Catholic Church in Rome shaped religious and intellectual life in Spain. Indeed, Rome claimed the final say on all matters pertaining to the mind. Its *List of Forbidden Books* of 1559 closed Catholic cultures to new ideas for centuries. The List banned nearly all the works of European scientific advance over the following centuries, including the crucial works of Kepler, Newton and Kant. Book banning became a crucial tool for protectors of the church. Even access to the Bible itself diminished across the Catholic world, as a prohibition on printed Bibles further removed laypeople from direct religious engagement. Priests celebrated masses in Latin rather than vernacular languages, offering much mystery, but little illumination.

While Protestant nations generally developed a culture of literacy and dissent by the 1600s, lower literacy rates prevailed in Catholic nations.

Protestants proved as willing as Catholics to kill for religious views, but in these centuries rising literacy resulted in more challenges to customary practices and perspectives. Even in 1500, before the Reformation, over 280 European cities had established printing presses that produced millions of works in the 1600s. Aside from questioning Catholicism, literate Protestants began to question Protestantism itself, prompting reformed churches to splinter into numerous sects. This left a loosely organized set of congregations free of any centralized authority, unlike either Catholicism or Islam.

Nor did Eastern Europe escape religious violence. Russian Orthodox rulers had long feared exposing their people to Catholicism, let alone Protestantism. During Russia's violent Time of Troubles (1598–1613), Catholics and Orthodox zealots fought each other for religious dominance in Russia. In Eastern Europe, conformist clerics generally obeyed tyrannical emperors. Though most European countries expected their clerics to be literate, the clergy in Russia were mostly illiterate. Russian or Eastern European peasants had little influence on cultural or intellectual life until the twentieth century.

Through the 1600s, religious fanaticism prevailed in Europe, prompting a particularly abhorrent persecution of women. From 1618 to 1648, the Thirty Years War brought great violence across most of Europe. The Holy Roman Empire, Holland, Belgium and the British Isles redirected resources towards religious warfare, and millions of people met famine or pestilence. Religious persecutors burned hundreds of thousands of women to death for alleged heresy as witches. In this period, European courts often allowed the use of magic and witchcraft, omens and superstition as evidence in disputes. Stomach-churning burnings, hangings and torture actually increased in the seventeenth century, as religious zealots targeted women who argued, were destitute, thought differently, or claimed to be healers. Over three quarters of accused witches were women, though other women frequently accused them. By 1700 Europe had tried over 100,000 cases of witchcraft. The outbreak of witchcraft scares declined by the turn of the eighteenth century as the Enlightenment approached to question such superstition.

Yet, amidst such fear, another social norm emerged in Europe, if slowly – one of acceptance and understanding. As early as 1563 the Dutch physician Johann Weyer had questioned the wisdom of invented accusations against witches. By 1700, many Europeans abandoned virulent disputes over which religion was the true one. **Anticlerical** attitudes thus grew in Europe in the eighteenth century. In particular, the north-western states of England and Holland focused energies on commercial activity rather than on enforcing religious orthodoxy. Perhaps not coincidentally, these countries experienced remarkable economic growth and improved standards of living thereafter.

Unexpected outcomes – Dutch tolerance and English inquiry

Amidst all this turmoil, some political and religious leaders in North-western European societies started to tolerate the spread of new ideas in the 1600s. The two countries most committed to exploring New World views were Protestant – England and Holland. Both would become dominant in producing new economic and technological ideas, both enjoyed high literacy rates and both began to look outside traditional aristocratic circles for decision-making.

The notion of tolerance was central to this new way of thinking. Dutch culture, more than any other, accepted a wide array of beliefs and worked to break the stranglehold of traditional authority. Early modern Dutch intellectuals like Erasmus (d. 1536) openly scorned the hypocrisy and corruption of the Catholic Church, using wit and satire to expose the virtues of a new way of thinking, **humanism**. This was a philosophy reinvented from its Greek origins that, though accepting of Christian teachings, prioritized the study of human matters over divine or supernatural ones. This culture of inquiry challenged the centrality of the Catholic Church in society and brought important questions of a secular nature to the fore.

In Holland after 1700, merchant leaders actively sought to overcome religious strife, partnering a commercial outlook with an acceptance of pluralism. Having fought off Spanish oppression, Dutch elites reversed Spanish attitudes towards Jews. A culture of acceptance towards traders of all groups, including Jews, therefore emerged. When Spanish elites in 1556 ruled that Jesuits could persecute Calvinists and force Jewish conversions (*conversos*), thousands of Jews and less zealous individuals moved north to Holland (and southeast to the Ottoman Empire), attracted by the promise of more tolerant societies.

Dutch thinkers freely discussed ideas seldom before broached in public. The Jewish intellectual Baruch Spinoza (d. 1677) decreed a return to pre-Christian classical thinking as a guide to life. For Spinoza, liberty could be attained only if humans lived free of fear and reasoned individually. Though his own traditionalist Jewish community rejected him, Dutch authorities found such questions unobjectionable.

In this period in Europe, more people questioned convention openly. But due to religious and political oppression, anonymity remained prudent. The 'Treatise of Three Impostors', first printed in 1598, openly criticized all three Abrahamic religions and their claims to holiness. Uncovered in the library of a German theologian, the text was supplemented by the Jurist Johannes Joachim Müller in 1753, who wrote:

Christians would rather adore this phantom than listen to the law of Nature which God – that is to say, Nature, which is the active principle – has written in the heart of man. All other laws are but human fictions, and pure illusions forged, not by Demons or evil spirits, which are fanciful ideas, but by the skill of Princes and Ecclesiastics to give the former more warrant for their authority, and to enrich the latter by the traffic in an infinity of chimeras which sell to the ignorant at a good price.[3]

Dutch tolerance developed alongside freethinking in England. But by 1750 England was both open to debate and more powerful militarily. The small island nation defined itself firmly against the Catholic Church once Henry VIII broke with Rome in 1534. Seeking a divorce from Catherine of Aragon (forbidden in Catholic doctrine), Henry challenged the papal hierarchy in Rome. After the Pope excommunicated Henry for marrying Anne Boleyn, Henry established a new church, the Anglican Protestant Church of England.

At the same time, influenced by the accounts of overseas travellers and explorers, English thinkers proposed radically new social hierarchies. In his celebrated *Utopia* of 1516, Henry's acquaintance Thomas More criticized the ritual worship of relics, but he also proposed a collective, more equitable approach to social and economic life (which would re-emerge in nineteenth-century socialist thought). *Utopia* proposed a nation with freedom of religion – or even none at all, suggesting radical propositions through the guise of fiction. More also condemned real-world England's gluttonous landlords, who enclosed their fields and expelled poor farmers.

By the 1640s, an increasingly literate population of commoners with a proclivity for protest began to gather, bring petitions or pass out pamphlets in open opposition to established customs in England. Challenges to authority became common, with groups such as the **Levellers** daring to argue for social equality, forcing those with wealth to at least consider their demands, if not to accept them. Even the splintered smaller Protestant churches (grouped together as **Dissenters**), protested the main establishment Church of England. Criticism in all directions fostered debate and a measure of open mindedness in seventeenth-century England.

A culture of reading encouraged questioning of accepted norms. Public opinion pressured clerics and princes. Inspired by the biting wit of William Shakespeare and other celebrated dramatists, a language of sarcasm and irony emerged in print and on stage, subtly and brazenly questioning authority. As in Holland, English officialdom either did not or could not counter this trend.

The first public library, the Bodleian Library opened in 1602, offering ideas and increased literacy to the wider population. Charles I's harsh censorship apparatus (the Star Chamber) was abolished in 1641. Thereafter printing boomed, which standardized language, facilitating easy dissemination of information and importantly, the safeguarding of new ideas about society and nature. By 1650 a group of natural philosophers founded the Royal Society of London, under a charter from

King Charles II, to promote useful technical and scientific knowledge. It is the oldest national scientific institution in the world.

In addition, seventeenth-century England saw a ready availability of newspaper periodicals, so that the small nation increasingly imagined itself as a secure island of 'Englishmen'. Numerous members of the English gentry displayed proud libraries of over 1,000 books by 1650; Samuel Pepys library alone contained up to 3,000 volumes. By 1700 more than half of Englishmen could read, an exceptional literacy rate in the seventeenth-century world.

So, in England, a revolutionary print culture emerged. With clear communication lines between various parts of the country, it was no longer possible to uphold the conceit that a single authority – a Catholic priest, a Protestant prince or a city leader – could explain everything. In other parts of Europe, such as Scotland, Holland and France, a vigorous print culture developed too, intersecting with England. Prior to 1500 around 20 million copies of manuscripts existed in Europe; between 1500 and 1600 over 150 million more were produced. By 1800 up to 1500 million copies of books shaped a culture of print literacy in Europe, unparalleled elsewhere on earth.

Speaking truth to power?

Intolerance on the part of some elites also stimulated dissent. Some devoted religious communities in England and Holland, unhappy with lax religiosity and liberal social norms, chose to leave, to establish socially and religiously homogenous societies in the Americas. The Thirty Years War (1618–48) pushed religious questions to the fore across Europe. It stirred one dissatisfied group of radical Protestants to separate themselves from the Church of England, departing on the Mayflower in 1620 and start a new life in the Americas – with great consequences for natives there. A larger group of Puritan dissenters followed them to New England in the 1630s, hoping to build an ideal Protestant community as a model for reforming an Anglican Church they saw as still too Catholic in style.

An austere Protestantism would dominate the culture of the New England colonies of America. The founder of Harvard University, John Harvard, was a Puritan who sponsored the training of ministers after 1636. In the colonies, the new Anglo-American world would be one of persecution, intolerance and suspicion. A pressure to conform to Puritan norms inspired the Salem Witch Trials in 1692, in which those who diverged from established norms found themselves accused and sentenced to death for consorting with Satan.

Yet, a culture of self-governance and more democratic social relations also developed in North America. Having escaped monarchical rule, various sects of religious groups in America rejected the unequal pecking order so prominent in Europe. In the American colonies, fervent Calvinists and other sects settled on vast lands free to think for themselves, which encouraged literacy and the exploration of spirituality, even within a culture of intolerance. Protestant religious thinkers debated and proposed new egalitarian ideas. By 1720 Methodists in both America and Europe disputed the Calvinist dogma of the elect going to heaven, arguing Christ saved all, and that mere repentance could save even the poorest souls. As the Methodist movement spread in America a spirit of criticism emerged in a more equal society than could be found in Europe.

The 1517 Reformation had undermined the prerogative of clerics to enforce religious dogmas. Then, in the Glorious Revolution of 1688, a political transformation in England limited the rights of the monarch, and elevated the power of parliament and the people. Though the seventeenth century was one of religious conflict in England as elsewhere, the country took a unique political path, ending the century with a weakened monarchy subject to strong parliamentary power. In the years after 1688 the seeds of popular agency were planted in public life, permitting parliamentary **representation** that, at least theoretically, gave a voice to the wider population. By 1700 England had established a balance of interests, between the monarchy, the noble classes and commoners, a balance that would tolerate some measure of protest.

The Glorious Revolution eliminated, once and for all, the idea of an absolute ruler in England. Thereafter a new philosophical debate stirred in the country, centred on the problem of who should make rules for society in the absence of a divine king. Some asserted that only those with property should hold political power, while others suggested that even commoners should be able to wield it. By the 1650s, John Locke and Thomas Hobbes were asking hard questions of English elites. Locke relied on reason to make the revolutionary claim that *all* humans have natural rights, and that they could work to improve society. Hobbes meanwhile took a more conservative approach: a strong king and state could lead all people in a secure society, maintaining firm absolute rule, as elsewhere, but in the interests of the people. Both of these were superior to the autocratic rule found in most places on earth.

Even as slavery expanded, John Locke argued that a variety of religious views should coexist on earth, and it was compatible with the message of Jesus to accept difference and not impose one view. In his 1693 'Letter concerning toleration' he wrote:

> The toleration of those that differ from others in matters of religion is so agreeable to the Gospel of Jesus Christ, and to the genuine reason of mankind, that it seems monstrous for men to be so blind as not to perceive the necessity and advantage of it in so clear a light.[4]

Such liberal thinking was, of course, incredibly intolerant by modern standards, and sat comfortably with racism, sexism and disdain for others in general. It may have emerged first in broad in Europe, but similar attitudes could be found elsewhere. Though the Muslim world rejected science and print technology,

Islamic scholars argued for tolerance too. One African Muslim scholar in Timbuktu equated intellectual exploration with virtue and piety, praising the ideas of renowned thinkers just as Europeans were being put to the stake for questioning dogma:

> A man of goodness, virtuous and pious, mindful of the Sunna, a very upright and distinguished man, full of love for the Prophet and devoting himself unceasingly to the reading of poems in honour of Muhammad . . . Lawyer, lexicographer, grammarian, prosodist and scholar, he occupied himself with the sciences all his life. He possessed numerous books, copied in his own hand with copious annotations. At his death he left about 700 volumes.[5]

By 1750, with the exception of North-western Europe, orthodoxy, illiteracy and acceptance of traditional views on power remained the norm across the planet. So, the intellectual potential of the vast majority of people, literate or not, remained confined, as it long had been. Traditional belief systems, reliant upon monarchical and sacred supremacy, persisted everywhere: nomadic chieftains, Chinese, Japanese, Ottoman, Indian and Russian emperors, the Habsburgs and Bourbons in most of Europe, lords of the manor and innumerable tribal chiefs across the world – all claimed control not only of the land and its resources but of existing power relations. None would countenance the impertinent views openly voiced by defiant English rebels or assertive Dutch merchants. While brilliant thinkers and dissenting peasants existed in all societies, most lived in repressive cultures that punished free thought.

Violent as it was, North-western Europe benefitted from three broad processes in this era, that created new intellectual possibilities. First, the discovery of the Americas from 1492 undermined conventional ideas of history, life on earth, and the cosmos. Second, if the incredulity at finding human beings in the Americas was not enough, the Reformation brought into question religious authority and encouraged a culture of protest. Last, an abundance of printed learning materials spread in the northwest of Europe in the seventeenth and eighteenth centuries to produce new philosophies that were humanistic, critical and inquisitive in a way that threatened traditional sources of religious and political authority. This modern way of thinking had only begun to develop by 1750. But it would open many new doors of perception, and scientific thinking, in particular, was soon to change the world in profound ways.

The scientific world view – Optimistic inquiry

Seventeenth-century Holland was an exceptionally liberal territory, where Jews escaped harassment so common elsewhere in Europe. It was in the Netherlands, in 1656, that the Jewish philosopher Baruch Spinoza first subjected the Bible to methodical literary analysis. Jewish authorities shunned him for his non-religious ideas. Yet by taking a secular approach to the past, he and others influenced by him nudged European minds towards modern scientific exploration – of society and the whole universe, not just historical scriptures. Spinoza notably condemned the 'occult qualities . . . and a thousand other trifles' found in traditional approaches to nature.[6] His work relied on a clear set of principles for understanding nature based on empirical analysis.

Driven by a new awareness of cultural and geographical differences on earth, thinkers like Spinoza leaned on experience and logic rather than divine scripture or ecclesiastical hearsay. Scientific minds did not reason from assumed basic principles – such as the supposed wickedness of heretics or divinely ordained weather events that ruined whole harvests and starved thousands. Instead, practical experience, trial and error, and, ultimately, evidence based upon reason came to predominate. Together these comprised a new form of knowledge organization, a way of ordering comprehension that could be applied to all aspects of life, whether the nature of community, the idea of political organization, social progress, motions of the planets or the effects of microbes in water and air.

Though humans would later prove capable of using science to commit major atrocities, its beneficial effects were vast. Geographical knowledge about nature, anthropological attempts to understand other cultures, biological awareness of the human body's complicated health systems, improved agricultural practices and advancements in education, law, political science and economics all improved human societies in different ways (Figure 7.2).

Figure 7.2 Brueghel, 1621. Record-keepers, accounting methods (Wikimedia Commons).

Science and truth

The juggernaut of science pervaded much of the developed world by 1900, but in 1500 traditional understandings of the earth appeared secure, eternal in their wisdom. Christianity, Islam, Judaism, Buddhism, Hinduism, Confucianism and other less prevalent belief systems had together elucidated life on earth for most of the last 2,000 years; their basic nostrums had been cemented as truths among power elites everywhere. Distributed downwards to the wider population through oral sermons, official proclamations and word of mouth, most believers accepted their faiths with little question. Traditions had gathered the power of certainty over time, providing religious elites with tremendous legitimacy harkening back for centuries, if not millennia.

Ancient traditions satisfied the needs of the majority of people. The only source of understanding for most people came from ancient texts mediated and interpreted by elites. One usually achieved literacy by learning to read sacred or orthodox texts, which explained the world in mystical or spiritual terms. Religious or cosmological truths were thus stamped over the centuries with the imprimatur of authority. Life's misfortunes, failed crops, personal failings or awesome storms all were attributed to gods or spirit forces.

Scientific truths, on the other hand, had to be tested and verified before even tentative claims could be posited. Empirically tested scientific conclusions applied to all cultures and regions; they were universal rather than specific. Though nearly all societies practised some form of scientific inquiry, it was the Anglo-Dutch assault on tradition that freed minds to push the limits of scientific investigation.

Precision became the new watchword of understanding in the 1700s, as mathematics, measurement and **metrics** began to explain reality and solve everyday problems. Science, of course, did not offer absolute truths. Scientists could only **theorize**, to provide guarded generalizations about the world that might hold up with repeated testing or experiment. But repeatable results tended to undermine ancient hypotheses about the origins and nature of the earth, about disease, reproduction or other fundamental aspects of everyday life.

The concept of science – from Latin *scientia*, or knowledge – ultimately rested on accruing information about the world. Its practice was hardly unique to Europe. As we have seen, Muslim, African, Asian and Hindu scholars had been developing scientific concepts for centuries and continued to do so in this era. Western Europe benefitted from its medieval Italian and Spanish heritage, some of which derived from the intellectual heritage of the Jews, Muslims, Indians and Chinese.

In all complex societies thinkers dissented, inquired or investigated, but it was in seventeenth-century Europe where we see the sharpest break with tradition and the development of the **Scientific Revolution**. Making use of concepts from Chinese, Arabs and Indians, Western Europeans put inherited Greek thought to use for new practical purposes. Questions discarded by Christian minds since the Greeks reappeared in this era: Does nature run like a clock, or machine? Can humans predict nature? How should investigators establish results?

Such simple questions inadvertently led some towards **scepticism** – inherent doubt – about any number of subjects or questions. Developments in the fields of navigation, medicine, botany, chemistry, geology and astronomy led to new systems of thought. Soon mathematicians across Europe used detailed records and data tables to challenge the geocentric view, assumed for centuries, which postulated incorrectly the earth was at the centre of the universe.

Science and the skies

Gradually, in the 1600s, scientific thought – and later, technology based on science – became a Western European impulse. The scientific view of the universe began in earnest when the Polish mathematician Nicolaus Copernicus (d. 1543) developed a radical new heliocentric model of the cosmos that placed the sun rather than the earth, at the centre of the universe – a model later understood to apply only to our solar system. Copernicus likely used data tables compiled by Muslim scholars. During this period Ottoman thinkers studied the skies from Islamic observatories, until Sunni orthodox clerics persuaded Suleiman the Lawgiver (d. 1566) to shut them down. Building on Copernicus's work, the Danish noble Tyco Brahe (d. 1601) in 1576 presented mathematical proof the heavens were dynamic – not static, as most believed – and moving of their own accord. The German Johannes Kepler (d. 1630) also argued the existing view was wrong because planets followed elliptical, rather than circular, orbits. These newly discovered laws of planetary movement countered the biblical view of geocentrism, and opened up the way towards modern physical sciences.

Understandably, many well-established interests resisted the new learning. Rome burned Giordano Bruno (d. 1600) alive for questioning the Catholic Church's view of the universe. Church authorities pressured countless others into silence, both through the formal Inquisition courts and the informal threat of torture or death. Yet, the new assessment of the universe only opened further doors of perception. Decades after Bruno's death, Galileo (d. 1642) used the newly invented telescope to notice mountains on the moon and sunspots.

A leading light in the development of observational astronomy and modern physics, Galileo was one of the earliest thinkers to argue that the laws of nature could be understood mathematically. He also articulated a vigorous defence of Copernican heliocentrism that put him at odds with Italy's religious authorities. When he publicized his ideas, he risked his life. Thrust before terrifying Inquisition courts in the 1630s, he famously recanted his heliocentrism to avoid violent punishment, but in a small act of rebellion purportedly muttered *Eppur si muove* as he left the courtroom.[7] Galileo's 1632 work 'Dialogue Concerning Two Chief World Systems' would remain on the Catholic Church's *Index of Forbidden Books* until 1835 (Figure 7.3).

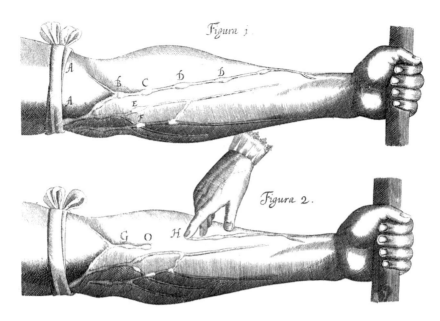

Figure 7.3 William Harvey (1578–1657) English physician. Blood Circulation (© Alamy).

The trial alarmed other innovative scholars like Rene Descartes (d. 1650), who wisely moved to Protestant parts of Europe so he could think and write without reservations. Descartes pushed Galileo's reasoning further to argue that *only* reason and logic could explain existence. For Descartes, logic was premised on **deduction** – where general theories were formed first to then test specific data – aiming to replace Aristotelian and scriptural explanations for nature. Descartes and his followers believed mathematics could explain truth better than the human senses. He proposed a systematic, mechanistic theory of the natural world, known as the Cartesian world view, inspiring fields of knowledge passed down as Formal Science.

Then, as now, science was messy. No consensus developed on how to best think scientifically in this period. Critical thinking not only challenged traditional ideas but new ones too, in a recursive process of new ideas. Descartes's system relied dogmatically on reason itself as a first principle of understanding, and was, in fact, not accepted by English intellectuals. The English privileged **empiricism**, which relied on experimentation rather than theorizing, with important consequences for both thinkers and tinkerers. Even within Europe, approaches to science were premised upon debate and evidentiary explanations.

Aptly, the Englishman Francis Bacon's (d. 1626) approach to knowledge conflicted with Descartes's view. Relying on visual evidence instead of general speculation, he argued in his 1620 *Novum Organum* that observation and research analysed with objectivity and inductive logic was a superior way to understand nature. Through **induction**, specific results could be used to build up theories or claims, not the other way around as with deduction. In practice, scientists used both systems together (and still do). But such open and rigorous ways of thinking had profound consequences for many knowledge systems ranging from the astronomical to the biological, as understandings of earth-bound organisms, like the human body, began to change radically and developed into the field of life sciences.

Science and health

In 1500, humans had little idea where they came from, though this slowly changed in the sixteenth and seventeenth centuries. The fallopian tubes were discovered in 1561, and a nascent sense of biological reproduction emerged. The Belgian Vesalius (d. 1564) began using cadavers to study the innermost regions of the body, dissecting humans to explore human anatomy and produce accurate artistic representations. Adding to this work, the Englishman William Harvey (d. 1657) determined the circulation of the blood and the heart's function.

These discoveries opened the door to medical knowledge that moved beyond dangerous practices such as amputations or leeches sucking blood. The French surgeon Ambroise Pare (d. 1590) crucially made inroads into understanding how to treat wounds and to help heal or treat broken or severed limbs. Such developments generally spread around various nations in Western Europe. As a result, public health slowly became a new social concern, which helped accelerate efforts to understand disease in the seventeenth century. Crucially, scientific inventions such as the microscope enabled the human eye to discern previously hidden microbes in water.

European global incursions brought not only material abundance but also new questions about other humans on earth, and subsequently, new ways to think about the human body and the world. Classifying and collecting flora and fauna from new regions changed understandings of history, geography and life's meaning. Scientific interests in the plants, animals and people of new places captivated minds at all levels of society. Aside from intellectual elites, countless amateur inventers also benefitted from a culture of trial and error, as more and more people heard or read about new cultures and scientific concepts.

The broad diffusion of information through pamphlets and books, particularly in Western Europe, also helped popularize science, making research on the body or nature more socially acceptable. By 1650 European thinkers could move around many centres of intellectualism, from Denmark to Italy to England or France. They could find like-minded innovators, creating networks of scholars in learned societies, disagreeing for the sake of knowledge, working free from persecution and pooling ideas. The ready availability of journals, published for peer review and openly shared, helped disseminate knowledge the production of new notions. Close relationships formed between intellectuals even in rival nations such as France, Holland and England. New comprehension fertilized Western European societies after the seventeenth century. England's Royal Society after 1660 and Frances Academy of Sciences from 1666 shared research based on questionnaires and surveys, provided funding for trips, spreading curiosity about anything and everything to counter inherited beliefs. In London, Amsterdam, Paris and other European cities, coffee houses became great centres of social interaction in the 1600s. In early modern coffee shops, a drink that originated in the Middle East prompted addiction not only to caffeine but also to loud conversation and debate about all manner of things.

Science, gender and authority

In this foment of new ideas, philosophers questioned not only the cosmos, they also inquired into the existing social order. If, some thought, new knowledge revised understandings of nature, then perhaps new explanations for social organization could be devised, too. In the 1600s, new ideas about political and economic philosophy emerged, with important consequences for those at the bottom of society, who could for the first time consider upward social mobility rather than mere survival.

England's John Locke (d. 1704) most notably debated conventions such as divine monarchy, arguing instead that the power to govern rested on the permission of the people and should protect the people's natural rights. Thus, his theory of a **social contract** between the powerful and the population planted the possibility of equality. This challenged the idea of aristocratic privileges and later influenced American revolutionaries like Thomas Jefferson and others. Locke's contemporary, the Italian Giambattista Vico (d. 1744) argued that government was not static but rather an evolving organism that grew and decomposed like humans. Hence, it could be improved.

By the 1740s, English politicians appointed a specific policymaker vested with authority free from monarchical or clerical purview. When Robert Walpole (d. 1745) became Britain's first Prime Minister, although extremely powerful, he helped develop a parliamentary system that institutionalized debate in England through a representative system of public discussion.

A middling class of people emerged in Western Europe in this era whose interests were not only economic and political but also intellectual, as they became consumers of philosophy, history, theology, music, literature and the arts. The growing education of the middle classes enabled more knowledge to trickle towards the common masses. Because those in power in England were more sympathetic to common people than in other European countries, English commoners were freer to challenge traditional values of obedience and piety.

Moreover, everyday leisure activities like festivals, jousts, animal fighting, ball games, sports and drama inspired a raucous, uncontrolled culture with freedom of action and ideas in England, where repeated complaints about the arrogance of young people suggested a society lacking in deference to authority:

In 1624, the Englishman Thomas Barnes griped, 'Youth were never more sawcie, yea never more savagely saucie . . . the magistrate is not dreaded.'[8]

Others began to question the historical oppression of women, arguing they also should be free to participate in the public sphere. Some, in Protestant and Catholic countries, countered the ancient dogma that women were mentally and physically inferior. Clearly the Silesian noblewoman Maria Cunitz was not inferior, when she had developed Kepler's astronomic tables. One in ten astronomers in Germany were women by 1700. Elena Piscopia earned the first ever doctorate in Italy in 1678, and the first female professor in Europe, the Italian Laura Bassi, took her position in 1732. Change came slowly, but the seeds of female emancipation and empowerment took root in Europe during the 1700s.

Scholars of literacy note that in this era, Europeans began reading and writing more, and doing both more than in other cultures. European women in particular achieved levels of literacy far above women around the world otherwise. In one Swedish diocese, an estimated 94 per cent of women could read in 1740; this while less than 6 per cent of men in northern India could as late as 1800. Between 2 and 10 per cent of Chinese women were literate in the late 1800s by comparison. Egypt's literacy rate in 1901 was only 7 per cent. Printed words, and the reflection they invite, shaped European culture far more than in others.[9]

In England in 1744, Eliza Haywood brought women's issues into the public sphere with the first periodical for women, *The Female Spectator*, which covered previously ignored topics such as childrearing, love, marriage and education. After 1750, during the Enlightenment era, accomplished women ran salons – vital sites of intellectual exchange – and so demonstrated that they were entirely capable of critiquing philosophies and changing world views. By 1750 women began to emerge as prominent writers and thought-shapers in England, particularly via the popular storytelling medium of the novel. Novelists, male and female, conveyed new realms of consciousness, empathetically exploring the thoughts and feelings of other people, with key protagonists often female. Widely read classics such as *Eloise*, *Pamela* and *Clarissa* helped men and women to question emotions, to experience others worlds and to commiserate with human beings not only locally but also globally.

Of course, while debating equality in salons was easy enough, agitating for it against entrenched interests was another thing altogether. Some women began to do this. Madame du Chatelet (d. 1749) dared to write to Frederick the

Great of Prussia that women were subject to unfair treatment in European society:

> Judge me for my own merits, or lack of them, but do not look upon me as a mere appendage to this great general or that great scholar, this star that shines at the court of France or that famed author. I am in my own right a whole person, responsible to myself alone for all that I am, all that I say, all that I do. It may be that there are metaphysicians and philosophers whose learning is greater than mine, although I have not met them. Yet, they are but frail humans, too, and have their faults; so, when I add the sum total of my graces, I confess I am inferior to no one.[10]

Elsewhere around the world, women challenged patriarchal norms. Nazo Tokhi (d. 1717) helped shaped the nation of Afghanistan. Tokhi, a Pashtun poet and warrior, depicted herself as the founder of the Afghan people, expressing an appreciation of the martial facets of existence but also the beauty of nature's mysteries:

> Dew drops from an early dawn narcissus
> as if tear drops from a melancholy eye,
> O beauty, I asked, what makes you cry
> life is too short for me, it answered
> My beauty blooms and withers in a moment
> as if smile comes and forever fades away.[11]

Tokhi drew inspiration from the sixteenth-century Roshanniya Movement in the Central Asian region, led by the revolutionary Pir Roshan, who called for absolute equality between men and women. Such ideas of equality would come and go through these centuries across the Muslim world. The Ottoman world at times invited tolerance, but since religious and secular power was combined in the sultan and his subordinates this generally inspired masculine venality. There were those though who wished to expose patriarchy and inequality. One eighteenth-century Turkish critic explained how corruption became endemic, accusing clerics of using tradition to justify covetous practices:

> And when the chief priest of a diocese dies, immediately the lobbying begins in force, some going to the patriarch, some going to the senior clergy, some to the notables and their wives, and often to the magnates, and of the many one is lucky and receives the office. Bu as much as he succeeds, any expenses are occasion by gifts to the go-betweens, some to the Porte, some to the higher clergy, all with iou's . . . and with this power, immediately he (the priest) arrives in the diocese, he begins to seek from the villages help for his new high priestly office . . . The poor cannot resist, fearful of excommunications, curses and exclusion from church, the notables are ashamed of the daily coffee and pipes and gifts. The (high officials) do not object, or he says to them, 'It is the custom, as my predecessor took it, so do I want it.'[12]

VOLTAIRE, N. 20 FEBBRAIO 1694, M. 30 MAGGIO 1778,
(Da un ritratto autentico di Largillière, fatto su Voltaire a 21 anni).

Figure 7.4 Voltaire (© Getty Images). The Art Archive at Art Resource, NY Image Reference: AA363381.

Science and perspective

European intellectual development tended towards a form of optimism. Both fictional and scientific inquiry into human emotions reveals the first attempts to consider the notion that all in society might aspire to happiness. The ideas of progress and happiness were not common in history. Spinoza argued for a life of joy, of living life to its fullest, not one fearing death or fate. He countered Descartes's notion of **dualism** – the view that a distinction existed between thinking beings and mere objects such as rocks – with a **monistic** view, claiming only one substance exists in the universe, one single form of matter. He advanced a philosophy of **materialism**, which countered conceptions of heavenly rewards, souls or joy in the afterlife, with the notion that physical matter is all that matters, here and now on earth (Figure 7.4).

Along with Spinoza's irreverence, satire and humour entered the public forum in Europe, often cutting the mighty to size through jest. Following Shakespeare's lead, the English philosopher Lord Shaftesbury (d. 1713) argued humour was the clearest expression of a common public sense of morality. The mocking of religion or authority was in this view justified and upright. European thinkers openly disagreed with one another through a mixture of rancour and merriment.

Voltaire was perhaps the most open critic of convention. In opposition to the philosopher Gottfried Leibniz (d. 1716), who made the claim that the cruelty and pain of life were central to the human condition, Voltaire's *Candide* parodied this view. In this hugely popular short novel filled with silliness and satire, he refused to accept the existing world of pain was the best one possible, simply because it was made by a good God, as Leibniz claimed. Voltaire criticized both traditional thinking and such trite positivity. He preferred to point to ongoing misery in the world, not only in Europe but also around the world from European colonization, thereby opening the door for future critiques of European expansion.

Less confrontational assaults on established world views came in other ways. New juridical principles emerged that would help shape international law in a European vein in coming centuries. Hugo Grotius (d. 1645), a Dutch natural law legal philosopher, argued that God's justice was not an entity to itself, or formed for the utility of rulers. Clerics, Grotius argued, must recognize correct moral precepts that they themselves were subject to. Grotius's influential ideas spread support for open markets, rule by reason, individual rights and the need for an open, civil society: 'Just as even God . . . cannot cause that two times two should not make four, so He cannot cause that which is intrinsically evil be not evil.'[13]

European confidence reached high. Intellectual determination to comprehend all of nature culminated in the greatest effort ever to compile information on all known subjects. Denis Diderot and other French intellectuals conspired against authorities to spend decades compiling the *Encyclopédie*, a Wikipedia for the eighteenth century. Leading intellectuals like Voltaire, Montesquieu and many others contributed to the project. Diderot and his fellow editors published seventeen volumes between 1751 and 1765, listing 71,818 articles by numerous authors – a magnum opus that aimed to gather all the world's knowledge in one place.

The study of so many diverse societies on earth was an important component of this quest for universal knowledge. Europeans began looking outwards to understand Islam, India, China and myriad indigenous populations. This aided Europeans not only in grasping cultural difference but also in their drive to dominate different cultures. By 1743, a Dutch bookseller and refugee from France went even further. He published the nine-volume encyclopaedic *Ceremonies et coutumes religieuses de tous les peuples du monde*, the first known attempt to distinguish all the world's religions.[14] When John Toland (d. 1722) published 'Christianity Not Mysterious' in England in 1695, he coined the new term **pantheism** – the idea of a spiritual energy that pervaded the whole universe – something that transcended mere cultural beliefs. From here, in the eighteenth century, Europeans began making a case for a world of nonspiritual, scientific principles that transcended traditional faiths.

Such new ways of thinking and acting influenced Isaac Newton's (d. 1727) revolutionary grand scientific explanation of the universe. Newton's three universal laws of gravitation, his studies of calculus and the laws of motion inspired a new way of seeing the world, whether or not he intended, though he himself was Christian. Leibniz challenged Newton's claims, offering his own view of the universe, writing fundamentally important works of mathematics, science, engineering and physics in use to this day. Both Leibniz's and Newton's views would remain the accepted explanation for space, time and the universe at large, until Albert Einstein's work in the early twentieth century.

Knowledge as power?

All of this theorizing, debating and experimenting impacted the real world far beyond universities and coffee houses. Francis Bacon's dictum that *knowledge is power* demonstrates the connection between learning and actual influence. The application of science made weapons on naval ships more powerful and accurate, and, therefore, made the colonization of native peoples all the easier and more effective. A peculiar mixture of progress and exploitation emerged from Western Europe in this era. Universally noble aspirations sat comfortably alongside brutal expansion.

Technically and scientifically advanced European powers would do great harm to societies all around the world after this era. Much would be lost worldwide in the coming centuries, as Europeans pursued global power, often in the name of progress and wealth generation. After English military strategies enabled victory over the ancient enemy France in the Seven Years War (1756–63), a century of British global domination and overseas expansion would oppress and humiliate ancient cultures worldwide.

By 1750, European thinkers began to apply systematic thinking to the field of economics. Theorists, soon called economists, asked new and broad questions about wealth. Could one calculate the main factors of production, land, labour and capital to purposely create prosperity? How should a civil government be run to enable efficient tax collection and revenue accounting? Such seemingly mundane questions influenced Europeans considerably in the eighteenth century, as they brought capitalism to every corner of the world and colonized even more regions in search of wealth. Interest in wealth generation at home motivated interest in foreign regions, bolstered by technical knowledge that would be turned into actual military power.

Important scientists like Robert Boyle (d. 1691) strove to analyse all atomic matter and determined the connection between the pressure and volume of gases. Mathematical calculations estimated air pressure and discovered the very existence of gas. Aside from inventing an adding machine in 1642, Blaise Pascal (d. 1662) devised theorems to forecast weather, by analysing air pressure and vacuums.

Information derived from such knowledge aided sailors, warriors and strategists as cultures clashed in the coming years. This further aided European technological and military superiority in the eighteenth century, as westerners began to exhibit open disdain towards other cultures. By the nineteenth century, European military technologies enabled global imperialism and the oppression of both non-literate and literate societies, usually in the name of economic necessity or cultural superiority.

The Scientific Revolution and its many associated transformations were not simply progressive movements of social justice, equality and tolerance for humanity. Few people suggested true equality or individual human rights. Though status, tradition and prestige were challenged like never before, behaviour was still regulated. Further, comfortable connections to family, village, tradition and local religious elites were now replaced by more individualistic, cross-cultural perspectives. Aligned with scientific knowledge, a new European culture of economic acquisition and religious condescension would alienate Eurasian and American societies through the eighteenth and nineteenth centuries. Overseas expansion through technical ultimately contributed to the new intellectual concept of scientific racism, whose effects are still very alive.

Many educated Europeans found solace in an intellectual world view premised on the inferiority of others. The Yale student David Brainerd wrote in 1745, upon encountering Native Americans, that their practices were monstrous, deriding Indian religious leaders who he claimed were:

Making all the wild, ridiculous and distracted motions imaginable; sometimes singing, sometimes howling, sometimes extending their hands to the utmost stretch . . . sometimes stroking their faces with their hands, then spurting water as fine as mist; sometimes sitting flat on the earth, then bowing down their faces to the ground; then wringing their sides as if in pain and anguish, twisting their faces, turning up their eyes, grunting, puffing, &c.[15]

Progress, reason and scientific progress soon succumbed to the human proclivity to dominate others. Indeed, in many ways, little changed. Europeans were not special. They continued to act hostile towards others, as societies had through centuries past. Slavery remained the most obvious moral blight on humanity, and saw its highpoint in the eighteenth century, while Europeans proclaimed liberal universal ideals. Slavery was supported and controlled by religious and secular people in the very European states that openly espoused the new ideas of freedom, liberty and justice for all. At the same time, Europeans also spearheaded the movement to abolish slavery after 1800. They introduced the new concept of **individual rights**, which exploded on the world scene in the American Revolution of 1776 and the French Revolution of 1789. The abandonment of fanatical institutions such as the Inquisition and the decline of burning live humans for supposed sorcery was surely a common good in human history.

Conclusion

In 1500, Europeans accepted astrology as an explanatory mechanism for the universe, whereas by 1750 leading European thinkers fundamentally condemned it. Traditional conceptualizations of nature failed to satisfy greater numbers of people. Reason came to the fore, enabling those who were allowed to think for themselves to try to live a more dignified life. After 1700 the idea emerged that there was only one type of human who, though living in various societies on earth, shared one human nature, one morality, one true understanding of justice and one explanation for the universe. In this conception, all societies all over the world, and all their rulers, were mere subsets of a common universal human nature. This idea came to fruition in the European Enlightenment of the late eighteenth century.

By then Voltaire spearheaded the crusade to shame the cruel and ignorant into reflection, and Immanuel Kant (d. 1804) ennobled reason by hypothesizing a cross-cultural, universal responsibility for all humans to uphold an ethical conscience towards others – he formulated this idea into his **categorical imperative**. Put simply, Kant argued, 'If we all acted that way, what kind of world would this be?' As the Enlightenment emerged in Europe, some sense of other people's well-being emerged as a fundamental world view. England stopped burning witches in 1716, and by 1749 the last witch was burned in Europe. Those who tended to light the match began to imagine their own bodies on fire, perhaps.

In 1750, as in 1500, European states had no more military or economic power than Asian empires. They were no more ethical or compassionate. They were no more productive economically, they were no healthier and they were certainly not superior biologically. What did set many North-western European societies apart, however, was that by the mid-seventeenth century they had begun to develop knowledge scientifically, gathering data and sharing information, applying ideas not only to the human body, the earth and its cultures but also towards industrial production and technological invention, as we will see in the next chapter.

Keywords

Indulgences
Predestination
Scepticism
Scientific Revolution
Humanism
Anti-clerical
Spanish Inquisition

Representation
Humanism
Levellers
Dissenters
Metrics
Theorize
Social Contract
Deduction
Empiricism
Induction
Dualism
Monism
Materialism
Pantheism
Individual rights
Categorical imperative

Further reading

Acemoglu, Daron and James A. Robinson. *Why Nations Fail: The Origins of Power, Prosperity, and Poverty*. London: Profile Books, 2013. An excellent study of political economy, showing that both before 1500 and today, nations rise or fall premised upon man-made political and economic institutions which either condemn or aid societies across the world.

Daly, Jonathan W. *How Europe Made the Modern World: Creating the Great Divergence*. London: Bloomsbury Academic, 2020. Latest research on Eurocentrism and European exceptionalism, putting Europe's rise in context of Eurasian societies while recognizing that Europeans did something different after 1700, for better or worse.

Huff, Toby E. *Rise of Early Modern Science - Islam, China, and the West*. Cambridge: Cambridge University Press, 2017. A thorough explanation of the role of universities, legal institutions and freedom to express that differed in Europe, China and the Islamic world in the early modern era.

Jin, Dengjian. *The Great Knowledge Transcendence: The Rise of Western Science and Technology Reframed*. Basingstoke: Palgrave Macmillan, 2016. . Original work recognizing the unusualness of European approaches to modern science and technology, offering explanations based on beliefs, geography and ideas.

Wiesner, Merry E. *Women and Gender in Early Modern Europe*. Cambridge: Cambridge University Press, 2019. A wide-ranging study of all aspects of women's life in the early modern era: including work relations, urban life, learning, literacy and art.

Interlude 4 – New types of knowledge

Though long-standing religious and philosophical traditions dominated most people's thoughts through our era, by 1750 new secular ideas, encouraged by print technology and growing literacy, were becoming prevalent. The *Encyclopédie* marked a turning point. This was a series of books published in France between 1751 and 1772, edited by the philosopher Denis Diderot and the mathematician-inventor Jean le Rond d'Alembert. Reaching close to 18,000 pages, it included images and text, intended to educate anyone who could read on subjects like philosophy, history, the arts and technology.

The *Encyclopédie*, of course, did not emerge out of thin air. First, it owed a lot to smaller reference works published in North-western Europe in the early 1700s. These included dictionaries like *A New General English Dictionary* (1735), or the *Lexicon Technicum* (1704–10), which illustrated the sciences and arts emerging in Britain, France and Germany in the 1720s and 1730s. The *Encyclopédie* was also born of growing interest in technology and new ideas spreading among a widening class of artisans and intellectuals in scientific societies. Last, it benefitted greatly from the increasing sophistication of print technology and the spread of literacy in Western and North-western Europe.

The subtitle of the *Encyclopédie* was 'Systematic Dictionary of the Sciences, Arts, and Crafts'. It was more than just a collection of entries; rather, it was actually representative of a new way of organizing and thinking about information that sought to systematize all known human knowledge. The entries were carefully ordered alphabetically, so that they would be easy to locate, and grouped in orderly manner into subjects. The *Encyclopédie* promoted ideas as products of *human* innovation, rather than as natural or divine inspiration. Thus, it represented a particular way of thinking that came out of the scientific revolution – empiricism. This was a process of experimentation, observation and understanding that proceeding through debate and brainstorming, supported by evidence, to reveal the way things worked. The authors and compilers of the *Encyclopédie* applied such reasoning to many new topics, such as the right of individuals to choose their religion, the virtue of increasing political rights and even the right to openly attack institutions like the monarchy or Catholic Church. In many ways, the *Encyclopédie* was the great intellectual product of the Enlightenment.

Aside from being, in and of itself, representative of the new technology of empiricism, the *Encyclopédie* also explored new technologies, spreading them in France, around Europe and then to the American colonies. These included glass-making, printing and weaving, among others, described in Chapter 8. The section on glass-making was especially extensive, and demonstrated both a rationalized system for organizing the workshop and individual steps in the process of making different glass products (Figure I.4.1).

The *Encyclopédie* represented a major change in ways of thinking about the world. It codified and spread new technologies of literacy. However, we should not overstate its immediate impact. The volumes had many detractors, including religious leaders who saw it as overly critical of the Church and conventional thought. Other opponents included philosophers and innovators who disagreed with some of the interpretations. Nevertheless, the *Encyclopédie* had a higher print run than almost any text written in this period, and was distributed widely enough to influence thinkers and tinkerers in much of the Atlantic world. It was the first widespread attempt to print total understanding of the world around us. Like Wikipedia today, it was imperfect, but it was a new way of finding information about the world.

Figure I.4.1 Sheet glass manufacture, 1765. Engraving showing men working with sheet glass in a glasswork (© Getty Images).

8

Technology in a maritime age

Chapter Outline

Situating the chapter

In this chapter we focus on technology in early modern history, with emphasis on two ideas: innovation and diffusion. **Innovation** is the process by which new technologies, techniques and material goods were created, while **diffusion** covers the spread of these goods and their adoption across regions and within societies. The invention of new technologies and their worldwide spread happened within historical context, and this chapter will outline technological change in the period between 1500 and 1750.

It's possible to say to some degree that technological developments, innovations and inventions occur in response to regional needs. If there is a problem to be solved or a new opportunity to be exploited, very often new technologies emerge or old ones are repurposed or improved to meet particular challenges. However, such a description of 'need driving innovation' fails to provide a sufficient explanation. Historians have learned long ago not to fall into the trap of **determinism** – believing that innovation or change *had* to happen because of some new situation. Different societies may in fact find different solutions to the same problem. Many innovations occur before they are needed, and the emergence of a new crisis or opportunity merely helps to make their adoption widespread. Societies sometimes reject useful new technologies for cultural or political reasons, even when they have a need in place or could benefit from the technology.

Although 'necessity' is not, then, the only cause of innovation and diffusion of technology, it remains an influential factor. The availability of materials and components necessary for the technology or for artisans who can work with materials is another important contributing condition – and that varies by location and geography. This is partly an environmental issue, so the environment can affect the geographic capabilities of a region for innovation. Another factor is the receptiveness of a particular society to a new innovation, an issue often shaped by cultural or

Figure 8.1 Colour woodblock print depicting a Dutch Ship of the Dutch East India Company. Dated 1860 (© Alamy).

religious considerations. Politics plays a role as well, especially in terms of the willingness of a government to sponsor or support particular innovations. Thus, technology does not stand alone as a theme, but rather is interwoven with various local and global contexts at any time (Figure 8.1).

In this chapter, we will look at the development and spread of new technologies in the early modern world. By the end of this chapter, readers should be able to:

- Interpret ways in which technology shaped the Atlantic slaving system, was used by abolitionists to end it and has played a role in how we remember enslavement.
- Hypothesize the relationship between technological development and the scientific revolution in this period.
- Explain the specific conditions that propelled or limited innovation and diffusion, whether in the development of the galleon, the use of clocks or the adoption of chintz-making in Europe.
- Compare and contrast new institutions that presaged the 'factory', including plantations, slave ships, silver mining refineries, sugar mills and cotton mills.
- Analyse ways in which technology and 'science' began to transform the daily lives of people worldwide.
- Debate both the benefits and costs of new technologies with regard to human dignity, safety and life.

Narrative

In this chapter, we explore the ways in which technologies were developed and spread around the world after 1500. Technological developments in the previous several thousand years created large landmasses of shared know-how that influenced early modern technological change. Among the largest of these was the iron-using zone that spread across almost all of Asia, Europe and Africa. Iron smelting technology had probably originated in only one or two places – Assyria and perhaps China and West Africa – but it spread widely across the connected regions of Eurasia and Africa. Much later in our era, technologies of gunpowder and movable-type printing diffused from China across to North Africa and Europe, although not yet to sub-Saharan Africa. Technologies of mathematics and medicine, devised in the Islamic world, but based partly on Greek and South Asian techniques, spread rapidly in the late medieval period and became widely available in Eurasia and Northern Africa.

The societies of the Pacific Ocean constituted a separate zone, sharing agricultural, canoe-building and architectural technologies widely among scattered islands inhabited over vast ocean expanses. People in the Americas constituted yet another zone, even more isolated from Eurasia. Here, too, however, there was widespread sharing. Pottery and agricultural techniques developed in central Mexico were adopted across Meso-America and up into the forestlands of the Mississippi river region. Across large areas of North America, communities shared a mound-and-canal building technology that allowed them to construct safe, elevated towns and cities as well as fields for growing crops. Peoples of the Andes region in South America also shared highly sophisticated weaving and transportation technologies.

Technology in a maritime age

In the early modern period, the Americas, Eurasia and Africa were brought together to a greater degree than ever before. The development of new technologies in the years before 1500, such as improved sailing vessels helped to create a new historical situation, and the opportunities that this connection offered helped spur on further technological development towards and after 1750. Thus, technological change was deeply linked to the Columbian Exchange and the new global connectivity that resulted in the early modern period. This was nowhere truer than in the building of sailing vessels.

Canouas, kora-kora and galleys

Just as broad zones of shared technology existed over land, so too did societies that bordered seas, oceans and lakes share maritime technologies that likewise allowed them to trade, migrate and travel around vast bodies of water. Perhaps the most ubiquitous type of maritime transport was the canoe, a narrow boat usually with pointed ends without a keel or rudder. Canoes were (and still are) generally propelled and navigated by humans using paddles. Such technology was found in various forms around the world at the beginning of the fifteenth century – from the round leather-covered coracles built of wicker in use in the Celtic societies of Ireland and Scotland to the dugouts used by the Yurok and other seagoing societies on the western edge of North America. In many of these societies, large cultural distinctions existed between communities that lived off the sea and those just inland who focused on land-based foods and products.

Along the western coast of Africa, numerous societies specialized in fishing and trading along the sea. These enormous canoes could carry relatively large loads of goods up and down coastlines. Some, carved from large trees, could carry as many as 120 people. Canoe-makers carved these out of hardwood like the silk cotton tree, and excavated the trunks with fire, which hollowed the interior and also drove out parasites in the wood. This caused it to leak a sap that acted as a pitch, sealing the vessel for the water. Such canoes were common from Sierra Leone all the way down to the Kingdom of Congo. These massive trading canoes had decks made of reeds, benches for paddlers and even hearths on which to cook. War canoes, used in battle, had built-up sides for defence against arrows and spears. Fishermen often used a number of smaller fishing canoes working together to allow for the netting of large schools. Still other small canoes were employed along streams, where they were more easily navigated.

Trading canoes also bound together the Caribbean region, which connected its many islands, not only with each other but also with the South American mainland. Indeed, the modern word 'canoe' is probably adapted from the word 'canoua', used by the Calusa people of the Florida coast. Most large vessels were made of a single trunk, often from the mahogany tree, although there is some evidence that planks were in some cases used to build above-water edges. The trunks were steamed and then spread to widen them, which in some cases produced a flat bottom, allowing for swifter travel in shallow water. Christopher Columbus claimed that most were not very large, but could move much faster between the islands than his own vessels. Many Taino and Carib canoes also had awnings of matting or leaves to protect the rowers.

Pacific maritime vessels, especially those from Polynesia and Melanesia, developed from canoe technology. In this region, however, the challenges of crossing the wide ocean had for centuries inspired the technological development of sails and outriggers. Sails reduced the effort necessary to propel sea craft, but they required a great deal of skill to use effectively. Outriggers – beams or logs attached to the side of the vessel at some length – made canoes far more stable in heavy seas. Unlike West African and Caribbean vessels, most of these trans-Pacific trading vessels were built from planks tied together with fibres. Many were double-hulled, with a platform stretched between them, adding to their stability and providing an enormous space for onboard activity. By the fifteenth century, very sophisticated types of rigging, that allowed for larger and better boats, spread out from the islands of Tonga.

Similar outriggers were in widespread use across Southeast Asia. Some canoes, like the kora-kora of the Maluku Islands, were probably developed from a common ancestor. The Malukans and their neighbours built outriggers into giant war vessels that could hold over 100 paddlers and warriors. These islanders could combine these vessels into fleets called *hongi*.

Even the fleets of the Malukans were no match for the massive armadas launched by the early Ming emperors of China. Well before 1500, Chinese sailed the seas in fleets consisting of more than 300 ships. The largest were 400-foot-long 'treasure ships' built of panels around interior frames and with sophisticated sails. The largest ships of the age, they were nonetheless abandoned in the mid-fifteenth century – partly because of the lack of sufficient timber, itself the result of a growing Chinese population – but also because of developments in its metallurgy industry. As a result, Chinese maritime activity by 1500 had moved away from the vast, government-built ships and into much smaller vessels owned by private companies or families and often built in Southeast Asia. Chief among these were *jongs*, which were built of many planks nailed together, navigated using rudders, wooden or metal devices at the rear of the ship, that could be turned to steer it. *Jongs* had multiple sails but no real rigging. Instead, their sails were divided into many pieces which could all be adjusted to the wind.

Jongs were used all along the Pacific coast of Asia and into Southeast Asia, but to the west the *dhow* began to replace them. These vessels were often constructed along the coast of South Asia, although were also used in Arabia and East Africa. *Dhow*-builders designed the vessel to take advantage of the strong winds and seasonal weather patterns of the Indian Ocean. Triangular, or *lateen*, sails allowed *dhows* to capture the wind and even to sail at an angle against it. Larger *dhows* had multiple masts, complex rigging and a hull sewn together with remarkably strong but not especially durable twine.

At this time, trade goods moving from East Asia to Europe along oceanic routes would typically been carried in *jongs* and *dhows* for part of their voyage. Once they reached the Mediterranean, however, they would have likely been carried in galleys. Although the African, Asian and European societies bordering the Mediterranean used large sail-driven vessels for carrying bulky goods, it was the many-oared galley that usually carried expensive, small items. Built for war, galleys had little cargo space but were well protected and moved fast. They might have a single sail, but it was ranks of oars that propelled them most of the time. Though lightly built for speed, galleys often boasted heavily reinforced rams at the bow. Perfect for the conflicts of the Mediterranean, they were not particularly useful trading vessels and were nowhere near durable enough to cross the Atlantic.

The new age of sail

With the above in mind, the key maritime development of the early modern age was in fact the three-mast, sturdily built trading ship. Early forms, such as the caravel, had been developed prior to 1492 and indeed made possible the fifteenth-century Portuguese and Spanish voyages of exploration and trade that would change world history. A widely shared Eurasian technological network helped make these vessels possible. Caravels combined European square sails with the lateen sail of the *dhow*, and their hulls borrowed from Mediterranean construction techniques used in the galley. Caravels were hardy and moved speedily, and since they didn't have to carry banks of oarsmen or paddlers they could carry relatively large amounts of cargo for their size. However, they could carry only light armament, and were still not sturdy enough for the storms of the wide Atlantic Ocean. So, while good starter vessels for trans-oceanic trade, they could not feed the voracious demands of the European public and Eurasian states eager for American metal and Asian goods.

Developments after 1500 soon propelled global trade forward remarkably. In order to bridge the vast distances of global trade routes, larger and faster ships were in constant demand. Durability and armament were also major concerns. Between 1500 and 1750, ships became larger and larger, culminating in the 600- to 800-ton **East Indiamen**, European-built ships that traversed the long distances from ports like London and Amsterdam to South and East Asia. Such ships were built more stoutly and somewhat lower in front than caravels, and could survive very rough weather. Their hulls were reinforced with **wales**, thick planks that ran longitudinally, and were internally braced. They had increasingly efficient pumps that sailors could man to remove bilge water. Their sails were larger and more carefully cut, and could be hauled or lowered only by use of massive blocks and pulleys that multiplied the work of sailors. These were sophisticated ships.

Because such ships proved difficult to build, in the 1600s some states began to sponsor the publication of technical textbooks for training shipbuilders in the many arts of naval construction. Builders across Europe made use of increasingly sophisticated mathematics, which by the eighteenth century helped them to engineer tighter and stronger ships. In the north-western parts of Europe, they also benefitted from state sponsorship of dockyards. Engineers built dry-docks that could be flooded when the ship was ready to float, reducing the need to move the huge ships from land to sea. Western European states benefitted greatly from the creation of colonies in the Americas, where vast forests with large, durable hardwoods provided an abundance of raw materials for ship building.

The *East Indiamen* and other large galleons gave Europeans an enormous advantage in achieving a position of dominance and control of trade routes around the world. Stable in rough seas, relatively fast, and able to carry huge amounts of cargo, these ships transformed the movement of goods around the world. The huge ships of the Portuguese East India Company brought control of the profitable routes linking China and Japan, while Spanish galleons linked Manila to Mexico and Spain. By the seventeenth century, large ships from Northern European states were competing to establish new routes or steal those dominated by Spain and Portugal.

Some societies pivoted quickly to emulate the Europeans so as to limit Western dominance. South Asian shipwrights quickly learned to build big ships modelled on the galleon. Many of these were purchased by the sultans of Southeast Asian island principalities like Aceh as well as mainland states like Johor. The rulers of these states also bought guns designed by Ottoman engineers to equip their vessels. As early as the mid-sixteenth century, these small states became effective competitors to the Europeans in this region. Still, in the long run it was Europeans, buttressed by the wealth of the Americas and early modern engineering technologies, who had the resources to consistently improve their ships and weapons and, eventually, to dominate global trade by the end of our period.

A scientific revolution in North-west Europe

After 1500, the wealth of the Americas helped to promote the development of new technologies in Europe and its American colonies. Many of these advances are connected to new, scientific ways of thinking introduced in the last chapter. The scientific revolution in thinking did not rapidly introduce new technologies for common household use, at least in the short term. Yet, it did help to promote the development of some basic scientific tools that would have major repercussions for technology and for global society in the long run. For instance, the use of astronomical knowledge enabled Europeans to more confidently sail around the world and dominate the indigenous peoples of the lands they conquered.

A revolution in basic tools

Perhaps the most important significance of North-western Europe technology in world historical terms was the ubiquitous development of basic tools and mechanisms that Europeans used to promote or contribute to the invention of *other*, more complex, technologies. The clock is a prime example. Timekeeping technology in Europe had developed rapidly in the late medieval period, with water clocks, sand hourglasses, sundials and, finally, mechanical clocks becoming widespread. Large clocks became features of urban life around Europe in this period, arranged around the centres of power – churches, palaces and town halls. In our period, however, a new seemingly minor innovation made the clock more portable, universal and thus ubiquitous in the lives of many Europeans. This was the **balance spring**, a coiled spring that could be wound up to propel the clock at a standard, constant rate.

Developed first by Robert Hooke in London in 1658, and then in even smaller form by the Dutch mechanic Huygens in 1674, the spring was truly revolutionary. Previously, all clocks had to be attached to the ground in a constant position, for they needed either a single orientation towards the sun or the pull of gravity to function. The balance spring liberated clocks from this need. As a result, clocks could be built smaller – and attached to people's wrists or pockets, allowing for the development of the watch! They could also be placed on ships, where, despite constant rocking by waves, they kept good time. Englishman John Harrison made the first such clock in 1761, and we should not underestimate its importance: shipboard clocks allowed sailors to determine the exact time of day, and together with sightings of the sun and the horizon, this enabled them to establish – for the first time in human history – their longitudinal position on the earth. As a result, British and later other European ships could navigate much more effectively and land where they intended. The impact was so vast that the British government awarded Harrison the huge sum of 10,000 British pounds for his innovation.

Another crucial technology developed in this period was glass lenses. It was already known across late medieval Eurasia that curved glass lenses could bend light and bring close or far away objects into focus. Islamic glass-grinders proved particularly skilled at developing such lenses for eyeglasses, or spectacles. In 1608, however, the Dutch spectacle-maker Johannes Lippershey put two lenses together in a tube in a way that magnified their power. This groundbreaking outcome led to the telescope, which became an essential tool of astronomy. With tweaking, the tube could magnify very close objects as well and by the late seventeenth century, Dutch and British mechanists were building compound microscopes. Perhaps the most important were Robert Hooke's 1665 mechanism and the Dutch scientist Anton van Leeuwenhoek's 1678 version (Figure 8.2).

In the early years of our period, technological innovators in Britain and the rest of Europe were not intellectuals, but rather artisans such as locksmiths. Indeed, artisan science has been shown as a primary motivator for change in technology. Artisans were often mobile, journeymen with a creative exploratory bent. They were not what we would think of formal scientists, but they did much of the arduous, experimental work that lead to what became a scientific revolution over time. Like state-sponsored scientists in recent centuries, these artisans worked through networked social relations, shared ideas and worked for freedom to explore nature's mysteries.

Tinkerers, gunsmiths, blacksmiths, glass-blowers and many obscure individuals knew already the skills of working with materials like metal, wood and sinews. As a result, they could carefully design and build the globes, clocks, quadrants, lenses and other parts necessary for complex instruments. Workers' guilds, such as the Worshipful Company of Clockmakers or the Spectacle Makers' Company, usually sponsored these innovators, rather than the Royal Society or kings and queens. Technological innovation in North-western Europe was often very much a middle-

Figure 8.2 A microscope built by Robert Hooke, 1675 (Wikimedia Commons).

class pursuit. More famous often well-connected, scientists whose names have filled textbooks for decades certainly played a role, but so too did many unknown, common artisans doing their work day by day in the interest of experimentation.

Politics and technological innovation

Still, by the mid-seventeenth century, governments began to play an important role in subsidizing innovation. Robert Hooke was a very important inventor and scientist who conducted experiments in the fields of chemistry, biology and astronomy, and built numerous significant tools besides the microscope. Yet he was not a rich man. His work, and that of many of his colleagues, depended on the support of the **Royal Society of London**, which in turn relied on the patronage of King Charles II of Great Britain. In a similar, if less organized, manner, scientists and technicians were sponsored by monarchs in the Netherlands, France and even the states of Scandinavia and German principalities. Galileo belonged to such societies, bringing sharp-eyed observation to human understanding of the skies. Indeed by 1750 there were more than ten connected Scientific Societies across Europe, from Dublin in Ireland to St Petersburg in Russia: this was an early internet of innovators.

Why were European rulers – exceptionally – willing to sponsor technological innovations? At least part of the answer resides in the peculiar politics of Europe in the early modern era, which we examined in Chapter 2. In the first place, there was already a good model in place. The Spanish and Portuguese had clearly reaped massive wealth from their American colonies, because of their rulers' sponsorship of risky overseas adventures. British, Dutch and French state officials sought to match their rivals by building better ships and by establishing colonies of their own. Indeed, they modelled their sponsorship of innovators directly on the Spanish crown's successful gamble on Christopher Columbus.

At the same time, the many small states of Europe were engaged in almost constant warfare during this period. So, they needed not only new weapons to fight with but also money to pay for them. Technological innovation promised both to improve weaponry and to beget economically promising industries that governments could tax, like textiles and mining. Violence begat innovation!

We should recall that many of these innovations were based on earlier Islamic and Chinese inventions, which often filtered into Europe through the countless trading voyages and religious missions that reported back after reaching Asia. Nor was Europe totally unique in the attention its governments paid to innovation in this period. Many West African rulers, for example, desperately sought to innovate in order either to meet the threat of the slave trade or to capitalize on it. Some innovations included moving communities to safer areas, building new types of armies and adopting new weapons like the flintlock rifle. However, since the Atlantic slaving system drained much of their population and disrupted society, there was limited opportunity to chart a course of technological development. In a similar way, the states and communities of the Americas during this period experienced both conquest and epidemics, and as a result, innovations developed on plantations and in mines mostly benefitted the European colonizers.

Asian societies were often more economically and politically stable than European ones in the early modern period. Asia had been the centre of technological development for centuries prior to this era. So why did the centre of technological innovation suddenly shift from China, South Asia, and the Islamic world to Europe? The wealth brought back from the Americas to pay for European innovation is one answer. Another is the continuing political struggles and wars that plagued the continent, which compelled invention. China, unified and preoccupied with the challenge of feeding and managing a vast population, focused more on agricultural policy and stability than on technological development. The Japanese government, embarked as it was on a campaign to unify the islands, focused on establishing order through appeals to tradition rather than introducing new technologies. There are many other examples, but in the end they all demonstrate that in the early modern period, European innovation benefitted from governments that were particularly willing and able to support technological experimentation and take risks. This state sponsorship of innovation owed largely to the ongoing political conflicts and religious rivalries between the continent's many small states. Of course, state sponsorship would have produced little on its own without the hard work of so many innovators, who could tinker without fear of repression, censure or censorship.

Technology and the development of an Atlantic world

The Columbian Exchange had done much to connect most of Africa, the Americas and Europe and had spurred development of the latter continent most of all. Indeed, the growing transatlantic world provided the context for many of the new technologies that benefitted Western European countries in the early modern era.

Technologies of the slave trade

Perhaps the first prominent technology of the Atlantic world was the plantation. It was at base a financial and organizational technology, though it was also an economic technology, which we discussed in Chapter 3. It's important to note how new it was in Atlantic and world history as a way of organizing production. A plantation was worked by hundreds of workers, usually organized into large gangs. They were awoken together and their time was highly regimented. They were often given specialized tasks, and they were controlled by overseers who reported to higher authorities, only sometimes to the owners of the plantation. In this it was more like a modern factory than any other site of economic production in the world at the time.

Moreover, the workers generally did not produce their own food or other subsistence goods. Whether Native Americans or indentured Europeans at first – and later and more prevalently – Africans, they usually relied on food brought in from outside. Security was always a major concern for those in power, both against raids by indigenous peoples or escaped former slaves and the flight of slaves into the countryside. On larger plantations, each of these jobs – work scheduling, victualing, security, storage, discipline and the eventual export and sale of goods – was overseen by experts.

The technology of the plantation was supported by an even more highly organized technology – the slave ship. This was a floating dungeon as well as an economic instrument. Slaving voyages could be immensely profitable to investors, but only if the enslaved human cargo survived the trip and did not escape. Thus, slave ships were carefully constructed to meet the needs of investors. For example, decks were often surrounded by extra nets and high rails in order to prevent suicidal slaves from jumping overboard. Installed chains, locks and iron bars prevented escape of millions of those enslaved as cargo.

To maximize profits, slave ships were packed with as many captives as they could carry. In the early modern period, before the slave trade was criminalized, slave ships were generally a mix of stability and speed. Because of the appalling onboard conditions for captives, many sickened or died on long voyages. But in vessels built for speed alone, the resulting instability often sickened or killed the captives. However, lengthy voyages also tended to result in high mortality rates among captives, so slave ships had to achieve a balance between speed and stability to maximize profits.

All of this required technological innovation that bordered on the scientific. Over time, slave-ship builders settled on common design specifications for completed ships and for their provisioning, including preferred height of decks, standard space for captives and types of food preparation. All decisions aimed at maximizing the number of captives who could be carried while minimizing escapes and deaths. Cost overrode compassion in this technological calculus.

Weaponry proved a key technology in helping to ensure the security and profitability of the voyage. Weapons – particularly cannon and guns – played three roles in the Atlantic slave trade. First, guns were one of the major goods exchanged in Africa for captives. Indeed, guns may have helped to stimulate the trade more than any other technology. When Europeans first arrived in regions of West and West-Central Africa looking to purchase humans for enslavement, they found trading partners who wanted guns in exchange. These guns, then, gave their new African partners a superior military technology, allowing them to raid other societies for slaves in turn. West African societies were then faced with a terrible decision: if they chose *not* to participate in the slave trade, as many preferred, they might become victims of better-armed rival neighbours. The only way they could get hold of these advanced weapons, however, was to participate in the trade themselves. This 'gun-and-slave' cycle was one of the major stimuli to the slave trade. Europeans retained superior guns to provide security on ships and to prevent raids and escapes once captives reached plantations in the Americas. Typically, Europeans traded older gun models for slaves.

Experiences of the enslaved

These new technologies – all of which were 'scientific' and 'rational' – transformed so many lives for the worse. One form of slave labour that required high levels of organization was the rowing of galleys in the Mediterranean. Even before the early modern era, such vessels, with their banks of rowers, required large pools of slaves from Southwest Asia, Europe and North Africa. This kind of slavery reached its height in the late sixteenth century before sailing ships replaced galleys.

Accounts from the 1571 Battle of Lepanto, between a Christian coalition and the Ottoman Empire, reveal the conditions in which galley slaves worked. Many of the rowers were war captives, although some were simply outcasts. Catholic ships, for examples, had many imprisoned Protestants and Jews as rowers, as well as homosexuals and debtors. They sailed exposed to the sun, often in sweltering conditions, and were poorly treated. For example, the food of Italian oarsmen:

> [C]onsists of 30 ounces of biscuits every day, in winter time they have water and soup on alternate days. . . . When they are in port, their soup consists of 3 ounces of fava beans with a quarter of an ounce of oil each; but they do not get it when they are at sea, to avoid stuffing them when they need to be extremely agile and ready to row.[1]

Conditions as a captive on an Atlantic slave ship 180 years later were even worse. Such ships were so unhealthy that mortality rates even among free sailors were incredibly high, although not nearly as high as for the captives. Olaudah Equiano detailed his experiences as a captive on board a ship in the 1750s:

> The closeness of the place and the heat of the climate, added to the number of the ship, which was so crowded that each had scarcely room to turn himself, almost suffocated us. This produced copious perspirations so that the air became unfit for respiration from a variety of loathsome smells, and brought on a sickness among the slaves, of which many died – thus falling victims of the improvident avarice, as I may call it, of their purchasers. This wretched situation was again aggravated by the galling of the chains, which now became insupportable, and the filth of the necessary tubs [toilets] into which the children often fell and were almost suffocated. The shrieks of the women and the groans of the dying rendered the whole a scene of horror almost inconceivable.[2]

As Olaudah explains, human captives suffered from sickness and death at terrible rates. European investors were not generally perturbed at this suffering, but they did recognize that mortality and sickness affected their profits. Thus, in the eighteenth century they developed an organized regime to keep the captives alive. These included routines in which the captives were fed, 'aired' on decks and forced to dance as exercise. Such dehumanization may have helped the slavers' economic bottom lines, but it did little to alleviate the captives' suffering.

Engineering – Technologies of domination

Of course, guns and cannon were available in many parts of the world in this period. In fact, fifteenth-century European guns were no better than those of the Islamic World or Asia. However, European military technology improved incrementally between

1500 and 1750 such that it was far superior at the end of our period. Sixteenth-century innovations like the wheel lock and the flintlock improved accuracy and made guns much easier to use. Still, most guns remained inaccurate enough that they needed to be used in large formations to be effective. By 1600, European experiments on new types of cannon resulted in the muzzle-loading cast-iron gun that came to dominate warfare in this era. By 1750, Europeans had made these guns better and lighter than those elsewhere in Eurasia, which resulted in a growing power gap by the eighteenth century.

The most important innovations were not in offensive armaments but in defensive fortifications. The late medieval period had proved that old-style castles with straight vertical walls and towers were vulnerable to cannon-fire. They also proved too costly to justify defending whole towns and cities. A series of Western European designers responded by developing new types of fortifications. Many were partially buried or composed of built-up earthworks that could better sustain bombardment. They were also laid out in careful patterns to make it harder for storming infantry to find cover from gunfire. These innovative patterns were among the most important works of engineering in Europe during this period, and were partly the result of mathematical calculations of men involved in other kinds of technological experiments and calculations at the time. Those who wished to fight and conquer relied on math and science to gain advantages.

European innovations in fortifications were again partly the result of the bloody conflicts that wracked the continent in this era. Such conflicts as the long revolt of the Netherlands against Spanish rule (1566–1609), the Thirty Years War (1618–48) and the Italian wars of the early sixteenth century were motivated in part by religious fanaticism and were accompanied by the widespread slaughter of town populations. Fortifying urban areas in such circumstances proved crucial. The bloodiness of these conflicts also helped to push forward medical innovation, as new techniques for surgery emerged from the treatment of wounded soldiers. Progress here was limited, however, and European ideas of medicine and health remained behind those of the Islamic world through our period.

Forts also served as power bases for protecting trading advantages and commercial ventures, including the slave trade. Of all the European outposts in the Americas that required protection, none was economically more important than the mines at Potosí in the Andes, the richest source of silver in the world and a key to the Spanish Habsburg Empire. The mine, the forts that protected it and nearby trading ports exemplified some of the most advanced engineering technology of the era.

Working the mines

Workers at Potosí and neighbouring mines were not formally enslaved, but were either wage labourers or drafted through the *mita* system. Still, they worked in dreadful conditions and were among the most highly organized of early modern labourers. Four thousand to five thousand people were organized into shifts and housed either in barracks or in small shacks. Antonio Vazquez de Espinoza, writing in the seventeenth century, described *mita* as a very corrupt system that Native Americans sought to evade and that caused the depopulation of entire villages. He also described the miners' working conditions:

> The ore was very rich black flint, and the excavation so extensive that it held more than 3,000 Indians working away with picks and hammers, breaking up that flint ore; and when they have filled their little sacks, the poor fellow, loaded down with ore, climb up those ladders or rigging, some like masts and others like cables, and so trying and distressing that a man empty-handed can hardly get them up.[3]

Aside from the rigours of labour, miners faced a great many dangers. Working with mercury caused dreadful burns and organ breakdown. Mines frequently caved in. Finally, the cold weather broke down their immune systems. Nor did they profit from their labour – pay was low, even for wage labourers, with most of the profits going directly to the Spanish crown, to investors and business interests in Spain, or to the big coastal ports of the Spanish Americas.

Mining was a relatively extensive technology worldwide at the beginning of the early modern era. In some areas, most people still collected metal from the surface or from rivers. Such techniques were extensive in Oceania, the central Pacific, and southern Africa as well as much of the Americas. However, somewhat more sophisticated underground mining was common across Europe, Asia and most of Africa. Copper mines from this period have even been excavated in North America. Yet no mines anywhere were as large as those that the Spanish constructed in their American colonies in the sixteenth century.

But the mines at Potosí were not technological marvels, rather just larger examples of older Eurasian mines. The processing of the silver, too, was largely based on older technologies known in Europe and adapted to some degree from even older Asian processes. An important new technology called **liquation** revolutionized the process. Liquation mixed ores with lead or mercury to separate the silver from the other metals with which they were mixed. This process was developed at the beginning of the early modern period in Germany, where miners often dug up copper and silver in a mixed alloy. Europeans thus created new labour-saving devices for mining, devising ways to refine metals and make pumps.

At Potosí, the silver refineries were composed of large buildings with stamp mechanisms for crushing the silver-bearing rock (or *ore*). Water wheels usually powered these stamps. Huge tanks then received the ore, where it was mixed with water, salt and mercury. The mixture then released the silver from the rock, combining with the mercury, which had to be distilled and the silver pulled out.

Yet, while the mining and processing technology were European (and Eurasian) in their origins, the system of labour organization technology used in the mines and refineries was a mix of European and indigenous Andean traditions. The Spanish recruited labour through the *mita* described in Chapter 5, a complex system long used by Inca rulers to build their own vast empire before the arrival of the Spanish. Under Inca rule, the *mita* required that surrounding communities provide a certain number of days of labour per year to keeping up the infrastructure of the state or working on communal fields. Under Spanish rules set up in 1570, the system became even more extractive, with local labourers required to contribute more and more hours. By 1600, about 5,000 labourers per day worked on the mines and in the refineries. But even this was not enough, especially as the indigenous American population in the region declined owing to epidemics and brutal labour conditions in the mines. The Spanish miners eventually turned to wage labour, offering payment in cash to voluntary workers who augmented the *mita* labourers.

The spread and mix of technologies in the Atlantic world

It seems apparent that sophisticated technologies developed in Eurasia allowed Europeans to dominate in the Americas. Yet, indigenous practices also contributed. As European mineral processing techniques merged with Andean organizational technologies in the mines of Potosí, the new commercial establishments Europeans developed in the Americas relied to a high degree on the mixing of Native American, African and European techniques and tools. Syncretism, as with religious and philosophical ideas, was the norm.

African pastoral and agricultural skills were in especially high demand. In the open grasslands of parts of North and South America, settlers paid a premium for enslaved Africans from northern Senegambia who were exceptionally skilled at working with horses. In the coastal Carolinas, the emerging rice farming economy of the late seventeenth century relied on the knowledge of expert rice growers from the African regions of the Casamance and Sierra Leone. Other Africans brought medical techniques. An enslaved African named Onesimus may have introduced the procedure of vaccination called variolation to Massachusetts, protecting the population from smallpox. Another, named Quassi, discovered a fever-reducing bark in South America.

Similarly, Africans and Europeans arriving in the Americas adopted or adapted Native American technologies. They came to rely on local crops to survive. Native Americans taught the new arrivals how to grow tobacco, and to integrate corn, beans and maize in combinations that retained soil fertility. The immigrants also learned fur-trapping and hunting techniques appropriate to the regions in which they now lived.

Africans and Native Americans who escaped from slave plantations and mines also combined many technologies or created new ones to defend their communities from re-enslavements. In Brazil, communities of escapees called **quilombo** included booby-traps, defensive ditches and walls, and special plantations that could grow abundant crops in small areas disguised to look like the surrounding forests. These communities grew everything they needed – cotton, foodstuffs like cassava and maize, and even sugar. The technologies they combined included some adapted from local Native American communities, some brought from Africa and others learned on European plantations.

Nonetheless, the movement of technologies and techniques around the world in this era clearly led to the decline or transformation of some American and African technologies. In parts of North America and Central Africa, for example, the arrival of cheap and well-made South Asian cotton cloth brought by European merchants essentially wiped out local cloth-making techniques based on bark or other fibres. European iron goods were especially desired in the Americas, where they represented an entirely new technology for natives. At the same time, imported guns began to replace local hunting tools and weaponry. Yet such transformations were only partial. In many regions, especially forested areas, guns were not adopted – local bows or spears remained better suited to the needs of the local population. In parts of Africa, similarly, societies retained local iron technologies and purchased only raw iron from Europeans.

Windmills, clocks and chintz: Three Eurasian technologies

The Atlantic was not the only zone of rapid technological exchange in this period. Along with manufactured products, new technologies increasingly flowed between Europe and large regions of Asia. This exchange was different than the Atlantic exchange, however, because European merchants and missionaries did not have the same power to dominate in Eurasia as they had in the Americas. As a result, the ways in which new technologies were accepted, embraced and rejected were very different.

Harnessing wind power

One of the most significant areas of technological innovation for widespread, everyday use in the period was the development of improved mills for doing work. Mills were large structures of wood that harnessed power to transform raw materials into products. Their most common use by 1500 was in grinding grain into flour. Medieval mills in many parts of the world harnessed the power of humans, animals, water or the wind to do such work. The earliest **windmills**, for example, originated in Persia early in the medieval era, and used large sails mounted to sticks to spin stones that ground anything put between them. By c. 1300, similar looking windmills had spread to parts of Europe. Yet, it was only in the late fifteenth century that a real revolution in windmills occurred, emanating from the very small region of the Netherlands in North-western Europe.

The Netherlands were so named because they were, literally, 'nether' lands, or low lands. Much of the region sits below sea level, and, as the population grew rapidly, land rose in value. This situation stimulated new inventions, and the most important was the adoption of an old technology – the windmill – to the draining of swamps. Between 1407 and 1650, the population of the Netherlands (the Dutch) invented a variety of devices that could be powered by windmills to drain water from sodden fields and increase land volume. Some of these involved attaching scoops to the ends of sails. Others harnessed wind power to screw-like devices that sucked water up and deposited it on the other side of dikes, or walls, built to keep out the sea. The combination of water-draining and dike-building rapidly transformed the Dutch landscape. Where once there had been large, boggy swamps there were now square or rectangular fields surrounded by dikes. These fields, soon known as polders, gradually spread across the Netherlands. In the process, the major rivers of the region were also surrounded by tall dikes. Over time, large areas of wetland wilderness transformed into carefully controlled farmland, grazing land and surrounding market towns – all below sea level!

With windmill technology now adapted to draining farmland, new uses soon followed. By the seventeenth century, the Dutch used windmills to grind pigments for paints (in the process stimulating an explosion in visual arts!), processing hemp and rope, sawing wood and grinding new food imports like chocolate. Different mills, built far away from towns, processed gunpowder much finer and more powerful than that produced by hand. By 1700, thousands of windmills dotted the Dutch countryside, and many of them had been transformed into large buildings with living quarters of the type we see today. Governments across Europe sent experts to learn how to build these technological marvels.

At the same time, Dutch merchants and administrators slowly came to control or influence large swathes of South-east and South Asia. In these territories, they began to introduce the windmill to grind spices and other goods for export to Europe. These windmills were intended to replace the existing local animal-powered mills based on Chinese technology. In the late seventeenth century, the Dutch East India Company built large numbers of windmills (and watermills) in Indonesia.

Local reaction to these windmills varied. Several rulers of provinces that neighboured Dutch colonies witnessed the efficiency of the mills, and laid plans to build their own, often with Dutch help. They included the sultan of the Javanese kingdom of Banten, Japanese officials and the king of Tonkin [Vietnam]. Yet there is some evidence that inhabitants of areas around the mills resisted new technologies like these for a very logical reason: the proficient mills required fewer labourers, and so threatened jobs.

Keeping time

By contrast, many Asian governments rejected the introduction of European mechanical clocks, although some private individuals embraced them. By the seventeenth century, portable clocks and watches brought about changes in some European societies. The technical necessities of producing tiny watch-parts stimulated advances in tools and techniques in London, the Swiss cantons and a few other urban regions. Public clocks began to regulate workdays, while expensive privately owned clocks enhanced the reputation of the growing middle class and inspired some to emulate their status.

Jesuit missionaries and Portuguese merchants brought the first European clocks to China. The clocks they brought immediately drew the attention of Chinese courtiers and even emperors. The emperor Kangxi even wrote a poem in praise of European mechanical clocks, comparing them to older water clocks. In fact, urban Chinese were fascinated by clocks, and immediately demanded them in great numbers. Europeans quickly found that they were one of the few goods that they could give as gifts to Chinese officials, as most European goods were seen as cheap and shoddy. They especially desired clocks with moving figurines, cuckoo-birds and other animated designs, in keeping with Chinese traditions of admiring mechanical people and animals. But though elite Chinese desired the mechanical clock as an exotic or entertaining artefact, Chinese society did not adopt the many social and economic changes that had accompanied the use of this technology in North-west Europe and Italy. There were many reasons for this. Chinese artisans hadn't been trained to make their own clocks, the Ming and Qing dynasties didn't see clocks as a necessary tool for the state and the system of marking twenty-four hours did not fit well with the Confucian-based rhythms of the Chinese day.

Yet the limits of Chinese interest in clocks was not unique. Similar scepticism marked the reception of clocks in Southeast Asia, Korea and the Islamic world, and even in many parts of Europe. Only in a few parts of North-west Europe, and especially Britain, did the clock create revolutionary changes in daily life before eventually spreading outside the region in later centuries.

Learning to make chintz

Not all new techniques and instruments in this period flowed from Europe to Asia. One set of technologies that flowed the other way involved clothes-making. As we have seen in Chapter 3, the trading explosion of the early modern era introduced much of Europe, the Americas, and Africa to textiles produced in India. Rather rapidly, South Asia began to clothe much of the world, expanding their already vast markets, as populations everywhere began to demand large quantities of cloth woven from cotton and other materials. Among the most popular was **chintz**, a glaze-finished and usually quite colourful cloth that used Islamic motifs and which was originally produced around the city of Calicut.

Chintz was a difficult-to-produce and highly specialized cloth. The designs were generally produced through the use of woodblocks dipped in ink, although in some cases they were painted onto the cloth. These designs were so intricate and colourful that, by the late seventeenth century, Europeans imported over a million pieces of chintz cloth every year. As a result, European textile producers sought to emulate the style. But they quickly found that this was almost impossible. Expert Indian producers used three different kinds of wood blocks, from large to small, and carefully produced inks using local products and sophisticated techniques that could not be reproduced in Europe. Moreover, Indian producers used special types of cotton that were not available to European producers.

European textile producers responded to South Asian superiority in the production of chintz in two ways. First, they lobbied their governments to ban the cloth, since it was outcompeting their own products. The French government obliged in 1686, and the English in 1720. However, fashionable men and women desired the cloth so much that the ban failed. So, beginning in the late seventeenth century Europeans sent artisans (or spies) to learn how chintz was produced. In the 1730s, French producers finally managed to reproduce the method, and soon after the government lifted the import bans.

These three examples show the ways in which technologies in this period were resisted, adopted or provoked reactions in new areas opened to them by the expansion of trade. In the Eurasian context, such technologies flowed back and forward largely because of the relative balance among these societies in the period prior to the Industrial Revolution. However, attitudes towards new technologies could differ across societies. In some cases, the states from which the technology was spreading or those receiving it viewed the technologies as having strategic and economic value. In others, the state ascribed little value to new technologies, but members of society disagreed and independently adopted them.

Towards the Industrial Revolution

In the seventeenth and eighteenth centuries, increasing demand for goods produced by mills drove innovations in milling technology. This would forever change production methods, eventually prompting the Industrial Revolution in eighteenth-century England.

New kinds of mills

Mill production also grew rapidly in this era in China, where new equipment in the sixteenth and seventeenth centuries increased the speed at which different kinds of textiles were produced. Chinese textile-milling machinery included mechanisms that separated cotton from seeds, and **calendar rollers** – giant machines that pressed cloth to improve its sheen. These processes allowed for more efficient processing of the cotton and hemp crops, which in turn helped to clothe and provide ropes for the huge Chinese population. Other innovations included new looms for processing silk, probably adapted from Persian models.

Machine innovations in China were important, but growth in productive capacities in the Atlantic world had a greater effect on the global economy over the long term. Sugar, more than any other product, drove new innovations. As we have seen, sugar was incredibly popular in Europe. So, sugar plantations exploded in the American colonies, beginning with Brazil, moving through Central America and the Caribbean, to Florida and Louisiana between the sixteenth and the eighteenth centuries. Profitable sugar production demanded huge labour gangs and efficient processing. The sugar in sugar cane deteriorated quickly, and so stalks had to be cut and transported rapidly to a mill near the fields. This was only the beginning, however, for processing at the mill required more technologically complex steps. The sugar-laden juice had to be pressed from the stalk and then boiled down and purified. Workers then carefully monitored the liquid as it crystalized. To grow profits from this labour-intensive process, sugar producers constantly updated and refined organizational processes and technology, introducing new machines like giant cane rollers and organizing the (mostly enslaved) labourers as specialists at each step of the process.

By the seventeenth century, early forms of factories emerged of the sort that became common in Europe and around the world in later centuries. Massive buildings worked by up to 300 labourers, using sophisticated technology for the time and creating a variety of products – crystal sugar, molasses, rum and other by-products. Plantations began developing into factories, the bane of nineteenth- and twentieth-century industrial workers (Figure 8.3).

Alongside the Caribbean sugar mill, another important innovation in our period was the automatic flour mill, built in 1755 by Oliver Evans of Delaware. The problem of expensive labour in the northern British colonies of North America helped spur this innovative technology. Cheap labour was not available there. As elsewhere, disease had decimated Native American populations, but settlers in these colonies had largely refused the importation of large slave or indentured servant populations, usually on moral grounds. Moreover, land was so plentiful that only a small rural working population sought wage labour. Evans sought to solve this labour shortage problem by automating the process of turning wheat into flour. He built a mill that used ancient devices linked together – bucket elevators (known in ancient Mesopotamia) to raise corn, the Archimedean screw (developed in ancient Greece) to move it to the grinding stones and large hoppers to spread out ground flour so it could dry. Historical technologies were now improved to increase productivity.

Figure 8.3 Sugar cane plantation in Havana, Cuba (© Bridgeman Images).

Sources of power

Still, the Caribbean sugar mill and the Evans flour mill both lacked a constant source of power beyond the work of humans. The windmill provided some additional power, as could water-driven mills which had been adapted by medieval Europeans from Islamic models. Yet these each had their own difficulties, depending as they did on the availability of constantly running water or blowing wind. In 1712 in Britain, however, the development of the steam engine brought to automated machines a revolutionary new source of power that was neither human- nor animal-driven. This promised to permit power production on earth to transcend muscle power and better exploit natural resources.

The first steam engine built by Thomas Newcomen in 1712 directed the pressure of steam, made from water boiled using coal. This pressure drove a piston that created an alternating cycle of high pressure, and employed vacuums that moved a rod back and forth. This versatile engine could be attached to just about any kind of machine to do work of almost any sort. By 1750 use of steam engines spread around England, a small country that in our period grew from peripheral irrelevance to central player in the world economy and in scientific thought.

Again, Newcomen's invention was merely a continuation of earlier innovations, and not even a particularly refined one. Within Europe, the creation of a vacuum using steam dated back to Italy in 1601. Their use in raising water from a low to a

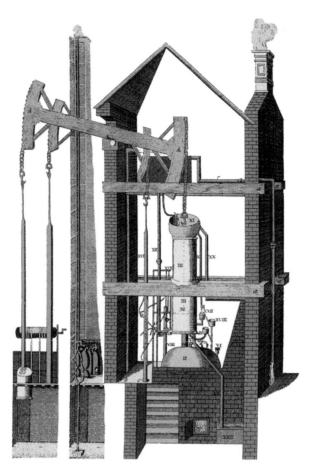

Figure 8.4 Engraving of a Newcomen steam engine in the eighteenth century (©
Alamy).

high spot had been shown possible in the 1660s. Pistons driven by heat had been
demonstrated as early as 1672 (Figure 8.4).

But Newcomen's engine was far more efficient than any earlier models. British
companies across the country soon employed it to drain water from mines. It was
still quite inefficient, because the engines required large amounts of coal to boil
smaller amounts of water so as to create steam. Newcomen was lucky that coal was
abundant in Britain, especially near the early mine sites in Staffordshire that used his
engines. This kept costs down, giving Newcomen and his workers time to gradually
improve the engine. The importance of this cannot be overstated. In Chinese textile
mills, energy continued to be produced mostly by humans, with some animal
assistance. In European mills and those in European colonies, burning coal slowly
replaced organic labour. Within fifty years, steam engines based on Newcomen's
invention revolutionized the world and helped usher in the Industrial Revolution.

This helped fundamentally shift the world balance of power and economic strength for the next 200 years or more, leaving Europeans and certain of their former colonies in positions of global dominance into the present era.

Life and labour

New technologies in the early modern era impacted the lives of most inhabitants of the world, though not everyone. Those groups most affected found their lives more tightly controlled than ever before, increasingly organized in a methodical, 'scientific' fashion. In industrializing regions, the watch and clock began to drive daily schedules, as work and meeting times became standardized and the movements of coaches and ships were scheduled. However, such changes were largely restricted to urban areas and the lives of everyday workers, particularly in Europe and its American colonies. The slave plantation and large mines in the Americas transformed the daily lives of those tied to them, usually in pernicious ways, especially for unfree Africans and indigenous Americans. New methods of organization built around the technology of the firearm transformed the way soldiers lived and fought, innovations that were later adapted to other aspects of modern life.

From the soldier to the worker

Early modern European states were consumed with ongoing wars, funded partly by silver and gold from American colonies and fought with larger and larger armies as populations grew. For European elites, military tools like firearms and armies themselves became essential attributes of a successful society. Engineers, mechanics and philosophers of the age increasingly imagined the movement of the human body as a machine, as it moved through the motions of loading and firing a gun.

The scientific study of human bodies, military organization and firearms technology merged around 1600 in the Netherlands, where the long war between Catholic Habsburg Spain and Dutch Protestant rebels provided a space for innovations in warfare. In an attempt to capitalize on the fast, easy-to-use, but inaccurate guns available to them, generals like Maurice of Nassau introduced a number of reforms. First, military intellectuals codified the motions necessary for firing muskets, and drilled soldiers to go through them as fast as possible. They also trained soldiers to do so in unison, so that large numbers of guns firing together could offset the inaccuracy of a single musket.

By the eighteenth century, this type of scientific organization was adapted to the processing of goods like textiles. In the 1730s, technicians even studied the movements of women working in textile mills in Britain, and made attempts to train them to use fewer motions, or to work together in unison. These same women were among the first large groups of workers to have their day organized by the clock, as well, working regular 'shifts' in what historian E. P. Thompson labelled 'Time-work discipline'. Working conditions for labourers in European factories were abhorrent, with no consideration paid towards health, safety or human rights. Child labour was normal until well into the late nineteenth century.

We have seen in Chapter 3 that life for slaves on plantations in the Americas was often horrifying. This was particularly true in the proto-factories where sugar was processed. That work was more mechanized than almost any other in the early modern world, with giant rollers blaring and boilers stifling workers lungs in miserable conditions. It was physically very demanding, as the refineries were immensely hot and the loads of cane and sugar very heavy. As a result, sugar refiners organized slave labourers into shifts, and even identified specialists at each stage. Conditions were so terrible, and the work with hot sugar so dangerous, that enslaved workers often became sick and died of overwork.

Slavery and the numbers

We can understand a great deal about how the slave trade functioned as an organizational technology through a vast collection of information about slave ship voyages called the Trans-Atlantic Slave Trade Database. Historians have tried to quantify the Atlantic slaving system since the late nineteenth century. It was only in the 1960s, however, that researchers committed to using this evidence to build a transatlantic 'census' that today helps us understand the mechanics of the whole system. In the decades that followed, historians began to describe such factors as where ships were built in Europe, where they embarked captives in Africa, where the captives were sold in the Americas, how many Africans had been enslaved and how many had died in the middle passage across the Atlantic. They did so by finding large sets of data like insurance records and port landing books.[4]

The information it contains helps us understand a great deal about how the Atlantic slaving system worked, including the technologies it used. For example, we are able to know with much greater detail now the regions where enslaved Africans were embarked and where they ended up.

We can correlate this information with evidence for how long it took to travel between different parts of Africa and the Americas. In doing so, we can see that new technologies that allowed for speedier ships enabled the slave trade to expand over time from the closest African regions to the Americas (like Senegambia and Sierra Leone) to more distant regions on the trunk of Africa.

Of course, this quantitative evidence cannot replace human stories in expressing the horrors of slavery. But it can complement the few first-hand sources we have of the transatlantic slave trade and help us to understand the broader trends that shaped the experiences of captives, crew and others. It also gives us a sense of how immensely widespread the trade was – from the manufacturing of ships, chains and other goods to the providing of foodstuffs, captivity itself and the plantation system in the Americas.

Slavery and ships

Some of the most important technologies of the early modern era were developed in Europe and the Americas to transport and imprison captive Africans forced into the Atlantic slaving system. This isn't surprising – the years 1490–1750 witnessed a great growth of maritime trade around the world, and perhaps the most profitable component of that trade was the Atlantic slaving system. Such vessels were truly Atlantic: largely designed in Europe, often built with American wood and designed to ply the trade routes between Africa and the Americas. Perhaps the most famous example is the ship *Brookes*.

The slave ship *Brookes*

The early slaving vessels of the sixteenth century were simply cargo ships turned over to the slave trade, and they were relatively inefficient. Designed with large holds to carry big bales and boxes, they could only imprison a small number of captive Africans. Because they were poorly ventilated, many captives died, which cut into the traders' profits. Moreover, holding large numbers of enslaved Africans in a single space allowed them to organize shipboard rebellions, dozens of which erupted in the passage between Africa and Europe.

By the late eighteenth century, slave ships were much better designed for their insidious task. Rather than large holds, they contained shallow decks equipped with metal rings to which the captives could be chained by their necks and feet in rows next to each other without any wasted space. Air holes cut to the exterior allowed ventilation of each row. Slaves were packed very tight. In many ships, each captive could occupy only eighteen inches from side-to-side, five-and-a-half feet in length and a depth of two feet in which to move. These decks were divided into rooms to make it hard for the African captives to organize. They also allowed the crew to bring small groups at a time onto the top deck for food and exercise.

The inhumanity of this system is obvious to us, though we often assume that European morals of the time made them generally immune to concerns about African captives being treated in this way. But this isn't entirely true for the whole period. By the late eighteenth century at least, many Europeans were becoming concerned about inhumane treatment involved in the slave trade. We know this, in part, because of the increased secrecy and security through which slave traders built and equipped ships. We also know this because when early abolitionists wanted to shock their countrymen about the horrors of the slave trade, they turned to images of the ships that carried them (Figure 8.5).

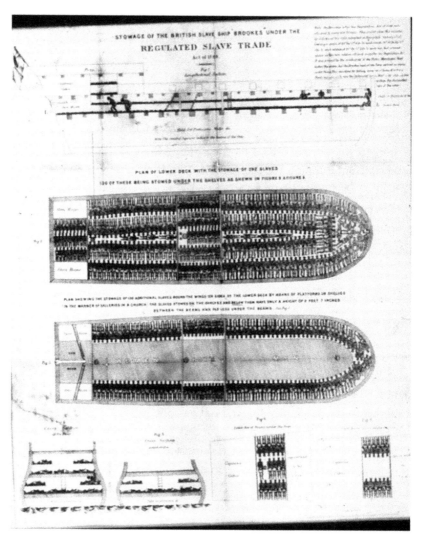

Figure 8.5 Stowage of the British slave ship *Brookes* under the Regulated Slave Trade Act of 1788. http://slaveryimages.org/s/slaveryimages/item/2553. Accessed 22 March 2021.

Probably the most famous abolitionist image of the late eighteenth century is that of the slave ship *Brookes*. This image is actually a series of slightly different images. The first was a large reproduction of the ship, with figures of enslaved Africans side-by-side, which was printed by the abolitionist Plymouth Committee in Great Britain. Text that called for the end of the slave trade (although not slavery itself) accompanied the arresting image. Within a year, a similar image and text had been distributed both in London across the Atlantic in Philadelphia and in New York, both important markets for British trade. Both Britain and the United States were among the most significant slave trading economies of the time. They were also, somewhat contradictorily, regions where abolitionism took hold, first among religious minorities like the Quakers but then more widely among the non-religious population, too. Powerful politicians and merchants were the groups that had to be convinced to abolish the slave trade.

The various images of the *Brookes* demonstrate the technological advances of their times. They were widely printed and distributed in a way that would not have been possible in earlier centuries. Developments in both paper production and the printing press in the eighteenth century caused an explosion in broadsheets and other publications. Abolitionists depended, in fact, on not just these kinds of images but also on published books by Africans like Olaudah Equiano, who told of the horrors they experienced in crossing the Atlantic. In many ways, this was the birth of propaganda for a cause, an early modern social justice movement.

Another technology of the time was the organizational methods used by abolitionist committees, a type of voluntary association common to the period and the forefathers of civic groups common in civil society today. They presented anti-slavery images using the scientific mindset that was becoming more common in the Atlantic world in this period. The reports contained in images of the *Brookes* shown in London, in particular, included precise mathematical details of the space available to humans, the impact of this on their health and well-being, all supported by eyewitness testimony from doctors.

Thus, the image of the *Brookes* gives us a sense both of the technologies of the slave trade as they developed from the fifteenth to the eighteenth centuries and of technologies that were allowing abolitionists to organize in this period. Eventually, their organization was successful. Buoyed by a publicity campaign that included both the appeals of British political and religious figures, abolitionism won widespread support from housewives and everyday people. Also, active advocacy by formerly enslaved Africans helped the abolitionists ban British participation in the slave trade in 1807–08, soon followed by the United States. Although both legal (using the flags of other countries) and illegal trade continued into the 1880s, this was an important first step, and the images of the *Brookes* played a large role in ending this immoral trade.

The *Brookes* image after abolition

The *Brookes* did not disappear from public view after abolition, however, and it has been brought back in the twentieth and twenty-first centuries to help keep memories of the Atlantic slaving system alive. The different versions of the images feature in many textbooks, for example, and they have even been recreated by groups attempting to demonstrate the experience of the middle passage. In 2007, the bicentenary of the abolition of the slave trade in Britain, both a university (Durham) and a museum (York Castle) in Britain laid out a life-size image of the *Brookes* and had students occupy the spaces on it. Durham University's 'slave ship' can be borrowed by schools who want to use it with their own students. The purpose of both organizations was to give the students a chance to reflect on the slave trade, but they also attracted criticism from activists and the public who saw the recreation as insensitive to the memories of Africans and as 'playing' a game about a very serious subject.

Experiencing the scientific revolution

On a global scale, only a relatively small number of people experienced genuinely substantial transformations in labour conditions and daily life from technological changes in this period. An even smaller group participated in the technological innovations that wrought the scientific revolution. Over the long term, however, all humans would be affected by these early modern processes.

A transatlantic society of letters

The scientific revolution was, in so many ways, truly revolutionary – but only for a relatively small group of people in our era. Mostly, the experimenters and thinkers formulating these new ideas came from a restricted class of aristocrats and a small number of men and women in the emerging 'middle' classes (or bourgeoisie). These people could read and write, and had access to each other's thoughts and findings. The emergence of the Royal Society and similar groups in France, Germany, Spain and the American colonies was significant, bringing changes that would come to the entire world in later era, like an intellectual and technological avalanche.

Such philosophers and technicians created a new society of letters, with thinkers sharing ideas that crossed international boundaries. Men like Gottfried Leibniz in the German state of Hanover and Isaac Newton at the Royal Society in London could argue across the early eighteenth century over the foundations of mathematics, their letters read and debated by fellows in Paris and Boston! As a result of the rapid spread of knowledge within and among intellectual societies, innovations could move speedily. Similarly, Benjamin Franklin, living in the British North American colonies, could conduct experiments and have his results read on the other side of the Atlantic Ocean. Indeed, from what we know of these early scientists, life often proved quite heady and stimulating, as new ideas arrived in the post monthly. This was a revolution in human communication and human intellectual endeavour, and collaborative technology was central to it.

From Spanish South America, intellectuals corrected European travellers' descriptions of the flora and fauna and the lives of the indigenous population. However, this exchange was not always even, even among Europeans. In a growing trend, over the course of the seventeenth and eighteenth centuries, the contributions of Spanish-speakers and especially of inhabitants of the Americas – even those of European birth – came to be viewed as less scientific and authoritative than ideas emanating from Britain, France and Germany. Spanish-speaking creoles in South and Central America were especially excluded, and, as we will see next, this trend only grew over time. The already common practice of excluding Africans, indigenous peoples of America and the Pacific, and even many Asians from the realms of science and innovation would become an entrenched, racist ideology of European superiority by the nineteenth century.

Gender and class in the scientific revolution

The majority of people saw the fruits of this research only slowly and in small doses. Studies of physics and metallurgy might help produce better watches and clocks, and innovations in chemistry might lead to better gunpowder, but dissemination into the public sphere often occurred slowly. We are, after all, discussing decades and centuries in these chapters. Thus, even within North-western Europe, people experienced the consequences of the scientific revolution differently and in ways shaped very much by class status. Though many middling folks began to use their time and material resources to tinker and study technology, the mass of workers, farmers and peasants had little spare time, few resources and merely worked to survive.

Technological change was also gendered – a very male experience, especially in Europe and particularly at the technological cutting edge, in male-dominated occupations like metalsmithing and glass-grinding. In fact, it was through the new philosophies of science that views of intellectual pursuits as masculine endeavours grew. Most European families – and society as a whole during this period – tried to prevent women from pursuing scientific experimentation, deeming such work as unfeminine. This was part of a wider suspicion among the upper classes towards their inferiors, but it took on a particularly gendered language – female involvement in science appeared to threaten traditional social and institutional practices of marriage and child-bearing. Social norms held that women should remain in the home, raising boys and families.

A look at perhaps the most accomplished female experimental scientist of the seventeenth century, Emilie du Châtelet, helps illustrate the gendered nature of scientific endeavour in this period. A French noblewoman, Châtelet largely trained herself in mathematics and the early sciences, eventually in partnership with the great philosopher Voltaire. While taking care of a growing family and a large household, she found time to duplicate and expand on experiments performed by members of the Royal Society in London and also to critique the work of the German mathematician Leibnitz in 1740.

However, her parents despaired of these pursuits. Early on, Du Châtelet's mother worried that 'flaunt[ing] her mind . . . Drives away suitors' while her father complained that he had 'argued with her in vain; she would not understand that no great lord will marry a woman who is seen reading every day'. This was a bind which would constrain female intellectuals for centuries, even into the present.

Most of those women who were involved in technological development and the sciences in this period came from regions where some measure of women's rights was more widely accepted. Anna of Saxony discovered many medicinal plants in the sixteenth century and wrote on their use. The Peruvian Countess of Chinchon learned that natives knew how to cure malaria through the use of a local bark. These women ran households at the same time as doing innovative work, an obstacle middle- and upper-class men did not face. Further down the class ladder, the need to take care of children and domestic duties excluded working-class women from any such pursuits, and hence most of these female innovators were from the upper classes. All women faced obstacles, however. Margaret Cavendish, the Duchess of Newcastle, wrote fourteen books on the sciences but was not admitted to any scientific societies!

'Visual' technology

Early modern technology affected people's views of the world in different ways. New artistic technologies and techniques of the period made the viewing and ownership of art available to more Europeans than ever before. When shared overseas, they did not much influence the artistic styles of other peoples. Yet, ideas centring on technology did begin to shape how Europeans viewed people in other parts of the world, and this mattered in the long run, as Europeans became convinced that they were somehow superior.

Inventing colour technology

Though much global trade moved from the Mediterranean to the Atlantic in this era, the Mediterranean Sea remained one of the busiest commercial zones in the world. Ships carrying goods from Asia, North Africa, and Europe crisscrossed the sea, their trade not yet heavily impacted by the growth of oceanic routes going around the tip of Africa and across the Atlantic. In this trade, Italian ports like Venice remained particularly important sites of exchange, and it was here that many artistic goods entered Europe from the Islamic world. These included highly desirable products like silks, glass, porcelain, metalwork, carpets and highly decorated books.

Italian artists of the fifteenth and sixteenth century learned a great deal from exploring Islamic products, especially in terms of the production of colour. Prior to 1500, the brightest colours available in European glass and paintings were largely imported from the Ottoman Empire and other regions of the Islamic world. In an attempt to capture part of the market, Italian painters, glass-blowers, dyers, dressmakers and tailors all experimented with pigments. In the sixteenth century, they learned to add ground metal and glass, minerals, and new types of plant dyes to their paints and pigments. The area that is now modern-day Afghanistan was the source Lapis Lazuli rock, a deep blue precious stone that when ground into a fine pigment produced a brilliant blue heavily prized by Renaissance artists. Other new colours arrived in Europe from the Americas, too, including scarlet red, derived from a Central American beetle that produced a deep colour never before seen by Europeans. The use of windmills to grind ingredients into pastes helped dramatically lower the cost of all of these pigments, especially in the Netherlands.

The availability of these new colours helped to produce a flowering of the visual arts in Europe, including a seventeenth-century period of painting in the Netherlands known as the Dutch Golden Age. Europeans produced millions of paintings in a short period, and because this pushed prices lower, many more people could own paintings than ever before. They could reflect on art and its meaning and explore all the complex imaginings that art brings out in humans. At the same time, this expansion of art helped to pave the way for art schools and apprenticeships, which raised the quality of the art and helped create new techniques, especially in painting. In another area of study, the demand for better colours drove experiments in chemistry, one of the key fields of the scientific revolution. So, art and science became tightly connected. Europeans borrowed colours and ideas from the wider world as always.

As paintings became more common and less expensive in Europe, Europeans began to carry them overseas. Settlers brought both paintings and the new artistic techniques to the Americas, while Jesuit missionaries brought European art with them to Asia. In general, however, European artistic styles did not heavily influence people elsewhere in the world. For example, while indigenous Californians living in Catholic missions were quick to use the new pigments brought by missionaries, and even to use them to depict such Christian subjects, they largely retained their own artistic styles and traditions.

Because Asians had their own long-standing artistic traditions, their royal courts were not impressed by European paintings. Both the Mughal emperors and those of Qing dynasty China viewed art brought to them by Jesuits, but these paintings had little influence on courtly arts in their realms.

Machines as the measure of men

European artistic techniques did not spread to Asia, partly because they did not appeal to highly developed local aesthetics and artistic traditions, but also because they did not appear to be superior or to address a real need. Even where Asian elites were attracted to European mechanical goods, like clocks, they rarely adopted them as a core cultural good in the early modern period.

Yet at the same time, Europeans began to judge other societies by their possessions, whether or not they owned technologies like clocks. This wasn't evident in the sixteenth or even early seventeenth centuries. European merchants, missionaries and explorers moving around the world in these years wrote more about their Christian faith than their technology as a way of distinguishing themselves from others. This was partly because their own technology was usually quite basic and the scientific revolution had yet to change their own mindsets. But gradually, these explorers and traders came to write about the technologies of other regions in disparaging terms, with a confidence soon bordering on disdain and prejudice. Whereas sixteenth-century Spanish travellers were impressed by Caribbean and West African canoes, by the early eighteenth century the Dutch trader Dierick Ruiters claimed that they were insufficient to fully exploit fishing opportunities. His contemporaries dismissed sub-Saharan African cultivation patterns as being too 'natural' and their mining techniques as crude. Europeans disparaged skimpy clothing appropriate for tropical weather as evidence of African and American primitiveness, and expressed delight at native peoples' fear of cannon and even how much musical instruments, like bagpipes, impressed them.

Europeans abroad soon began to develop a similarly negative view of North African and Asian societies, whose technology was similar to that of Europe and often as sophisticated. They disparaged the military technology and artisan tools of South Asian societies and the *jongs* of the East and South-east Asian trade. In particular, eighteenth-century Europeans in Asian commented on local societies' unwillingness to adopt the clock to regulate their daily lives.

As a result, by 1750 Europeans had begun to formulate a sense of themselves as superior to other societies because of their material technologies, military power and faith. This was not the fully formed idea of a civilizational hierarchy that emerged in later periods. Nevertheless, it demonstrates the role that technology had begun to play in shaping a distinct European identity by around 1750. This developed into an ideology – founded on racism, imperialism, capitalism and European civilization – that in later years would help to shape the modern world, with Europeans holding immense power in the late 1800s.

Conclusion

In the two and a half centuries leading up to 1750, new technologies such as shipbuilding and basic tools helped to link the world together. New technologies flowed across regions of the planet and helped to promote trade. Some exploited and used new environments by creating new labour regimes. They also helped set the stage for the Industrial Revolution, which had just begun to emerge as the early modern period ended. While drawing the regions of the world closer in trade and communication, many of these technologies helped to create serious global inequalities – both real and perceived. This had a real and meaningful impact on the way people in different parts of the world experienced the new 'global modernity', and how they were affected by it, particularly in the eighteenth and nineteenth centuries.

Keywords

Balance Spring
Calendar Rollers
Chintz
Determinism
Diffusion
East Indiamen
Innovation
Liquation
Quilombo
Royal Society of London
Balance Spring
Wales (on a ship)
Windmill

Further reading

Adas, Michael. *Machines as the Measure of Men: Science Technology, and Ideologies of Western Dominance*. Ithaca: Cornell University Press, 1989. Adas describes an important connection between culture and technology in the way people came to view the world in the modern era. The first two chapters are of relevance to the early modern period.

Goldstone, J. A. (Jack A). *Why Europe? The Rise of the West in World History, 1500–1850*. Boston: McGraw-Hill Higher Education, 2009. A concise and readable study of the technological and economic inequalities that emerged between Europe and the rest of the world after 1500.

Headrick, Daniel R. *Technology: A World History*. La Vergne, TN: Oxford University Press, 2010. Wide ranging study of technological invention in world history.

Jacobs, Margaret C. *The Scientific Revolution: A Brief History with Documents*. New York: Bedford St. Martin's, 2009. This is a useful introduction to this era that deals well with experimentation and technological development in the historical setting of this era.

Marcus, Rediker. *The Slave Ship: A Human History*. New York: Viking, 2007. This is both an erudite and a moving exploration of the technology that moved millions of enslaved humans from Africa to the Americas in the early modern period and beyond.

Epilogue – Assessing the early modern era

Early modern outcomes

How might we assess the early modern period? What were the mentalities of early modern humans? Were they just like us? Or were the most powerful people more like cantankerous teenagers by our standards? Was there a widespread compulsion towards violence we can barely conceive of today? We can't really know, but we do know that, in 1492, the meeting of two radically different worlds in the Americas quickly led to violence. We also know that sophisticated understanding or compassion was mostly absent, and that bitter enmity developed among peoples, with repercussions that reach down to this day.

The sources of the early modern era provide only a glimmer of the world views of most people and societies on earth. But they do tell us something about acceptable attitudes and behaviours. They show that by the 1600s some thought-shapers were beginning to recognize a common humanity, and the depth of the shared human past. Others, of course, remained committed to disdain, bigotry and rivalry, which would increase through to the last century. The early modern era can seem like it was another world and in so many ways it was. But there is much continuity, too.

Indeed, we can marvel at centuries of population growth, cheer the proliferation of ecological knowledge and applaud advances in medical knowledge. We can celebrate the development of the first open, tolerant societies, and we can credit those elites and commoners who questioned political and religious corruption. We should be appreciative of technological developments that set us on the path to our mostly comfortable techno-life today.

Yet we can also dismay at the incessant war, famine, disease, inequality, fear and loathing that the centuries between 1500 and 1750 epitomize; this was a world of unimaginable violence and ignorance, where natural disasters wrecked the lives of all who lived, suffered and died, and where pandemics went wholly unchecked and misunderstood. We can find particular horror in the Atlantic slave trade, which forced over 10 million unfortunate souls into a life of misery or early death. We can bemoan the ecological genocide in which Eurasian diseases struck down over 15 million Native Americans. We can ponder the less despairing, but equally disagreeable, lives of peasants and villagers all over the world who continued to live under the thumb of a small number of elites, and who often *lost* freedoms as political centralization increased the control of the powerful over their populations. Infectious and parasitic diseases added pain to social diseases such as addiction, violence and oppression worldwide.

But by any measure, there was progress – in understanding the environment, creating wealth, questioning spiritual and traditional authority, innovating technologically and perhaps most importantly for humans in this period, in political rights. Of course, this progress, however measured, was uneven, and this is important. Common people in North-western Europe enjoyed more rights by 1750 than in other societies. By then, the previously irrelevant western edge of Europe was becoming a global player, and this was in no small way because of the way these societies employed manpower – peasants, women, workers, all of society. There was no reason Western elites should have let go of the reins of power and allowed for individual rights or arguments for fairness to flourish. Clearly though, around the world in 1750, authoritarian rule was more the norm than the exception.

So, it is notable that before he died in 1661, the Scottish theologian Samuel Rutherford had railed against absolute monarchy and the supposedly 'divine right of kings' for decades, in concert with many others. In countries like Britain and Holland, even the religiously inclined allied with the masses to counter political absolutism. This was exceptional. A century later in Japan, the imperial ruler, Tokugawa Ieshige – like those in China, South Asia, the Muslim world and the rest of Eurasia – had little interest in either representative rule or the views of social inferiors. This attitude failed to appreciate how the world was changing (Figure E.1).

Change over time

Reflecting upon the previous chapters, we see that between 1500 and 1750, environmental understandings of the earth, of planetary and of human bodies, increased considerably. By 1750 the mathematical sciences of cartography and astronomy provided new knowledge of territories worldwide. Europeans grew to understand the earth better, and they subsequently claimed lands with brute force from 1750, until well into the twentieth century. Many people across Eurasia benefitted from the huge energy subsidy derived from the Americas and Africa. But for Europeans, this new power would later define for them those who were civilized and those who were not.

Population patterns around the world were transformed in this new, tightly connected world. Of the roughly 500 million humans alive in 1500, most lived across Eurasia. Two other major empires, the Azteca and Inca, populated the Americas, with much of that hemisphere otherwise sparsely populated. South Asians constituted about 20 per cent of world population, while in the Middle East, Africa and other regions, smaller numbers of myriad populations existed in minor settlements. China represented about 40 per cent of humanity, Europeans about 20 per cent. By 1750, however, Europeans grew to

Figure E.1 Tokugawa Ieshige (1712–61), ninth ruler of the Tokugawa shogunate (1751–60), Japan (© Bridgeman Images).

around 30 per cent of world population, while China and India remained roughly the same. Europeans were spreading to all continents by the eighteenth century, increasing in number and in power, growing faster than any other group.

We have also learned that control of land facilitated the imposition of political power upon millions of people, both in traditional societies and in rural areas. People worldwide who had existed in symbiotic relationship with nature, separate from urban centres, were by 1750 increasingly bound up in the tentacles of centralized imperial and national states. As Europeans vanquished indigenous Indians, Chinese and Russian leaders sent officials, soldiers and adventurers into Central Asia, dominating less complex societies and subjugating whole populations in a similar vein. Nomadic populations who had roamed Central Asia for millennia were subsumed by the two agrarian states in the seventeenth and eighteenth centuries, forced into subject roles as the growing empires enveloped the steppes.

The Chinese state conquered millions of people, including Muslim Uighurs, Tibetans and other diverse tribes, who still today consider themselves separate from the dominant Chinese Han. Other nomadic groups had long lived on marginal lands, comprising steppe, mountains and partial desert. But from 1550, the Russian state expanded across to Siberia – from a small region around Moscow – to end ancient lifeways for many, building forts and settlements to control a vast portion of Eurasia. Similarly, to the south, Ottoman Turks subjugated Arab and African nomads in these centuries. Those that remained independent from Istanbul would in the eighteenth and nineteenth centuries meet colonization and impoverishment at the hands of European soldiers and settlers.

Political power brought economic gain. In Europe, the new tendency towards marketable valuation of land and property brought great profits. Labour was increasingly measured with precision, and workers were pressured to perform to the point of abuse. Capital formation became extensive and widespread through imaginative financial instruments derived in Europe. In the medieval era, people had been exposed only marginally to foreign attitudes or goods, but by 1750 they were aware of products from faraway markets, and consequently of the customs of distant people. Perhaps most importantly, around the world, people began to spend their days producing for global markets, measured by numerical revenues, as opposed to working merely for home-grown subsistence. By 1750 more workers toiled for bosses and supervisors rather than labouring with those with whom they had long-standing social relations. This industrial economic transformation would change human life and the natural environment immensely after 1750.

This was also an era in which religious and intellectual paradigms would change in societies worldwide. Christian nations brought their ideas to ancient peoples worldwide, impacting countless traditions and changing lifeways. Christianity spread from Europe to the Americas, Africa and into Asia, and Islam also spread widely into Southeast Asia. The other major civilizations did not grow in scope, remaining only in regions where they had long been dominant. Towards the end of our period, secular, scientific, ideas – soon to coalesce into the intellectually modern Enlightenment era – also entered the world view of many people globally.

But even with a common Christian culture and similar traditions, European nations were not one unified, orchestrated people acting in conformity. They did not know they were crossing the Atlantic Ocean any more than Africans or Indians expected their arrival. These bodies of water, and the lands they surrounded, would over time be named by Europeans. There were no actual Africa's, Europe's, Asia's or Americas in the early modern mind. But Europeans would get to label all these continents and regions, owing to their newfound power, which derived chiefly from their greater military and industrial technology. As an indication of this technological and environmental power, for instance, the time zones used internationally today begin in Greenwich, London, because of overwhelming global British power in the nineteenth century.

In these centuries, across vast, newly claimed and newly named expanses, hundreds of millions of early modern people would be forcibly transported. They would shape new nations and environs, they would produce countless items to fill homes and dreams, and they would succumb to immeasurable disease microorganisms. All these changes would prompt new approaches to life, mostly inconceivable in 1500, that would help modern humans imagine the world to come after 1750, which is explored in Volume Two of this series.

Glossary

acephalous societies Roughly egalitarian societies without a single ruler or clear government.

anti-clerical Indicating opposition to the power or influence of the clergy, especially in politics.

Asiento system A licensing system established in sixteenth-century Spain in which the Crown granted licenses to other countries for the trading of slaves in Spanish colonies.

Atlantic economy A transatlantic economic system that grew as European colonies in the Americas developed beginning in the sixteenth century. This economy was characterized by the transatlantic trade in goods; the production of valuable commodities like precious metals, sugar, coffee and tobacco; and the migration of peoples – especially the forced migration of enslaved Africans.

balance spring A spring attached to a balance wheel in mechanical timepieces. This innovation allowed clocks to be manufactured in a smaller, more portable size and to run more accurately.

big men Local or regional African chiefs who sought to undermine the economic power of central rulers who aspired to build large empires.

capitalism An economic and political system in which a country's trade and industry are largely controlled by profit-seeking private owners, rather than by the state.

calendar rollers Large machines, first developed in China, that pressed cloth allowing for the more efficient processing of cotton and hemp crops into clothing and ropes.

categorical imperative Developed by eighteenth-century German philosopher Immanuel Kant, this describes an unconditional moral obligation which is binding in all circumstances and is not dependent on a person's opinions, preferences or purposes.

centralization A process of state development in the early modern world in which more power accrued to central governments. Centralizing governments ruled over states with more rigid borders, more formal and uniform laws, and highly organized bureaucracies.

chartered companies A new form of European trading group in the early modern world in which governments granted chartered companies exclusive trading rights and privileges through a written grant called a 'charter'. These chartered companies often played a crucial role in the early colonization efforts of European states.

chattel slavery A form of slavery in which the enslaved person is legally rendered the personal property of the slave owner.

chieftaincies A political order, usually in socially stratified tribal societies, where larger groups of people are ruled by elected or hereditary leaders, but without the professional bureaucracies or rigid set borders of a state.

chintz An intricate, multilayered cloth with a glazed finish first developed in south-central India in the sixteenth century.

Columbian Exchange Describes the widespread transfer of plants, animals, human populations, diseases, culture, technology and ideas between the Americas and the so-called Old World of Africa and Eurasia following the voyages of Christopher Columbus.

confederations A form of political organization in which power is balanced among several different families, tribal groups or regional governments.

consanguinity The fact of being descended from a common ancestor. Under the influence of the Catholic Church, most European societies had particularly stringent rules against intermarriage between close cousins.

consumerism A theory that spending money and consuming goods is good for an economy. Consumerist societies often enact economic policies to encourage consumption in order to drive economic growth.

deduction A form of logical reasoning in which one begins with a general statement or hypothesis and then examines the specific premises that

must hold in order for the general statement or hypothesis to be valid. Scientists use such reasoning to apply hypotheses and theories to specific situations.

determinism A philosophical and historical doctrine that all events, including human action, are ultimately determined by causes external to the will of human beings.

diffusion A process in which ideas, goods or technologies spread to other regions or peoples.

diplomatic system A structure of international relations in which professional diplomats conduct professional, official dialogue and negotiations between states with the ostensible goal of avoiding military conflict.

Dissenters Members of nonconformist Protestant churches in England who refused to recognize the supremacy of the established Anglican Church.

dualism A theory developed by seventeenth-century French philosopher René Descartes which holds that the mind and body are two distinct forms of reality and so, theoretically, it is possible for one to exist without the other.

East Indiamen General name for large trading ships that sailed under license of the various East India trading companies of the European powers in the eighteenth and nineteenth centuries.

economic growth An increase in the sume of economic goods and services that a nation or society produces and consumes. This is a very recent idea historically and one not common to the early modern era.

empiricism A philosophical theory that all knowledge is derived from sense-experience. It challenged the importance of received wisdom and helped stimulate the development of experimental science.

enclosures A process undertaken in England and Wales after 1600 in which landlords asserted exclusive property rights over lands traditionally held in common and worked by peasants. The 'enclosure' of these lands allowed landowners to introduce more efficient, profitable and less labour-intensive agricultural methods. Many displaced peasants fled to towns and cities seeking work.

endogenous Describes something as having an internal cause or origin.

exogenous Describes something as originating or developing from external influences.

expansion The political strategy of extending a state's territory by encroaching on that of other states. This strategy includes policies implemented to establish control of new territories by extending the reach of imperial institutions and other power structures.

ghost acreage Land in a colonized country used to provide food and resources for the benefit of the colonizing power.

governance Encompasses the range of strategies by which social elites created, managed and implemented laws and regulations to better govern a state. The tools of governance include the operation of state institutions like armies, police,

tax collectors, royal courts, even education and hospital systems, as well as individual politicians, ministers and monarchs.

hadiths A collection of traditions containing the sayings of the Prophet Muhammad. Next to the Koran, they constitute a major source of religious guidance for Muslims.

humanism A philosophical approach or system of thought that attaches primary important to human affairs over divine matters or supernatural forces.

indentured A form of servitude in which a labourer is contracted to perform service for a fixed period of time to pay of a debt or obligation.

individual rights Rights held by individual persons regardless of whatever group affiliation they may have.

induction A form of logical reasoning in which one argues from a set of specific premises towards a general conclusion. Scientists use such reasoning to form hypotheses and theories.

indulgences A corrupt religious practice in which the Catholic Church would absolve the sins of the wealthy who contributed money to the church.

innovation To make improvements on something established by introducing new methods, efficiencies, products or ideas.

intercropping The agricultural practice of growing one crop among others of a different kind, usually with aim of making optimal use of the soil's nutrients.

kaozheng A Chinese term, meaning 'search for evidence', describing a scholarly approach to study and research in the early seventeenth the mid-eighteenth centuries under the late Ming and Qing dynasties.

legitimacy The ability to defend the right to rule of a monarch or government. Defending legitimacy often included traditional or religious displays or ceremonies meant to reinforce power and authority.

Levellers A groups of radical dissenters in the mid-seventeenth-century English Civil War that advocated the abolition of the monarchy, religious freedom and social and agrarian reforms.

liquation A metallurgical technology developed in late-fifteenth-century Europe that allowed for the more efficient separation of metals from ores and alloys.

Little Ice Age A period of regional atmospheric cooling affecting primarily Europe and North America between the fourteenth and nineteenth centuries. It shortened growing seasons, undermining agricultural productivity and leading to increased food competition and human migration.

Maroons Members of any of various communities, especially in parts of the Caribbean, who were originally descended from African slaves who escaped captivity.

materialism A philosophical doctrine that physical matter is the only reality and that everything – including the workings of the mind – can be explained in terms of the physical world.

metrics Standards of measurement, especially ones that aid in the assessment of a complex process or system.

Mestizos A category used to describe those born of native mothers and Spanish fathers in Spanish America. Mestizos occupied a middling status in harsh racial caste system in Spanish America known as *las castas*.

millets Independent courts of law in the Ottoman Empire that allowed religious communities largely to govern themselves as long as they paid taxes and acknowledged the ultimate authority of the sultan.

monism A theory that counters the dualism of René Descartes by arguing that all of reality is reducible to a single substance.

monoculture An agricultural practice of growing a single crop or livestock species at a time. This practice can increase efficiencies in planting and animal husbandry, but at the risk of soil degradation, higher risk of disease and less diversity of ecosystems.

mulattos A term, dating to the late sixteenth century, and used across European colonies to describe those born of European fathers and African mothers.

ontological A branch of philosophy that studies the nature of being, most notably concepts such as existence, being, and reality.

pantheism A doctrine that the universe is identical to God, or is the ultimate expression of God's nature.

political culture The set of interactions and practices in any particular society that structure the ways in which individuals and groups of people participate in political decision-making.

predestination A doctrine of Christian theology that God knows all that will happen. It is particularly associated with the belief that God knows which human beings will achieve salvation before they are even born.

progress An emerging doctrine of the early modern period that focused on the improvement of the human condition over time. Proponents of progress tended to hold an optimistic view of the ability of human beings to understand their world and shape it for the better.

Price Revolution A series of economic events occurring from the late fifteenth to the mid-seventeenth centuries that led most notably to a high rate of inflation across Western Europe during this period. The influx of precious metals, population growth and urbanization all contributed to this long-term rise of prices.

proselytize The process of converting or attempting to convert a person from one religion or belief or to another.

public sphere An area of social interaction where people can come together to freely discuss political and social problems, and through that discussion possibly prompt political action.

quilombo Portuguese name given to independent, self-sufficient communities in Brazil established by escaped African slaves.

racism A belief that groups of human beings possess different behavioural traits, cognitive abilities and physical appearances, and that these groups can therefore be classified in a way that distinguishes superior races from inferior races. Beginning in the early modern world Europeans used such racist thinking to justify their colonial ventures and control local populations.

rationalization The action of organizing government authority and power in a more logical, consistent and efficient manner, usually through the development of a permanent governing bureaucracy.

reason The capacity of the human mind to consciously apply logic in thinking, understanding and making judgements.

representation When political actors speak, deliberate and act with regard to public affairs on behalf of others in a political arena.

Royal Society of London A learned scientific society founded in England in 1660 under a royal charter and funding by King Charles II. It is the world's oldest extant national scientific institution.

scepticism An intellectual approach emphasizing that nothing can be known with certainty.

Scientific Revolution A series of developments beginning in the early modern period that led to the emergence of modern science. The use of experimentation and empiricism led to radical developments in the fields of mathematics, physics, chemistry, astronomy and biology.

social contract A political theory originating in seventeenth-century Europe concerning the origins and legitimacy of government. It posits that individuals consent, either explicitly or tacitly, to surrender some freedoms to a governing authority in exchange for the protection of remaining freedoms and the maintenance of social order.

sovereignty Supreme power or authority within a state. In a functioning diplomatic system, states recognize each other's sovereignty over their territory.

Spanish Inquisition A religious court established in Roman Catholic Spain in 1478 and tasked with maintaining religious orthodoxy. It initially targeted heretics among Jewish and Muslim converts to Christianity but later used to combat the Protestant challenge.

state A nation or territory considered as a distinct political entity under the ultimate authority of a single government.

theorize To provide tentative generalizations about the world that might prove correct with repeated testing or experiment.

usufruct The right to use of another's property short of the destruction or waste of its substance.

utilitarian Indicating a belief in the view that the morally right action is the action that produces the most good.

viceroy A ruler who exercises authority in a colony on behalf of a sovereign power. Some viceroys ruled elaborate colonial governments called vice-royalties.

volta do mar A Portuguese term, meaning 'return from the sea', referring to a navigational technique that allowed mariners to swing out into the Atlantic, sail south towards the Cape of Good Hope, and then use Atlantic wind patterns to return safely.

wales (on a ship) An especially thick plank that ran horizontally along a ship's hull and was thicker than other surrounding planks. A wale provided extra stiffening and strength to the hull.

windmill A milling technology using wind power to process grain first developed in ninth-century Spain. In the early modern period, European countries adapted the windmill to drain farmland, to process hemp and rope, and to grind gunpowder, among other uses.

Notes

Chapter 1

1 https://archive.org/stream/fumifugium00eveluoft#page/n15/mode/2up/search/lond on+does+environ. Accessed 22 March 2021.
2 Nicholas P. Canny and Philip D. Morgan, *The Oxford Handbook of the Atlantic World, c.1450-c.1850* (New York: Oxford University Press, 2011), Map 7.
3 Mark Pendergrast, *Uncommon Grounds: The History of Coffee and How It Transformed Our World* (Basic Books, 2010), 17.
4 http://afe.easia.columbia.edu/special/china_1000ce_mingvoyages.htm. Accessed 22 March 2021.

Chapter 2

1 K. Klein Goldewijk, A. Beusen, M. de Vos and G. van Drecht, 'The HYDE 3.1 spatially explicit database of human induced land use change over the past 12,000 years', *Global Ecology and Biogeography* 20, no.1 (January 2011): 73–86, doi:10.1111 /j.1466-8238.2010.00587.
2 William Theodore De Bary, Irene Bloom, Wing-tsit Chan, Joseph Adler and Richard John Lufrano, *Sources of Chinese Tradition* (New York: Columbia University Press, 1999), 175.
3 Cited in Shireen Moosvi, *People, Taxation and Trade in Mughal India* (Oxford: Oxford University Press, 2008), 281.
4 Hilda L. Smith, *Women Writers and the Early Modern British Political Tradition* (Cambridge: Cambridge University Press, 1998), 72.
5 Cited in Thomas Benjamin, *The Atlantic World, Europeans, Africans, Indians and Their Shared History, 1400-1900* (New York: Cambridge University Press, 2014), 175.
6 George C. Kohn, *Encyclopedia of Plague and Pestilence: From Ancient Times to the Present*, 3rd ed. (New York: Facts on File, 2008), 261.
7 Daniel Defoe and Louis A. Landa, *A Journal of the Plague Year*, rev. ed. (Oxford: Oxford University Press, 2010), 74.
8 Cited in Nicholas P. Canny and Philip D. Morgan, *The Oxford Handbook of the Atlantic World, c.1450-c.1850* (Oxford: Oxford University Press, 2011), 22.

9   Cited in William H. Worger, Nancy L. Clark and Edward A. Alpers, *Africa and the West: A Documentary History* (Oxford: Oxford University Press, 2010), 46.
10 Hispanic Anthology: Poems Translated from the Spanish by English and North American Poets. Ed. Thomas Walsh. New York: G. P. Putnam's Son, 1920. http://mit h.umd.edu/eada/html/display.php?docs=sorjuana_arraignment.xml&action=show. Accessed 22 March 2021.
11 Cited in Worger, Clark and Alpers, *Africa and the West*, 46.

Interlude – Population problems

1   http://www.nbcnews.com/science/human-challenge-continuing-civilization-indefi nitely-2D11785380. Accessed 15 May 2021.

Chapter 3

1   Excerpt from *Historia de Congo by Visconde de Paiva-Manso*, translated in Basil Davidson, *The African Past* (New York: Grosset & Dunlap, 1964).
2   David J. Lu, *Japan: A Documentary History* (Armonk: M.E. Shapre, 1997), 213–14.
3   Juan Gonzalez de Mendoza, *The History of the Great and Mighty Kingdom of China and the Situation Thereof*, translated by R. Parke and edited by Sir George T. Staunton (London: The Hakulyt Society, 1854), 67.
4   C. T. Forster and F. H. B. Daniel, eds., *The Life and Letters of Ogier Ghiselin de Busbecq, Vol. I* (London: Kegan Paul, 1881), 220.
5   Bartolome de las Casas, *A Short Account of the Destruction of the Indies* [1542], Preface. http://www.thelatinlibrary.com/imperialism/readings/casas.html. Accessed 22 March 2021.
6   Venture Smith, *A Narrative of the Life and Adventures of Venture, a Native of Africa: But Resident above Sixty Years in the United States of America. Related by Himself* (Middletown, Conn.: J. S. Stewart, Printer and Bookbinder, 1897), 11–12. https://do csouth.unc.edu/neh/venture/venture.html. Accessed 22 March 2021.
7   http://www.gutenberg.org/files/2801/2801-h/2801-h.htm. Accessed 22 March 2021.

Chapter 4

1   Margaret Rich Greer, Walter Mignolo and Maureen Quilligan, *Rereading the Black Legend: The Discourses of Religious and Racial Difference in the Renaissance Empires.* (Chicago: University of Chicago Press, 2007), 31.

2   Tomé Pires and Francisco Rodrigues, *The Suma Oriental of Tomé Pires: An Account of the East, From the Red Sea to Japan, Written in Malacca and India in 1512-1515* (London: The Hakluyt Society, 1944), 226.

Chapter 5

1   Cited in William Cronon, *Changes in the Land: Indians, Colonists, and the Ecology of New England* (New York: Hill and Wang, 2003), 80.
2   Robert Dankoff, *An Ottoman Mentality: The World of Evliya Çelebi* (Leiden: Brill, 2004), 63.
3   Thomas Mun, *England's Treasure by Forraign Trade* (London, 1664), 220. http://www .fordham.edu/halsall/mod/1664mun-engtrade.asp. Accessed 22 March 2021.
4   Cited in Paul F. Diehl, *The Dynamics of Enduring Rivalries* (Urbana: University of Illinois Press, 1998), 52. Referring to 'open seas' and 'closed seas'.
5   Cited in Jane Whittle and Elizabeth Griffiths, *Consumption and Gender in the Early Seventeenth-Century Household: The World of Alice Le Strange* (Oxford: Oxford University Press, 2012), 63.

Chapter 6

1   Cited in Adrian Hastings, *The Church in Africa: 1450-1950* (Oxford: Clarendon Press, 1994), 76.
2   http://www.constitution.org/bacon/nov_org.htm. Accessed 22 March 2021.
3   http://www.gutenberg.org/files/43627/43627-h/43627-h.htm#chapter-51. Accessed 22 March 2021.
4   Constantine Nomiko Vaporis, *Voices of Early Modern Japan: Contemporary Accounts of Daily Life during the Age of the Shoguns* (Santa Barbara, CA: Greenwood, 2012), 202.
5   Cited in Jerry H. Bentley, *The Oxford Handbook of World History* (Oxford: Oxford University Press, 2011), 20.

Chapter 7

1   Oliver Cromwell and Thomas Carlyle, *Oliver Cromwell's Letters and Speeches: With Elucidations*, 2nd ed., enl. (London: Chapman and Hall, 1846), 380.
2   Cited in Russell Thornton, *American Indian Holocaust and Survival: A Population History since 1492* (Norman: University of Oklahoma Press, 1987), 71.

3   http://infidels.org/library/historical/unknown/three_impostors.html. Accessed 22 March 2021.
4   http://www.constitution.org/jl/tolerati.htm. Accessed 22 March 2021.
5   Cited in Adrian Hastings, *The Church in Africa: 1450-1950* (Oxford: Clarendon Press, 1994), 59.
6   http://plato.stanford.edu/entries/spinoza-physics/. Accessed 22 March 2021.
7   'Yet it moves' – meaning the earth *does* move around the sun irrespective of church doctrine.
8   Griffiths, Paul, *Youth and Authority: Formative Experiences in England, 1560-1640* (Oxford: Clarendon Press, 1996), 111.
9   Cited in Jonathan W. Daly, *How Europe Made the Modern World: Creating the Great Divergence* (London: Bloomsbury Academic, 2020), 107.
10   Samuel Edwards, *The Divine Mistress* (New York: David McKay Co., 1970), 1.
11   http://en.wikipedia.org/wiki/Nazo_Tokhi#Special_dream. Accessed 22 March 2021.
12   Cited in Andrew Wachtel, *The Balkans in World History* (Oxford: Oxford University Press, 2008), 60–1.
13   Hugo Grotius and William Whewell, *Grotius on the Rights of War and Peace: An Abridged Translation* (Clark, NJ: Lawbook Exchange, Ltd., 2009), 30.
14   'Rituals and religious customs of all the world's peoples'.
15   Cited in Nicholas P. Canny and Philip D. Morgan, *The Oxford Handbook of the Atlantic World, c.1450-c.1850* (Oxford: Oxford University Press, 2011), 444.

Chapter 8

1   https://commons.wikimedia.org/wiki/File:Hooke_Microscope-03000276-FIG-4.jpg. Accessed 15 May 2021.
2   Pannera, *Dell'armata navale* [Mrts (February 1, 2004) Arizona Center for Medieval and Renaissance Studies (ACMRS)], 129, translation in *The Journal of Aurelio Scetti: A Florentine Galley Slave at Lepanto (1565-1577)*, 15.
3   Olaudah Equiano, *The Interesting Narrative of the Life of Olaudah Equiano or Gustavus Vassa the African* (1789; repr., London: Penguin Books, 2003), 58.
4   Antonio Vazquez de Espinosa, *Compendium and Description of the West Indies* (Washington, DC: Smithsonian Institution, 1942).
5   At first, they collected these data sets in the technology of the time – books. In the 1990s, however, they began to digitize and combine their data and to make it available on CD-ROM two decades later, and the CD-ROM is now available on the internet as the Voyages project (www.slavevoyages.org. Accessed March 22, 2021). The database available through the Voyages website is searchable, can be queried through defined parameters and is constantly changing as new information is entered. Moreover, unlike books and CD-ROMs, it is free and available to anyone around the world.

Index

www.ingramcontent.com/pod-product-compliance
Ingram Content Group UK Ltd.
Pitfield, Milton Keynes, MK11 3LW, UK
UKHW010023280225
455688UK00006B/258